AF262600

BLANCHE HOSCHEDÉ-MONET

IN THE LIGHT

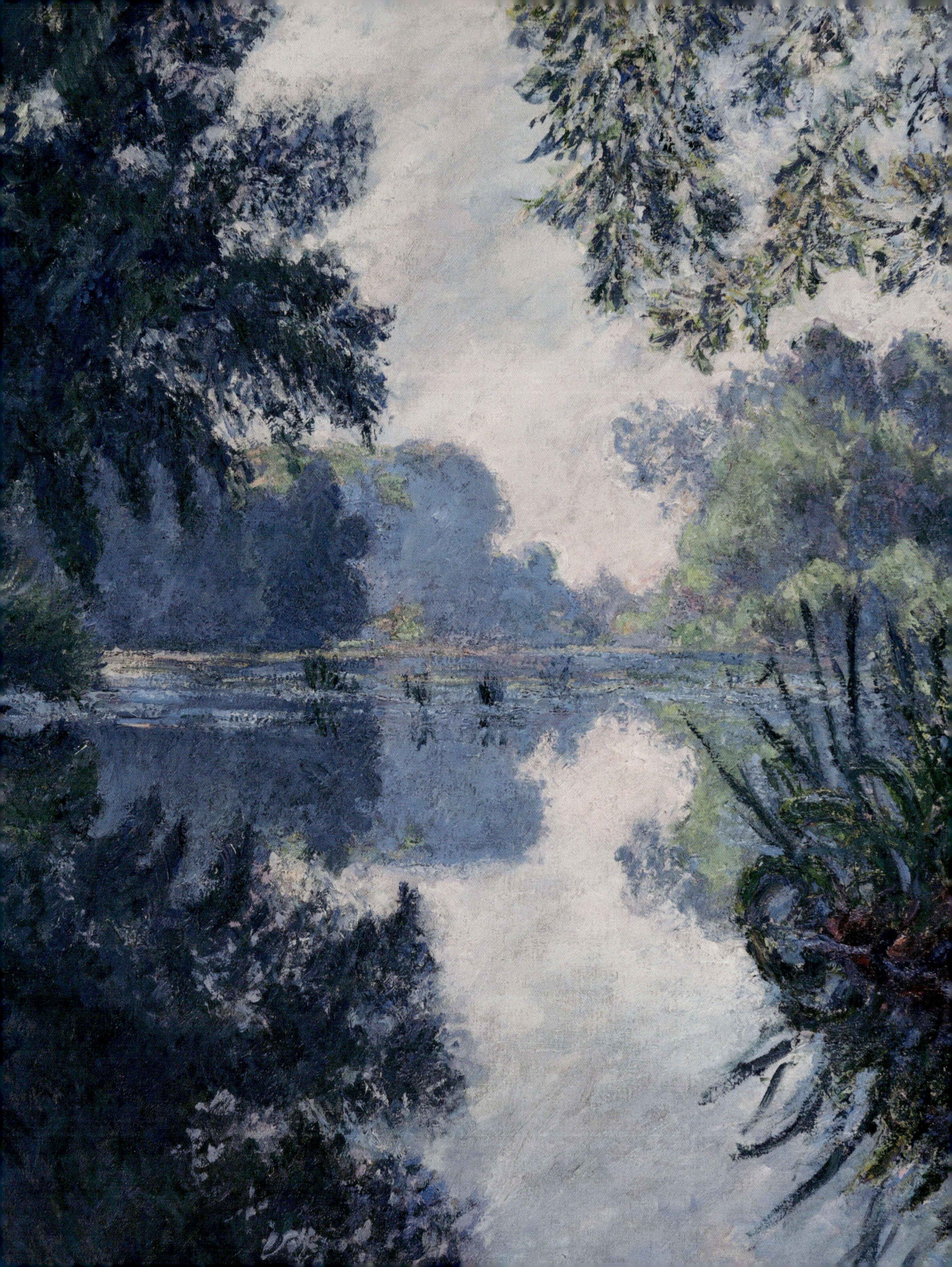

BLANCHE HOSCHEDÉ-MONET
IN THE LIGHT

Edited by Haley S. Pierce

Contributions by Nicolas Bondenet, Nancy Mowll Mathews,
Galina Olmsted, Haley S. Pierce, and Philippe Piguet

Foreword by David A. Brenneman, former Wilma E. Kelley Director, Sidney
and Lois Eskenazi Museum of Art, Indiana University

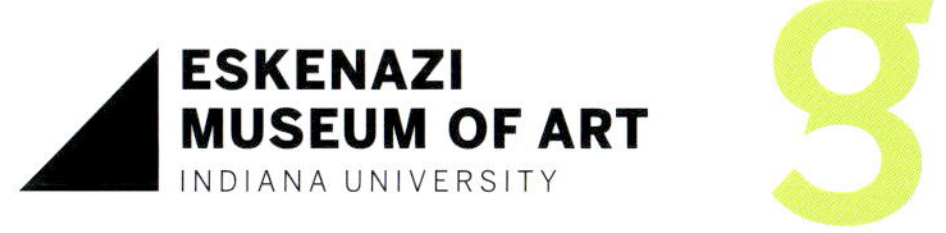

Sidney and Lois Eskenazi Museum of Art, Indiana University, Bloomington
in association with D Giles Limited

Blanche Hoschedé-Monet in the Light is made possible by generous support from Alice and Rick Johnson, Gary J. and Kathy Z. Anderson, Nancy L. McMillan, Susan C. Thrasher, Paula W. Sunderman, PhD, the Jane Fortune Fund for the Advancement of Women Artists, and members of the Henry R. Hope Society.

This catalogue accompanies the exhibition *Blanche Hoschedé-Monet in the Light* at the Sidney and Lois Eskenazi Museum of Art, Indiana University, Bloomington, IN, February 14–June 15, 2025.

First published in 2025 by GILES
An imprint of D Giles Limited
66 High Street,
Lewes, BN7 1XG, UK
gilesltd.com

ISBN Hardcover: 978-1-913875-71-8

All measurements are in inches and centimeters.

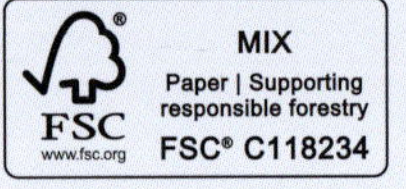

For Sidney and Lois Eskenazi Museum of Art:
Mariah R. Keller, Interim Director, Sidney and Lois Eskenazi Museum of Art, Indiana University
Haley S. Pierce, Assistant Curator of European Art, Sidney and Lois Eskenazi Museum of Art

For D Giles Limited:
Copy-edited and proofread by Sarah Kane
Designed by Alfonso Iacurci
Produced by GILES, an imprint of D Giles Limited
Printed and bound in Europe

Sidney and Lois Eskenazi Museum of Art Indiana University
1133 East Seventh Street
Bloomington, Indiana 47405
https://artmuseum.indiana.edu/

Front cover: Detail of Pl. 25
Back cover: Detail of Pl. 23
Frontispiece: Detail of Pl. 13
Pp. 10–11: Detail of Pl. 5
Pp. 68–69: Detail of Pl. 4
Pp. 114–15: Detail of Pl. 23

Photograph Credits:
© Agence Albatros / Réunion des Musées Métropolitains de Rouen Normandie: fig. 28; The Art Institute of Chicago / Art Resource, NY: pl. 2; © BnF, Dist. RMN-Grand Palais / Art Resource, NY: fig. 22; Courtesy of Bonhams, 2024: fig. 15; CC0 Paris Musées / Petit Palais, Musée des Beaux-Arts de la Ville de Paris: fig. 8; © 2024 Christie's Images Limited: fig. 7, pl. 18; Courtesy of Columbus Museum of Art: pl. 12; Digital Image © 2024 Museum Associates / LACMA. Licensed by ArtResource, NY: fig. 5; Courtesy of Eskenazi Museum of Art, photo by Shanti Knight: figs. 3, 21, 23-24, 37, pls. 4-5, 13, 17, 20, 22, 26, 35, 38; Courtesy of Eskenazi Museum of Art, photo by Kevin Montague: pl. 16; © Collection du village de Giverny / photo: Jean-Charles Louiset: pl. 40; HIP / Art Resource, NY: fig. 27; Courtesy of Institut national d'histoire de l'art, Paris: fig. 18; © Valérie Kattan. Musée Blanche Hoschedé-Monet, Ville de Vernon, 2024: figs. 10-14, 16-17, pls. 23, 25, 30; © C. Lancien, C. Loisel / Réunion des Musées Métropolitains de Rouen Normandie: pls. 33, 41; Courtesy of Musée Clemenceau, Paris: pls. 24, 27-28; © Musée Marmottan Monet / Studio Christian Baraja SLB: fig. 25; Photo © 2024 Museum of Fine Arts, Boston: fig. 38; © Paris, Lycée Claude-Monet / photo: Jean-Charles Louiset: pl. 29; © Collection Philippe Piguet: figs. 2, 6, 9, 19, 26, 29-30, 32-35, 39-42, pls. 3, 6-11, 14-15, 19, 21, 31-32, 34, 36-37, 39, 42-43; © Collection Philippe Piguet / photo by Jean-Charles Louiset: fig. 31, pl. 1; © RMN-Grand Palais / Art Resource, NY: fig. 20; Photo courtesy of Sotheby's, Inc. © 2024: fig. 4; Terra Foundation for American Art, Chicago / Art Resource, NY: fig. 36; Courtesy of The Walters Art Museum, Baltimore: fig. 1.

CONTENTS

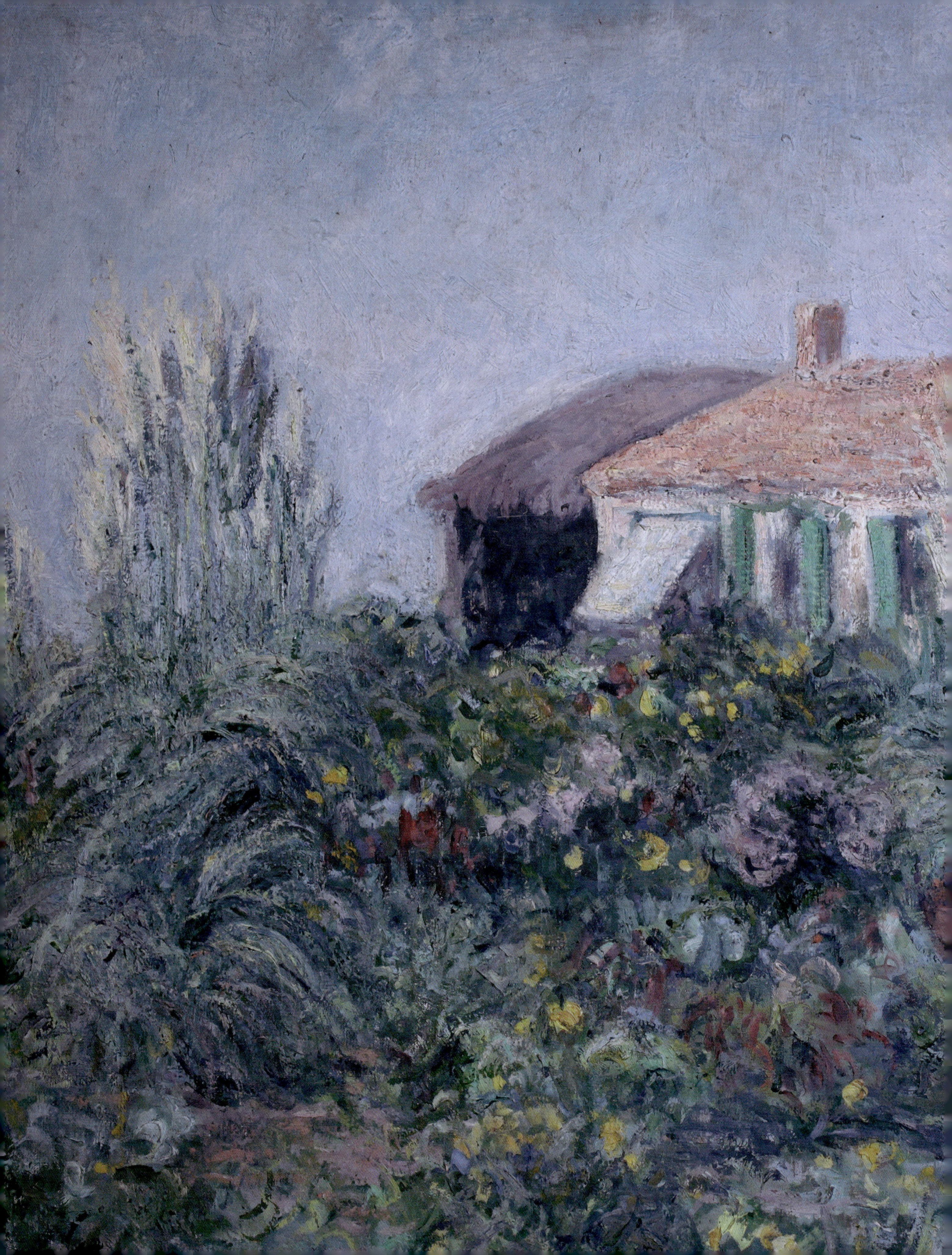

DIRECTOR'S FOREWORD

I take great pleasure in writing a few words of introduction to this catalogue that accompanies the exhibition *Blanche Hoschedé-Monet in the Light*. This project was the result of several factors that happily came together at Indiana University. The first was a visit eight years ago to IU alumni Alice and Rick Johnson's home to see their collection of European and American art, where I was surprised to encounter a painting by Blanche Hoschedé-Monet. As I explained to the Johnsons at the time, I had heard of the artist through work on Claude Monet earlier in my curatorial career, but I had not until then seen a painting by her. This serendipitous experience stuck in my mind, and I sensed that, like me, others would be interested to see more works by Hoschedé-Monet and learn about her.

A few years later, I was able to visit the Johnsons again with Dr. Galina Olmsted, who had joined the museum's staff as an assistant curator. Olmsted had recently finished her doctoral dissertation on the work of Gustave Caillebotte, the Impressionist artist and friend of the Monet family. We first discussed the idea of organizing a small focus exhibition on Hoschedé-Monet, but as Olmsted studied the artist further, we expanded our thinking to a larger exhibition that would present the work of Hoschedé-Monet for the first time to an American audience. I would like to thank Dr. Olmsted for laying the groundwork for this exhibition and its accompanying catalogue.

After Dr. Olmsted accepted a position at the Minneapolis Institute of Art, we were fortunate to find Haley S. Pierce, who had recently finished working on the exhibition *Manet/Degas* held at the Metropolitan Museum of Art in New York. Pierce ably took over the project, secured the loans, and brought the exhibition and this publication to a successful conclusion. I would like to thank her for her enthusiastic and highly professional management of this complex project. She worked closely and very effectively with Danielle Johnson, the museum's director of curatorial affairs, to whom I would also like to offer my sincere thanks.

Another important factor in bringing this exhibition to life at Indiana University is the Jane Fortune Fund for the Advancement of Women Artists. Thanks to a generous estate gift from the late Jane Fortune, we were able to move this project forward with a sense of confidence that it would be fully realized.

I would like to acknowledge and thank Alice and Rick Johnson, whose interest in Blanche Hoschedé-Monet provided the initial impetus, and who encouraged us at every step along the way. I am deeply grateful for their support on many different levels.

Finally, I would like to acknowledge the support and scholarship of Philippe Piguet, Blanche Hoschedé-Monet's grandnephew and author of the artist's forthcoming catalogue raisonné; Nicolas Bondenet, the director of the Musée Blanche Hoschedé-Monet in Vernon, France; and Dr. Nancy Mowll Mathews, the esteemed former curator of the Williams College Museum of Art, Mary Cassatt scholar, and now resident of Bloomington, Indiana. These individuals, working closely with Galina Olmsted and Haley S. Pierce, have helped to bring into the light the work of an artist who deserves to be seen and understood on her own terms.

David A. Brenneman
Former Wilma E. Kelley Director
Sidney and Lois Eskenazi Museum of Art
Indiana University Bloomington

ACKNOWLEDGMENTS

Often lauded for her modesty and humbleness of spirit, Blanche Hoschedé-Monet was an artist of considerable and celebrated talent. From being surrounded as a child by the modern masterpieces in the art collection of her father, Ernest Hoschedé, to family visits with such renowned artists as Édouard Manet, Auguste Renoir, Gustave Caillebotte, and of course, Claude Monet, Hoschedé-Monet came of age at the center of the movement that would later become known as Impressionism. The only one of her siblings to pursue painting, she possessed a keen eye and dedication to her craft. Early drawings from 1882–84 reveal closely observed studies of her family and immediate surroundings, in addition to landscapes created during excursions into the Normandy countryside.

The carefully framed points of view that filled the pages of her sketchbook were echoed in her later practice as a painter, when she joined a professional network of exhibiting artists in Giverny, Vernon, Rouen, and Paris, remaining active until her death in 1947. Despite taking a step back from her work to care for Monet towards the end of his life, Hoschedé-Monet was largely responsible for the preservation and continuation of his legacy, especially throughout the turbulent years of the Second World War. It has been a privilege and an honor to learn about Blanche Hoschedé-Monet's life and work, and it is our hope that this exhibition and catalogue will help to shed further light and encourage future scholarship on this important artist.

A project like this would not have been possible without the contributions of many individuals. First and foremost, my sincere thanks to David A. Brenneman, former Wilma E. Kelley Director of the Sidney and Lois Eskenazi Museum of Art, for recognizing the potential and importance of this exhibition as the first monographic show of Blanche Hoschedé-Monet's work in the United States. Danielle Johnson, Director of Curatorial Affairs, provided endless support and encouragement, and ensured the exhibition's success at every step. Galina Olmsted, now Associate Curator of European Art at the Minneapolis Institute of Art, spearheaded this project from its early days, and remained a vital collaborator throughout its realization.

This exhibition would never have come to fruition without the generosity of exceptional donors and loans from public and private collections. Our sincere thanks go to Alice and Rick Johnson, Gary J. and Kathy Z. Anderson, Nancy L. McMillan, Susan C. Thrasher, Paula W. Sunderman, PhD, the Jane Fortune Fund for the Advancement of Women Artists, and members of the Henry R. Hope Society. For their trust and support, I warmly thank Azize Atif, Nicolas Bondenet, Michel Cervoni, Marie Delbarre, Érik Desmazières, Jacques Doucède, Aurélie Gavoille, Gloria Groom, Catherine Fernandez Herry, Jean-Noël Jeanneney, Claude Landais, Lise Lentignac, Edwige Lequesne, Daniel Marcus, Sophie Mary, Catherine Minot, Brooke A. Minto, Astrid Piguet, Boris Piguet, Gérard Piguet, Marc and Nicole

Piguet, Philippe Piguet, Valérie Ries, Nicole Rome, James Rondeau, Cyrille Sciama, Pascaline Verrier, and Annie Wallington.

This singular project is indebted to the foundational studies and previous exhibitions that have helped bring the work of Blanche Hoschedé-Monet to light, including *Blanche Hoschedé-Monet, 1865–1947: Une artiste de Giverny* (Musée Municipal A.G. Poulain, 1991), *Blanche Hoschedé-Monet: Un destin impressionniste* (Musée de Louviers, 2010), *Blanche Hoschedé-Monet: Un regard impressionniste* (Musée Municipal A.G. Poulain, 2017), and *Saga familiale: Monet, Hoschedé-Monet et les Butler* (Musée Municipal A.G. Poulain, 2022). For their integral collaboration and collegial support, I am grateful to Philippe Piguet, Nicolas Bondenet, and Nancy Mowll Mathews, whose insight and research has contributed significantly to the scholarship on Hoschedé-Monet, and the success of this exhibition. Mariah Keller, Director of Creative Services, was instrumental in shaping this catalogue and ensuring its development. I likewise thank the Publishing and Editorial team at D Giles Limited for their expertise in guiding this book through production, including Dan Giles, Liz Japes, Susan Kelly, Allison McCormick, and Louise Ramsay.

Finally, I thank my colleagues at the Eskenazi Museum of Art for their hard work, patience, and attention to detail which made this all possible. Emma Fulce, Registrar, adeptly oversaw the logistics of all loans with focus and tremendous organization. We depended upon the essential fundraising efforts undertaken by Christine Baldwin, Director of Development. Special thanks to Steve Cook, Assistant to the Director, for his help in myriad ways; Jennifer McComas, Curator of European and American Art; Julie Ribits, Beverly and Gayl W. Doster Paintings Conservator; Pete Nelson, Chief Preparator; Laura Greenwood, Senior Preparator, and the rest of the Installation team; Shanti Knight, Photographer, and Jessie Waymire, Graphic Design Manager; Jean Graves, Patricia and Joel Meier Chair of Education, and Ben Gardner, Andrew W. Mellon and Anthony J. Moravec University Experiences Manager; Richard Valdez, Finance Manager; Jane Gilbert for her help with translations; and the vital Security and Guest Services staff, who ensure the success of this project and others at the museum every day.

Haley S. Pierce
Assistant Curator, European Art
Sidney and Lois Eskenazi Museum of Art

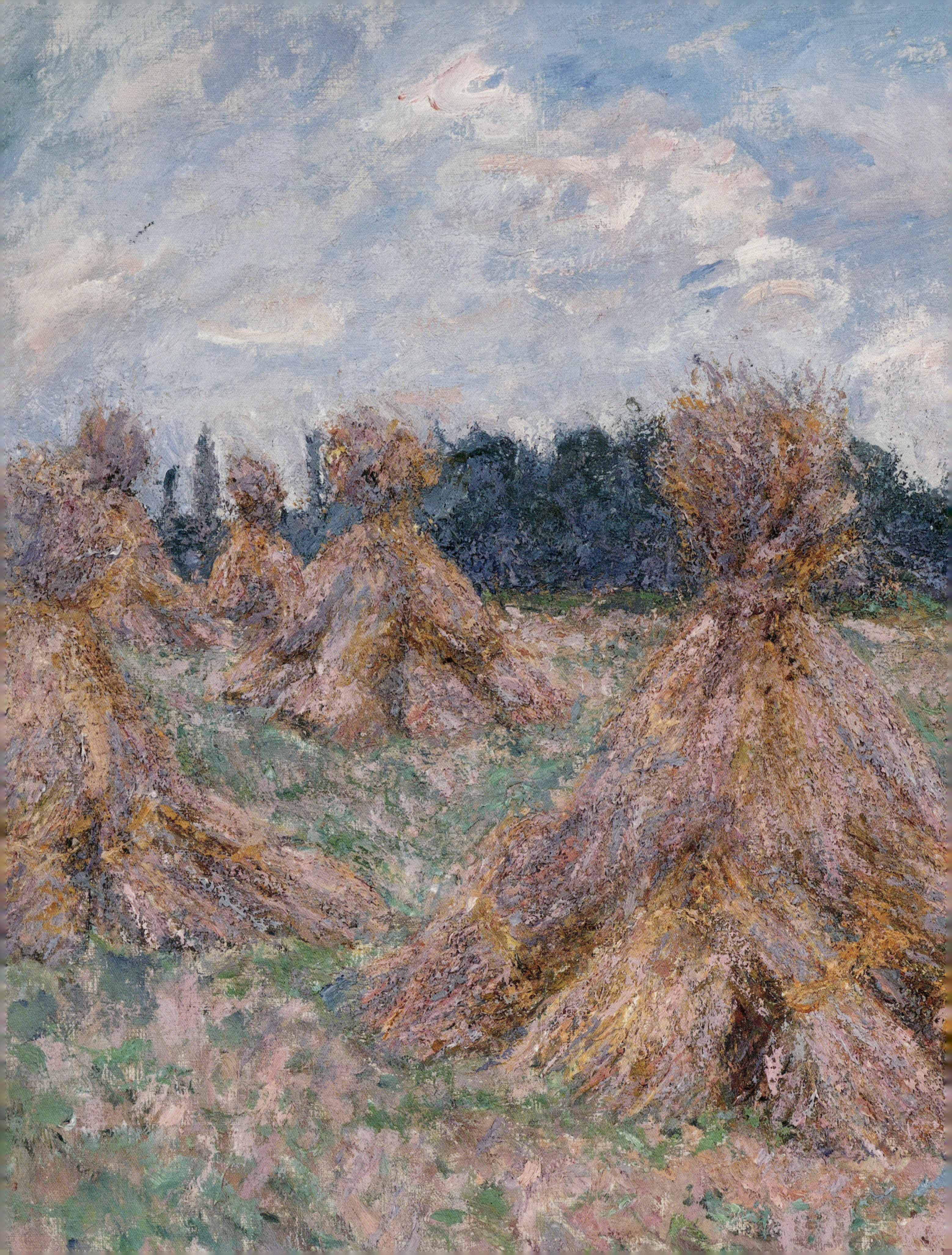

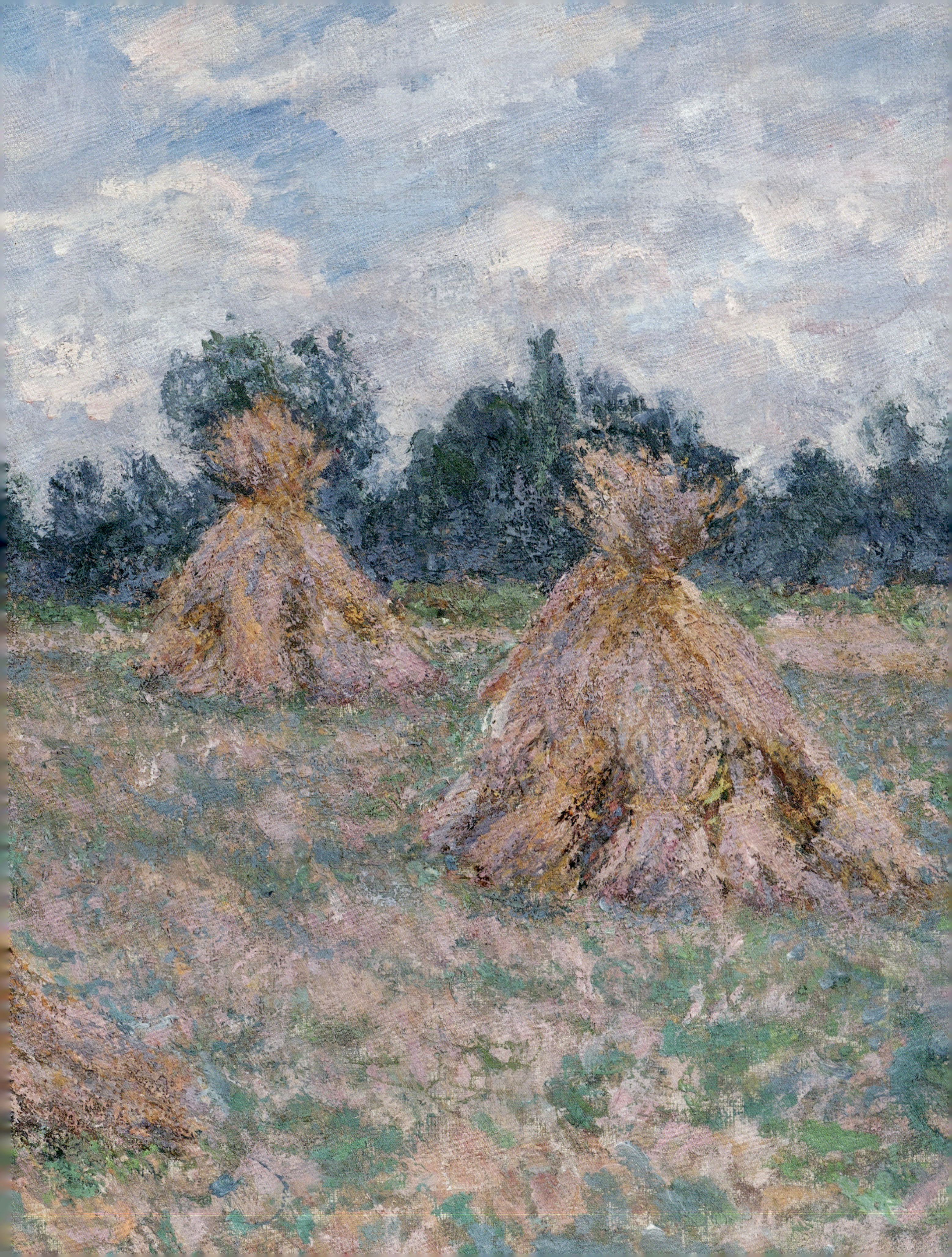

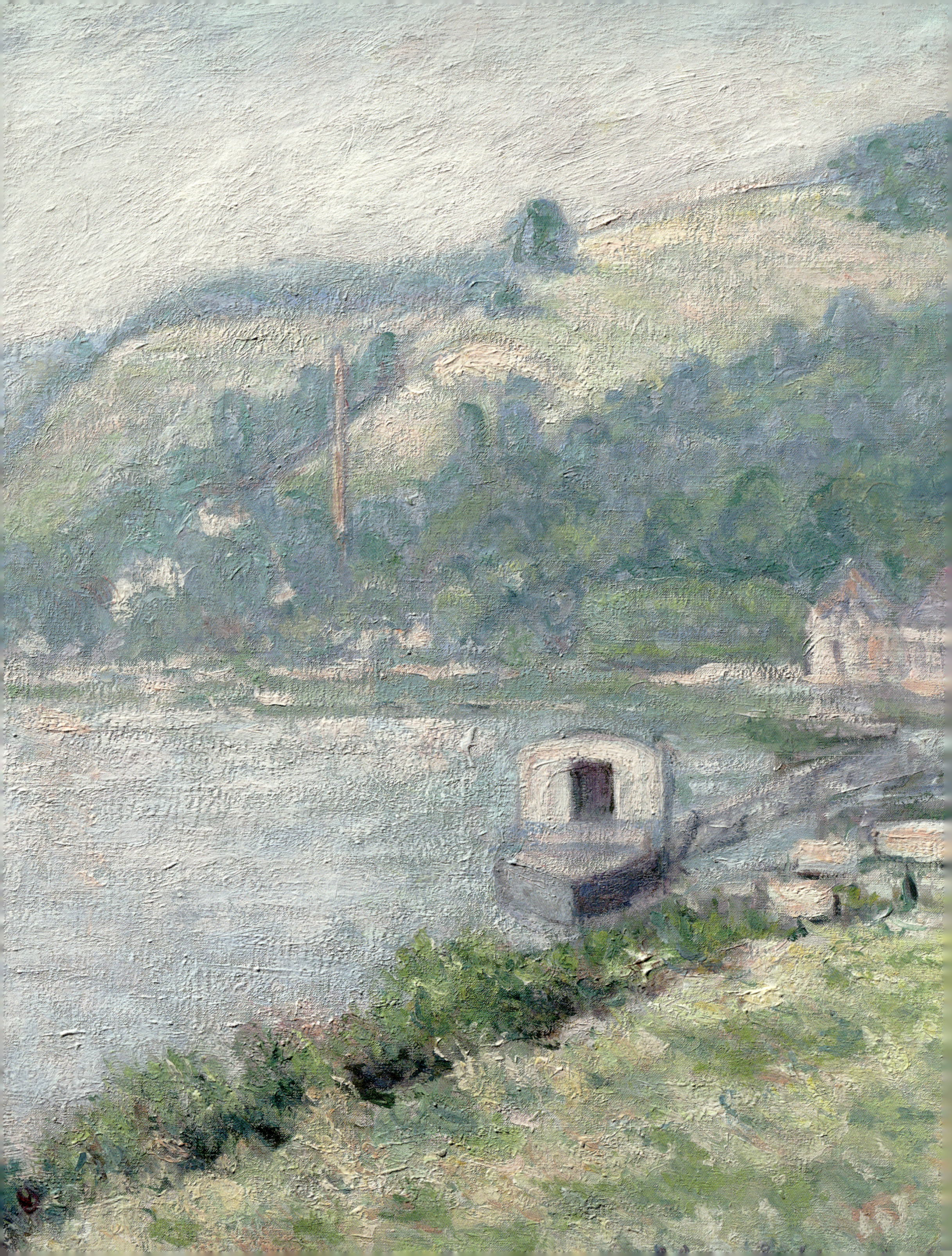

PEINTRE IMPRESSIONNISTE

Galina Olmsted

In the spring of 1867, a group of French artists dreamed of an independent exhibition outside the auspices of the state-sponsored Salon. The group—which included Frédéric Bazille, Paul Cezanne, Claude Monet, Camille Pissarro, Auguste Renoir, and Alfred Sisley—found themselves at the center of debates about the inconsistencies of the Salon's policies and sought a new venue to exhibit their pictures. Delayed first by financial constraints and then by the Franco-Prussian War and its aftermath, the first independent exhibition of the group that would become known as the Impressionists opened in the spring of 1874 with the name "Société anonyme des artistes peintres, sculpteurs, graveurs, etc." In the 1870s and '80s, the group organized eight independent exhibitions, as well as dealer-sponsored exhibitions in Paris and London.

In April 1886, *Works in Oil and Pastel by the Impressionists of Paris* opened at the American Art Association in New York City, the first exhibition of Impressionist art in the United States.[1] The exhibition was a success, and one of its co-organizers, the dealer Paul Durand-Ruel, opened a gallery in New York City the following year. By 1897, Impressionist paintings had been exhibited as far west as Denver. Claude Monet quickly became synonymous with French Impressionism, as American painters traveled to the small village of Giverny to paint *en plein air*, with the hope of catching a glimpse of the artist. One critic for the *Art Amateur* described the "American colony" that had gathered there in 1887, "seventy miles from Paris on the Seine, the home of Claude Monet. . . . A few pictures just received from these men shows that they have got the blue-green color of Monet's impressionism. . . ."[2]

Monet's fame continued to grow, and so did the colony at Giverny. As Katherine M. Bourguignon notes in her study of artistic activity in Giverny, over 300 artists made extended trips to the village between 1885 and 1915, traveling primarily from the United States and elsewhere in France, but also from Argentina, Australia, Austria, Canada, Germany, Great Britain, Norway, Poland, and Sweden.[3] At the center of this group of international artists was a young woman, an artist herself: Blanche Hoschedé-Monet. Despite her role in the artist's colony at Giverny, her success as a painter who exhibited regularly in Paris and Rouen, and her status as the stepdaughter and eventual daughter-in-law of France's most famous painter, Hoschedé-Monet is almost entirely unknown to American audiences. She has been the subject of solo exhibitions in

France and her work has been included in studies of Monet's family and circle, but her paintings are rarely found in American public and private collections. *Blanche Hoschedé-Monet in the Light* and its catalogue mark the first monographic consideration of her work in the United States. Together with this introduction about her early years, the essays that follow take full measure of Hoschedé-Monet's life and career and situate her work in the broader context of Impressionism.

MEETING THE IMPRESSIONISTS

In November 1885, Blanche Hoschedé-Monet received a gift from a fellow artist. A simple inscription—"Given to Blanche for her twentieth birthday"—on the original stretcher of Gustave Caillebotte's *Riverbank, Morning Mist* (*Bord de Rivière, Effet de Brume Matinale*, 1875; private collection) affirms Hoschedé-Monet's place among the Impressionist painters of the 1880s.[4] Hoschedé-Monet and Caillebotte had met for the first time nearly a decade earlier; Hoschedé-Monet spent her childhood summers at the Château de Rottembourg in Montgeron while Caillebotte frequently visited his family's estate in Yerres, just a few kilometers away. Caillebotte's painting of the Yerres river and its parallel walking path, curving gently before receding into the early morning mist, must have evoked Hoschedé-Monet's memories of the summer of 1876,

experiences that would shape the course of her personal and artistic life.

Claude Monet first arrived at the Château de Rottembourg, the summer estate of the Hoschedé family, in July 1876. A department store magnate and art collector, Ernest Hoschedé had commissioned the thirty-five-year-old artist to paint four decorative panels for the dining room. The commission proved transformative for Monet, who completed a group of large decorative works including *The Turkeys* (*Les Dindons*, 1876; Musée d'Orsay, Paris) and *The Pond at Montgeron* (*L'Étang à Montgeron*, 1876; State Hermitage Museum, St Petersburg), as well as several views of the nearby Yerres river.

On his walks to the Hoschedé family fishing cabin on the river, Monet became better acquainted with Caillebotte. The two artists had participated in the second Impressionist exhibition that spring, and, just before its opening, Caillebotte purchased three paintings from Monet.[5] When Monet returned to Paris in early 1877, Caillebotte secured an apartment for him at 17 rue Moncey and encouraged him to paint the nearby Saint-Lazare train station, works that would become the basis for Caillebotte's triumphant installation of city paintings at the third Impressionist exhibition in the spring of 1877.[6] The summer of 1876 was a catalyst for the success of Monet and his group at that exhibition, the first at which they adopted the name "impressionnistes."

A biography published after Hoschedé-Monet's death by her brother Jean-Pierre Hoschedé relays

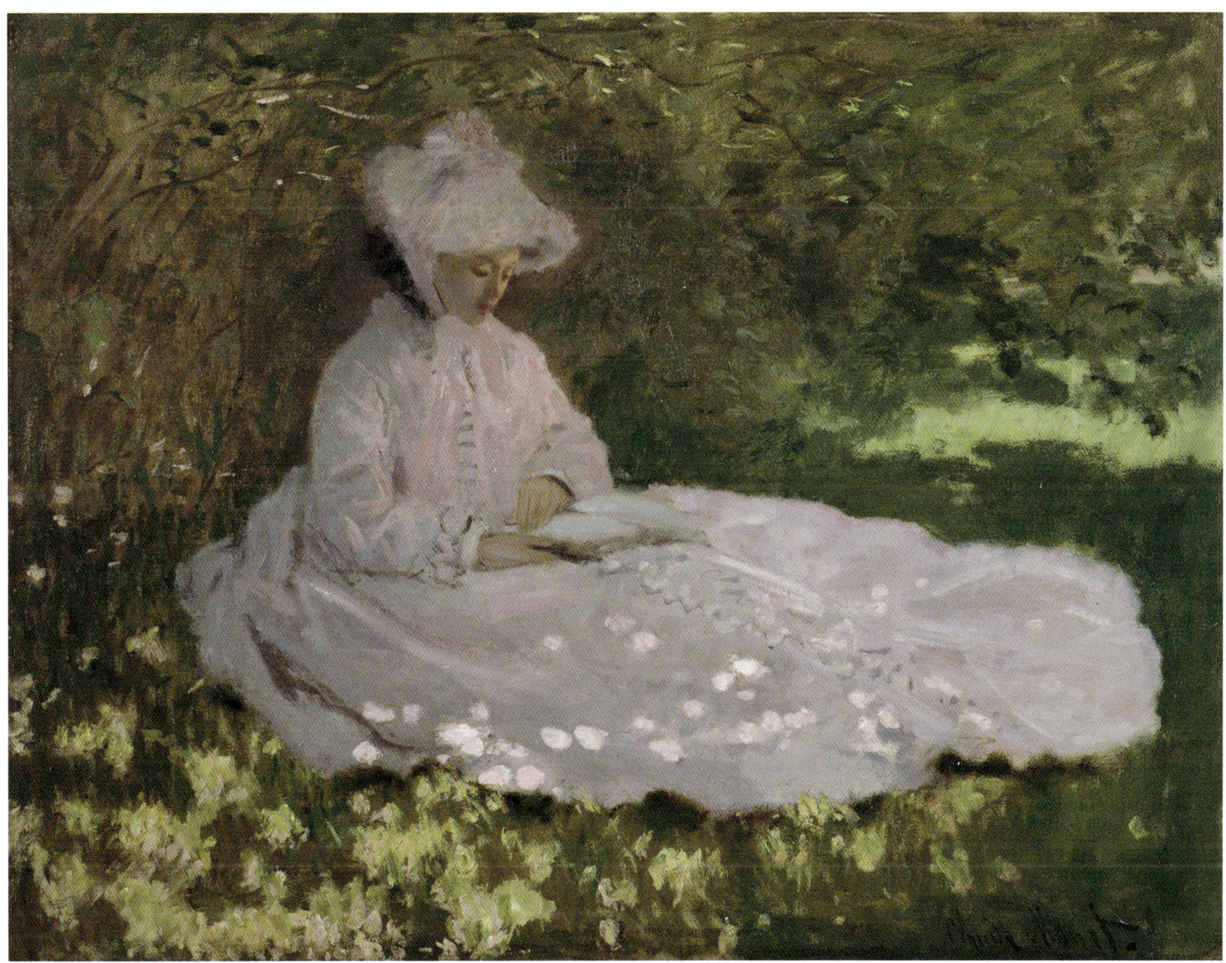

Fig. 1 Claude Monet, *The Reader* or *Springtime* (*La Liseuse*), 1872. Oil on canvas, 9 11/16 × 25 13/16 in. (50 × 65.5 cm). The Walters Art Museum, Baltimore (37.11)

her memories of meeting Monet for the first time that summer: "I was just eleven years old but I remember his arrival at my parents' house in Montgeron. He was introduced to me as a great artist, and he had long hair. That struck me, and I immediately had sympathy for him because we could tell he was fond of children."[7]

The young daughter of a prominent collector, Hoschedé-Monet had met many artists, and her brother's biography describes dinners and studio visits with Édouard Manet, Renoir, and others, but it was Monet's work that defined her earliest childhood memories. Of the twenty or so paintings by Monet owned by her father, she admired *The*

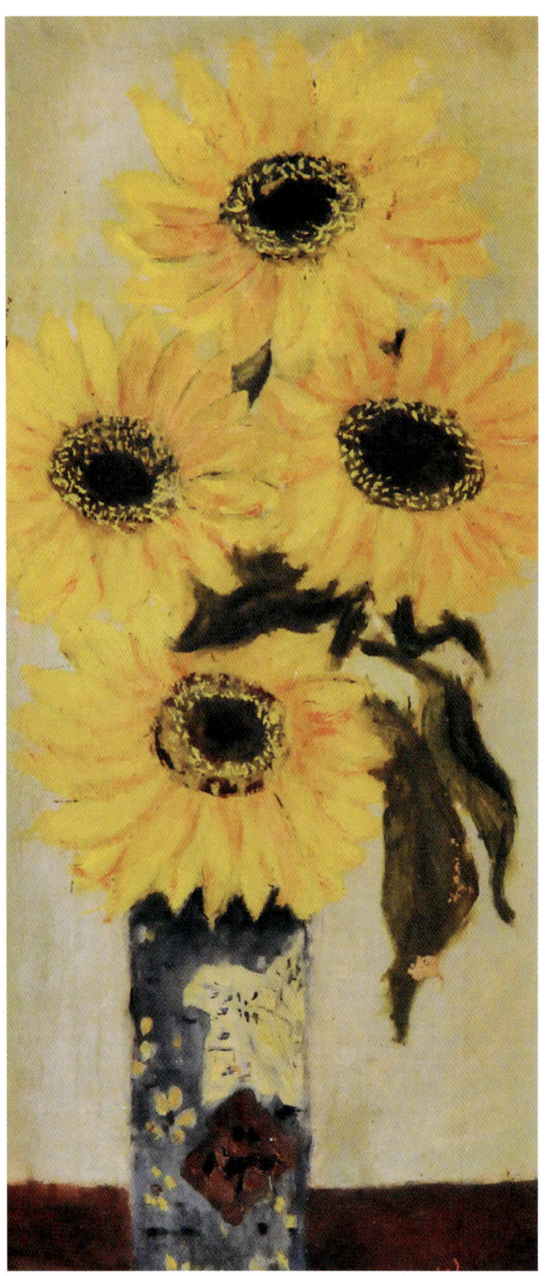

Reader (*La Liseuse*) (fig. 1) above all others, writing that she was "deeply struck" by the touches of sunlight on the skirt of Monet's first wife, Camille Doncieux, who was the model.[8]

Monet went to Paris in December 1876, and the years ahead were tumultuous for both the Hoschedé and Monet families. After the close of the third Impressionist exhibition in the spring of 1877, Monet returned to Argenteuil to reunite with his son Jean and with Camille, who was suffering from a prolonged illness. In early 1878, the Monets moved to Vétheuil and welcomed a second son, Michel. Ernest Hoschedé faced mounting financial pressures in the mid-1870s and was forced to sell most of his collection in 1878, as well as the estate in Montgeron and his apartment in Paris.[9] Monet invited Hoschedé, his wife Alice, and their six children (Marthe, Blanche, Suzanne, Jacques, Germaine, and Jean-Pierre) to live with his family in Vétheuil, bringing four adults and eight children together under one roof. Camille's health continued to decline until her death in September 1879. By 1882, Alice and Monet had entered into a domestic partnership, although they did not marry until 1892.

Just thirteen years old when the families first merged, Hoschedé-Monet was the only of the Hoschedé or Monet children to show a sustained interest in art. Her earliest known painting, *Four Sunflowers in a Vase* (*Quatre tournesols dans un vase*) (fig. 2, pl. 39), is better understood as an artistic artifact of childhood than a finished work, but it is evidence that her artistic ambitions were taking root just as the Monet and Hoschedé families came together. Jean-Pierre would later write that Hoschedé-Monet had little time for painting in those early years, as the Hoschedé sisters were preoccupied with chores around the house and the care of Michel, the younger Monet son, and of Jean-Pierre himself, the youngest of the Hoschedé children.

In the summer of 1882, the Hoschedé and Monet families rented a small house in Pourville, the Villa Juliette. Painted that summer, Monet's *Cliff Walk at Pourville* (*Promenade sur la falaise, Pourville*) (pl. 2) captures Hoschedé-Monet and her older sister Marthe facing a rocky outcropping suspended near the edge of the water. Like Monet, Hoschedé-Monet was inspired by the landscapes of Pourville and filled a sketchbook with views of the cliffs and the surrounding villages (pl. 1). In his account of Hoschedé-Monet's adolescence, Jean-Pierre writes that she began painting *en plein air* in 1882. Few canvases can be definitively assigned to this earliest period in Pourville, and it was not until the Hoschedé and Monet families moved to Giverny in the spring of 1883 that she began to paint consistently, accompanying Monet on his daily walks through the countryside, canvases and paints in tow.

HAYSTACKS IN GIVERNY

At first glance, Hoschedé-Monet's paintings from the 1880s and '90s are most striking in their resemblance to the better-known canvases by Monet: *The Small Grainstacks* (*Les Moyettes*) (pl. 5) and *Morning on the Seine (Matinée sur la Seine)* (pl. 13) share viewpoints with the *Small Grainstacks* (*Les Demoiselles de Giverny*, 1894; Israel Museum, Jerusalem), and the *Morning on the Seine* series (1896–97, see figs. 37 and 38).[10] Jean-Pierre describes the *plein air* practice shared by Hoschedé-Monet and Monet during those early years in Giverny:

> She helped him in all circumstances, whether in the studio or in the garden or accompanying him to various sites, transporting his canvases and easel as well as her own. She did it all with the help of a wheelbarrow, following elusive paths, across fields and meadows sometimes drenched in dew. That was the case, for example, with his morning views of the Seine. Here again, she would help her stepfather by taking up the oars of the canoe.[11]

In the absence of any published diaries or memoirs, family letters and Jean-Pierre's biography remain the primary texts for understanding Hoschedé-Monet's ambitions and interests during this early period in Giverny. His description of his sister's painting practice in the 1880s and early 1890s is singularly focused on her role as a companion of and assistant to Monet, but her paintings reveal a nascent artistic independence.

In the spring of 1893, Hoschedé-Monet and Monet painted the haystacks in the meadow just

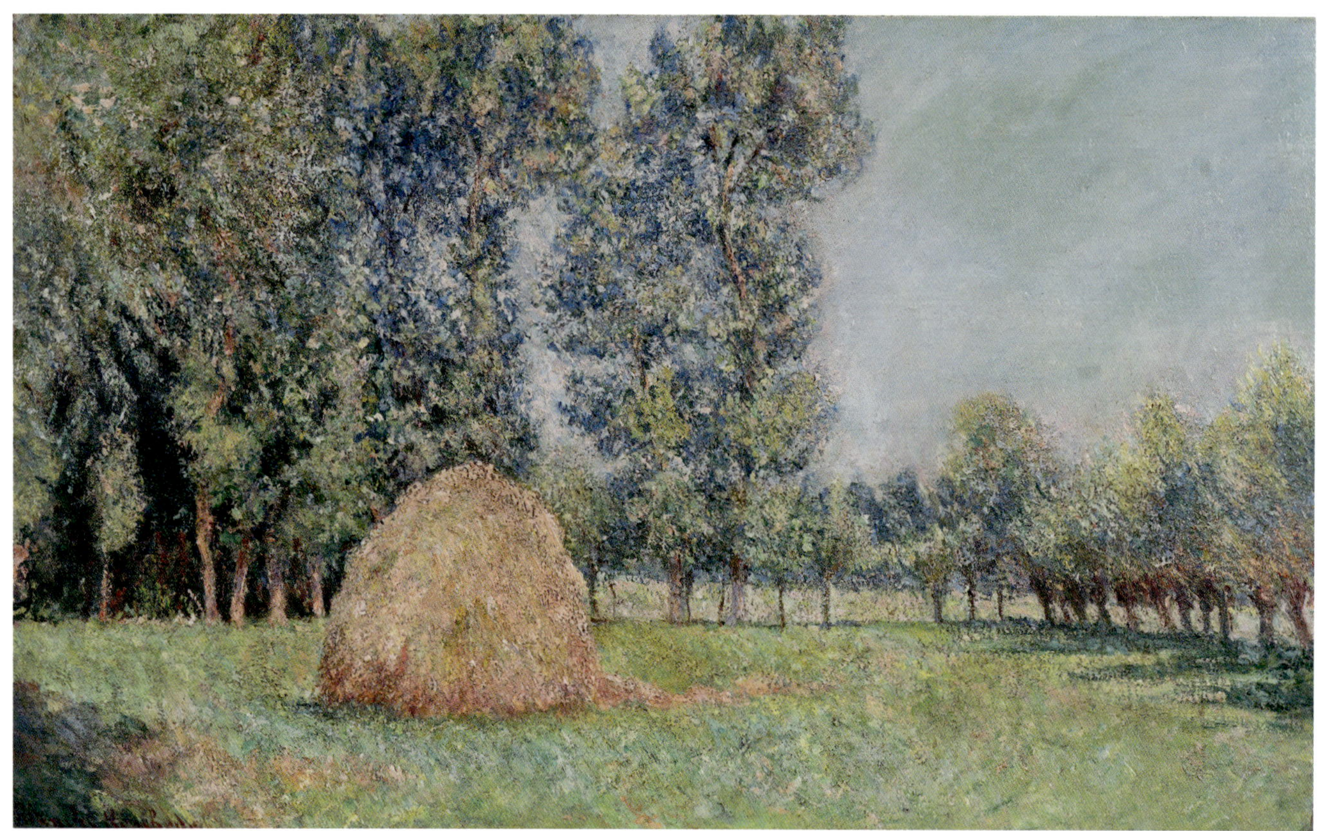

south of the shared family property in Giverny, where Monet would later excavate the water lily pond and plant its surrounding gardens. Monet's versions vary in their palettes and atmospheric effects, but all three present the same composition: a single haystack at or near center, with a row of trees just below the horizon line and haystacks dotting the meadow beyond.[12] One of Hoschedé-Monet's compositions, *Haystack at Giverny* (*Meule à Giverny*) (fig. 3, pl. 4), now in a private collection, pictures the monolithic haystack from a side angle. The row of trees that fills the horizon of Monet's paintings runs diagonally on the right, with the haystack positioned off-center to the left. By moving her easel to show the haystack from the side as compared to Monet's versions, Hoschedé-Monet isolates the stack, further simplifying the motif. A band of blue sky and clouds above the trees fills the top quarter of Monet's canvases, but in her version Hoschedé-Monet reserves a large square

Fig. 3 Blanche Hoschedé-Monet, *Haystack at Giverny* (*Meule à Giverny*), ca. 1893.
[See pl. 4]

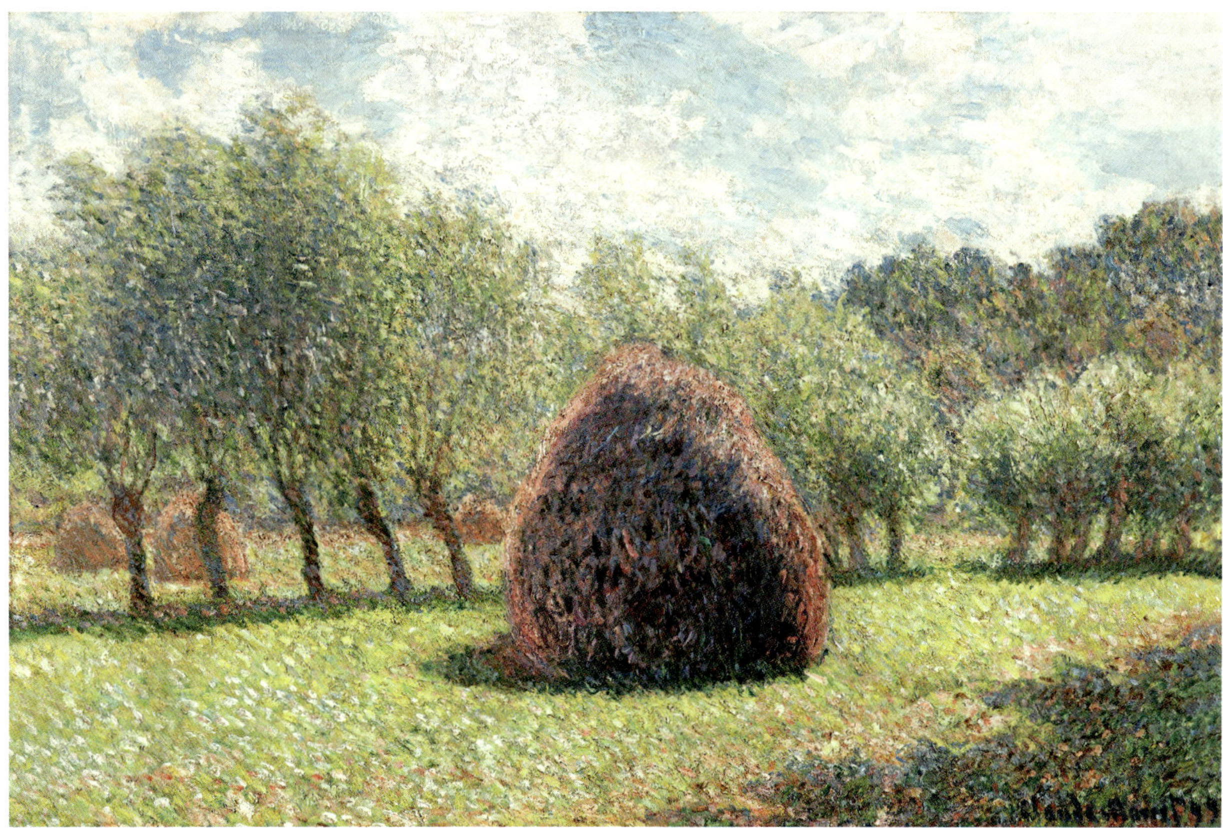

of clear blue sky in the upper right corner. While her handling of the haystack, trees, and meadow is similar to Monet's brushwork in *Haystacks at Giverny (Meules à Giverny)* (fig. 4), the sky is worked up as a whole, with even color applied in overlapping brushstrokes.

Although her artistic practice was still shaped by her daily excursions with Monet, Hoschedé-Monet was developing a style that was recognizably her own. Compositional shifts to open the sky in *Haystack at Giverny*, or to fill all four corners of the canvas with foliage in *Morning on the Seine*, are evidence of her attention to compositional balance and her commitment to the motif, even as Monet was willing to subsume the subject in color and light. Monet took Hoschedé-Monet's ambitions as an artist seriously, instructing her to draw and to "get used to putting things in the right place," and even depicting her at her easel in an 1887 portrait of her and her sister Suzanne (fig. 5).[13]

Fig. 4 Claude Monet, *Haystacks at Giverny (Meules à Giverny)*, 1893. Oil on canvas, 25⅞ × 39½ in. (65.5 × 100.2 cm). Private collection

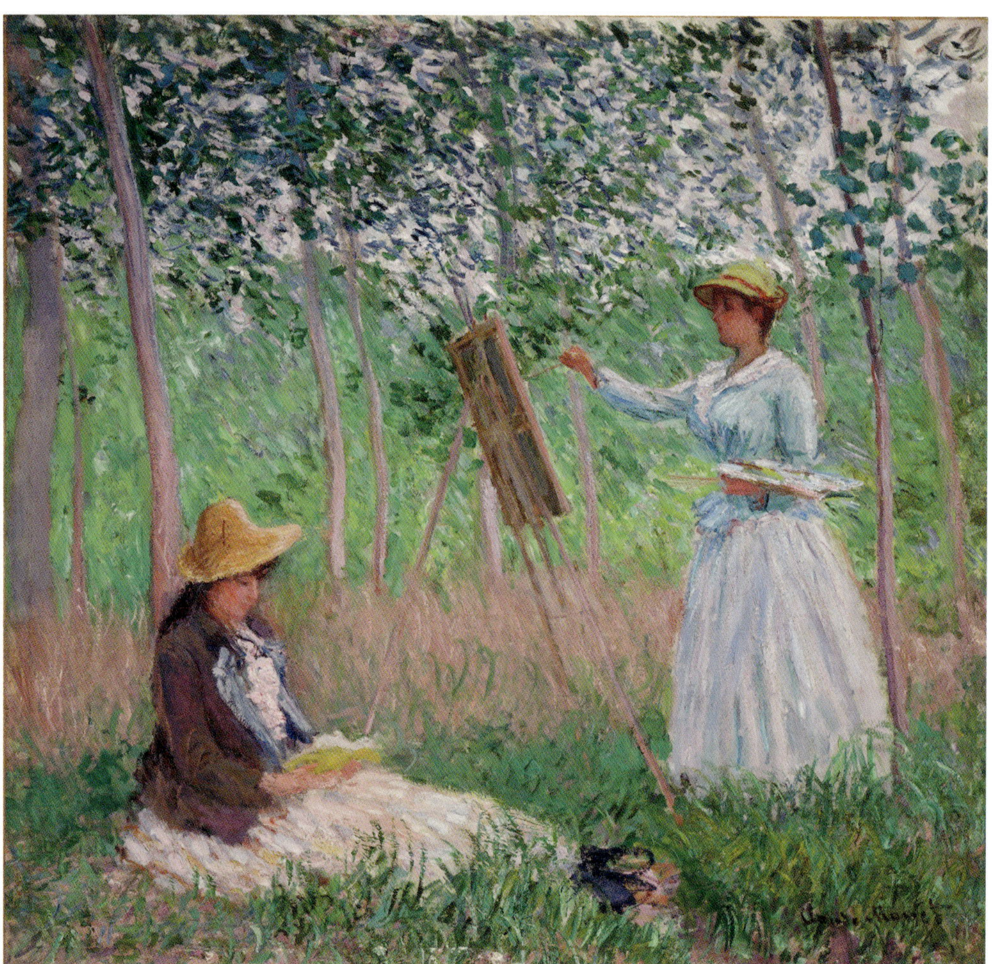

By the early 1890s, Hoschedé-Monet had begun to cultivate a reputation for herself outside of her immediate family. In her memoirs, Julie Manet (daughter of Berthe Morisot and niece of Édouard Manet) described seeing Hoschedé-Monet's paintings on a visit to Giverny in 1893, and in 1892 the American artist Theodore Robinson wrote in his diary: "I saw some things by Mlle. Blanche, she has improved greatly since I saw her work last—a spring landscape, sold to Potter Palmer quite charming. . . ."[14]

Fig. 5 Claude Monet, *In the Woods at Giverny: Blanche Hoschedé at Her Easel with Suzanne Hoschedé Reading* (*Dans le Marais de Giverny, Suzanne lisant et Blanche peignant*), 1887. Oil on canvas, 36 × 38½ in. (91.4 × 97.8 cm). Los Angeles County Museum of Art (M.46.3.4)

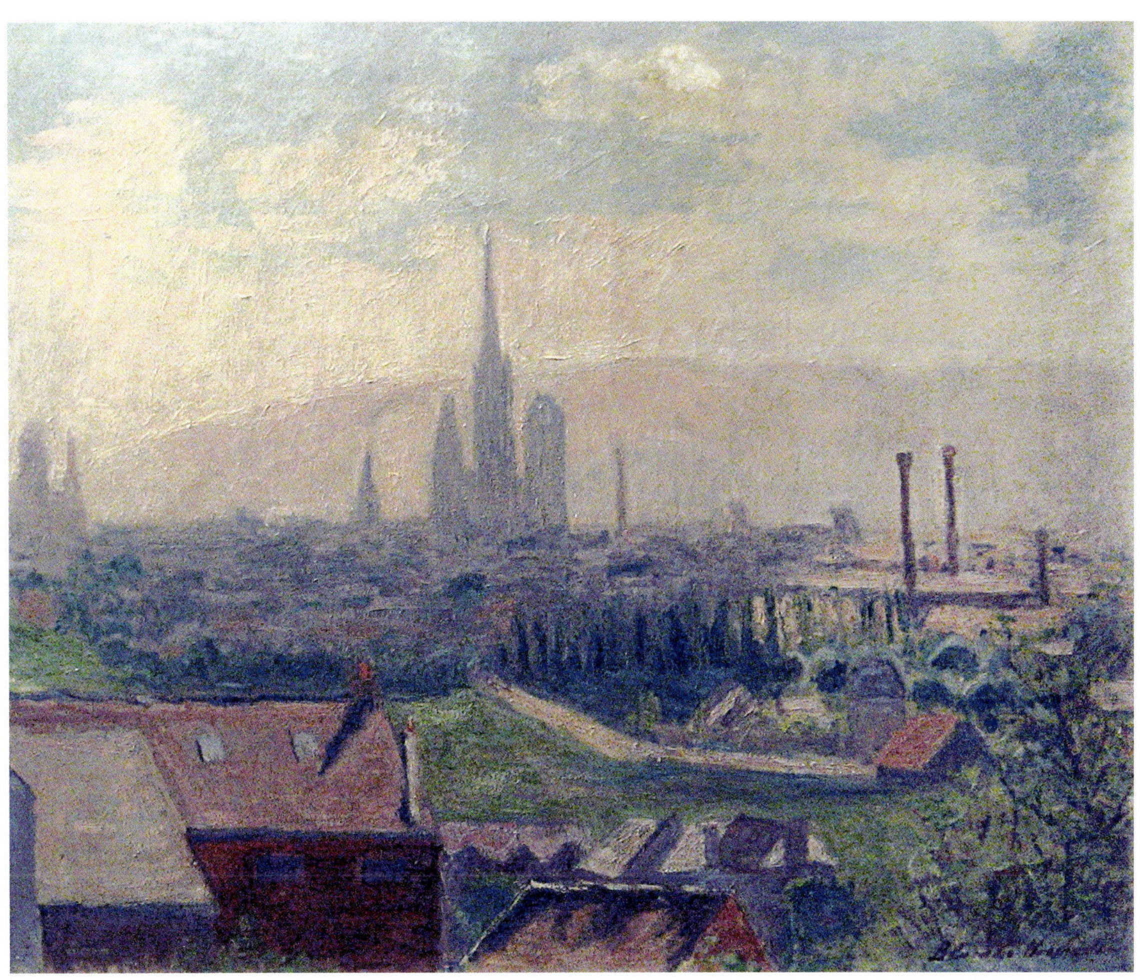

MADAME JEAN MONET

In 1897, Hoschedé-Monet married Monet's eldest son, Jean. The couple moved to Rouen, where Hoschedé-Monet found new subjects for her paintings, including the city itself. This period was one of meaningful productivity for Hoschedé-Monet, who was captivated by the intersection of the natural and industrial worlds. She made cityscapes from her window, depicted her garden in all seasons as well as views of meadows and pine trees in nearby villages, and painted ambitious landscapes in the neighboring towns of Croisset, Eauplet, and Saint-Adrien. In her *View of*

Fig. 6   Blanche Hoschedé-Monet, *View of Rouen* (*Vue générale de Rouen*), ca. 1900. [See pl. 14]

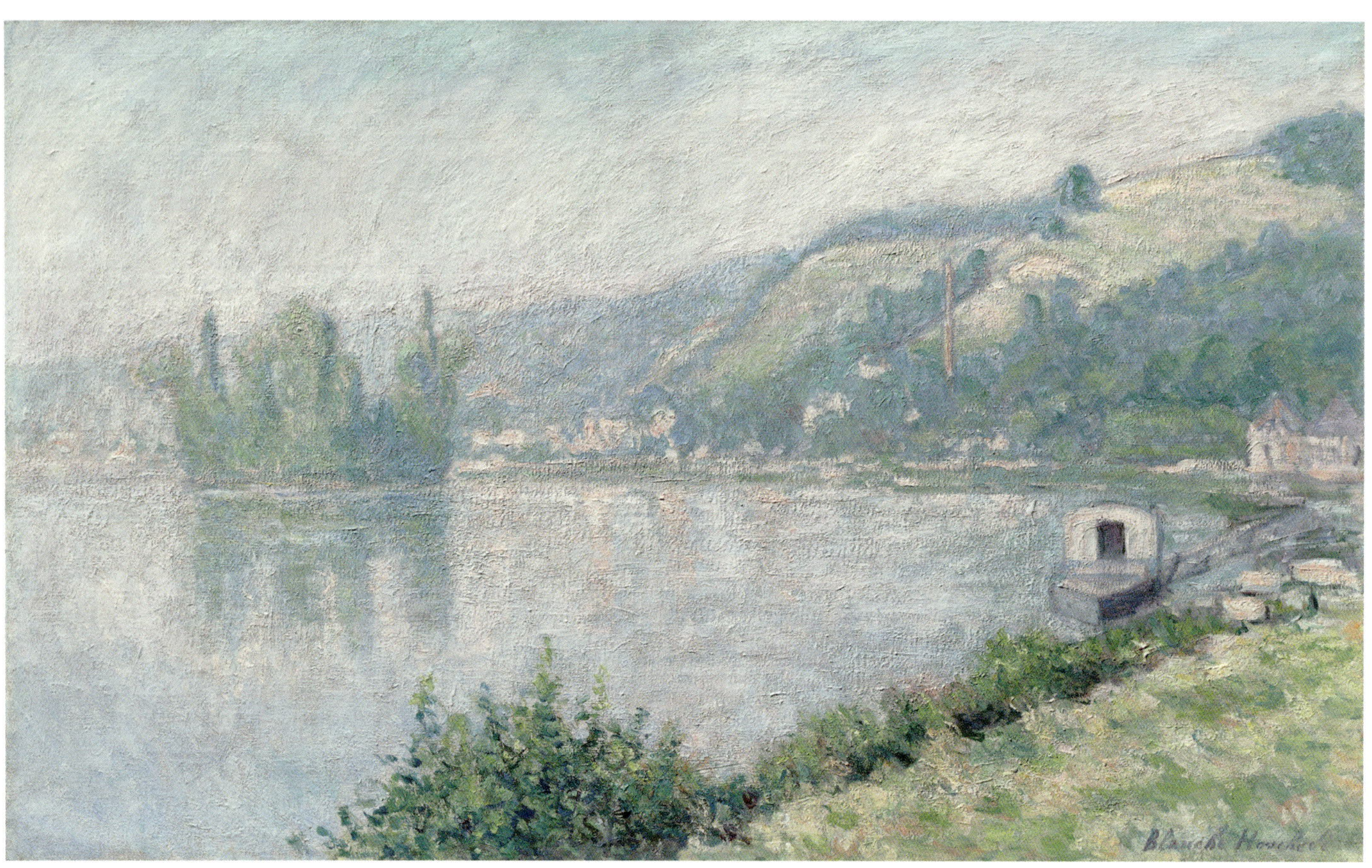

Rouen (*Vue générale de Rouen*) (fig. 6, pl. 14), from around 1900, she pulls the bottom third of the canvas into focus, delineating nearby houses and trees, with two industrial smokestacks close to the horizon line at right cast in bright sunlight. Whereas Monet had focused on the effects of light and atmosphere on the ornate façade of Rouen Cathedral, painting over thirty canvases between 1892 and 1894, Hoschedé-Monet pushes the cathedral's spire and towers into shadow, rendering the whole as a hazy silhouette against the distant hills.

Around the same time, Hoschedé-Monet painted several versions of a view of the Seine from Croisset, a small village on the right bank just west of Rouen (including pls. 17 and 18). Like the *View of Rouen*, they are part of her wholly independent painting practice and do not correspond to any work by Monet. One version, now in a private collection,

Fig. 7   Blanche Hoschedé-Monet, *The Seine at Croisset* (*La Seine à Croisset*), ca. 1897–1910. [See pl. 18]

shows a dock and the *bateau omnibus* that connected cities and towns on the Seine (fig. 7). While the painting demonstrates the clear influence of the school of Impressionist painters in Giverny, it resists characterization as a mere imitation of Monet's style. The palette of blues and cool greens is typical for Hoschedé-Monet during this period, as is the careful attention to the horizon and the reflection of sky, hills, and trees. Painted just as she was beginning to establish a reputation for herself among the small group of artists known as the École de Rouen, Hoschedé-Monet chose a view of the Seine favored by Rouennais artists such as Albert Lebourg (fig. 8) and Léon-Jules Lemaître. This period of productivity and independence from the Giverny school corresponds with a commitment to the public exhibition of her paintings. Hoschedé-Monet had participated in the Salon des Indépendants in Paris in 1905, 1906, and 1907, and between 1907 and 1913 she exhibited regularly with the Société des Artistes Rouennais. She showed substantial groups of pictures in Rouen, sending six in 1908 and 1910, and another five in 1911.[15]

After a conflict between Jean Monet and his uncle Léon Monet over the family business in Rouen in 1910, Hoschedé-Monet and her husband moved to Beaumont-le-Roger. There, she found new subjects for her paintings, venturing out into landscapes similar to those in Giverny but crafting compositions entirely her own. Paintings like *Meadows downstream from Rouen* (*Prés en aval de Rouen*) (pls. 19 and 20) show the lingering influence of Monet and his circle, with the palette of bright blues and greens, but the bird's-eye view is evidence of her close ties to the circle of painters in Rouen. Synthesizing styles from the artistic communities that were so central to her practice as a young artist in her twenties and thirties, Hoschedé-Monet was making her own way as a painter, often repeating compositions before arriving at the right one. But just as she was settling in as a midcareer artist, sending paintings annually to the Salon de la Société des Artistes Rouennais, the Hoschedé and Monet families were upended by loss. Soon after the death of Alice in 1911, Jean suffered a stroke and Hoschedé-Monet became his primary caregiver. In the spring of 1913, Monet bought a house for Hoschedé-Monet and her husband in Giverny, the Villa des Pinsons, where they lived together until Jean's death in February 1914. Soon after, Hoschedé-Monet returned to the family property to care for the home and for Monet. The artist that she had first met as a young girl was now seventy-four years old.

HOSCHEDÉ, MONET, HOSCHEDÉ-MONET

In the preface for an exhibition at the Charles E. Slatkin Galleries in New York City in 1960, Jean-Pierre Hoschedé wrote:

> Why is the talent of Blanche Hoschedé, which has not been in doubt for some time, still ignored? Why aren't the works

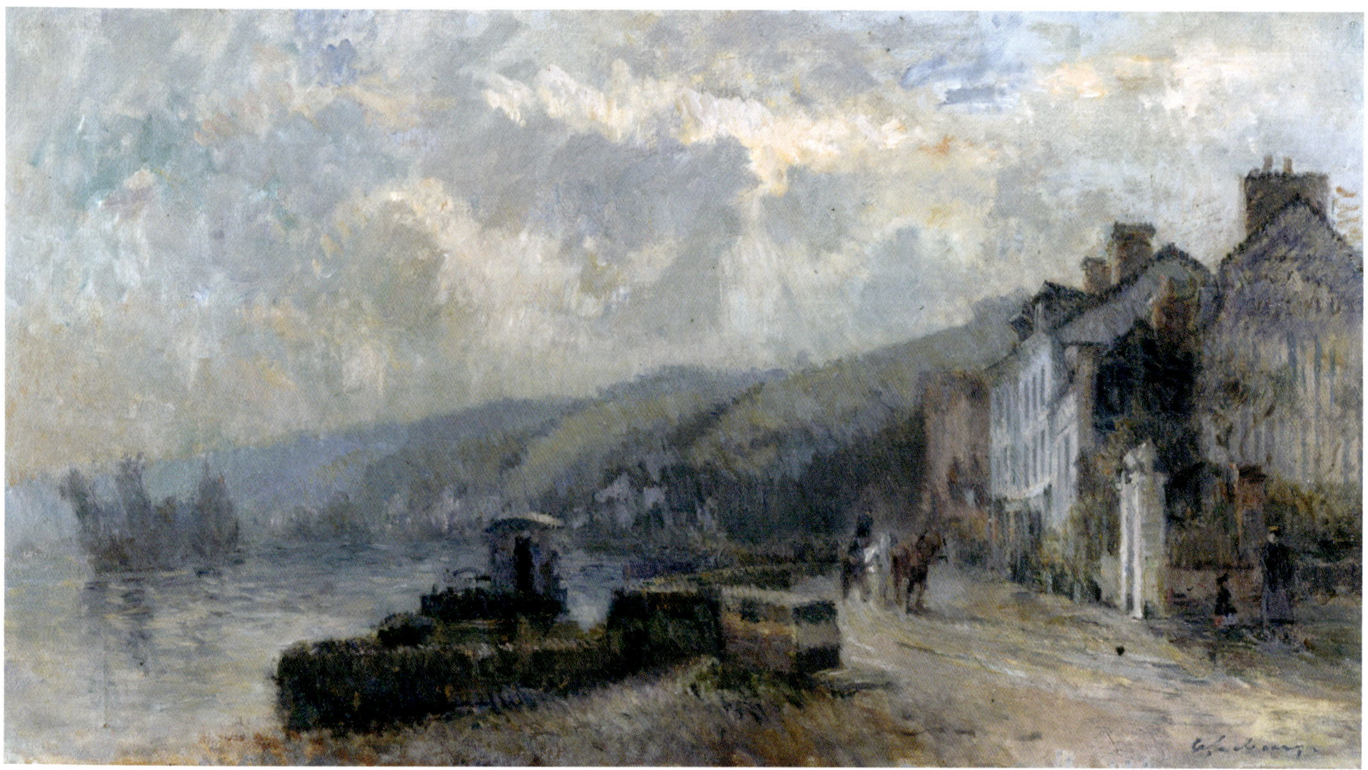

valued at what they should be? It is easy to answer these questions: a) because Blanche Hoschedé never had the slightest ambition; b) because being Claude Monet's daughter-in-law was precisely why she never benefitted from his protection, nor from the great name that also became hers; c) because she painted solely for her own pleasure.[16]

As Nicolas Bondenet, Nancy Mowll Mathews, and Philippe Piguet explore in their essays,

Hoschedé-Monet's ties to Monet defined her personal and artistic life. Her work is inseparable from the community they built in Giverny, from the years she spent traveling across Normandy to visit family, and from the final decades of her life spent living with and later without Monet in the shared family home. The exhibitions and books that have presented her paintings to the public have understandably focused on those ties, and Jean-Pierre's supposition that her relative obscurity can be blamed on "the great name that also became hers" rings true.

Fig. 8   Albert Lebourg, *Rainy Weather*
(*Temps de pluie*), ca. 1901. Oil on canvas,
18⁵⁄₁₆ × 33¹¹⁄₁₆ in. (46.5 × 85.5 cm). Musée des
Beaux-Arts de la Ville de Paris, PPP82

But while Jean-Pierre may have understood his sister as never having "the slightest ambition," her paintings reveal an undeniable passion and determination. An unambitious artist would not fill each day painting *en plein air* alongside her stepfather, cultivate buyers for her pictures, exhibit large groups of canvases in Paris and Rouen, or travel extensively throughout France and beyond, relentless in her pursuit of new motifs and inventive compositions. And while her family name has certainly shaped how her work was and is received, her family life also shaped her career as an artist. Like so many women artists, Hoschedé-Monet spent decades of her life caring for others. As Jean-Pierre notes, in her adolescence she was responsible for the younger children in the Hoschedé and Monet families, and at the midpoint of her artistic career she began to look after her ailing husband. Following his death, she devoted herself to Monet's care and, after 1926, to the house and gardens at Giverny. All the while she painted, and her works attest to her talents, her creative spirit, and her commitment to her art.

Hoschedé-Monet's last painting, *Cyclamens* (see fig. 33), recalls her earliest sunflower painting from 1878 (fig. 2, pl. 39); in each, an arrangement of flowers in a vase placed on a table, a lifetime between them. In addition to her talents as a painter, she was, as her brother described, the "guardian of the many sentimental memories she found everywhere, among the flowers, in the garden, among the water lilies."[17] Through her

art, surviving letters, and her brother's biography, this exhibition and accompanying catalogue takes measure of seventy years of painting and brings to light the life of Blanche Hoschedé-Monet, a critical figure in the artistic colony at Giverny and a remarkable artist in her own right.

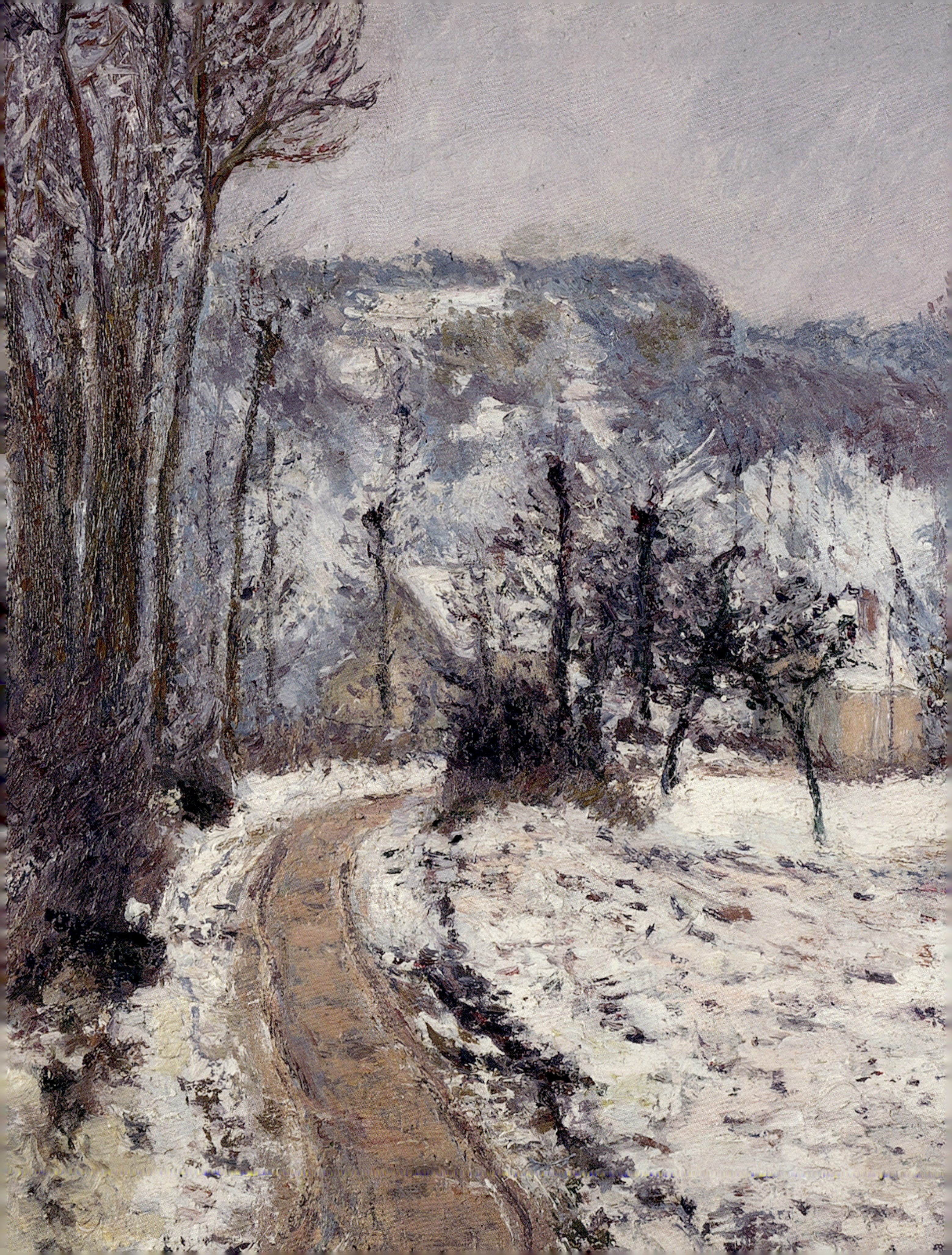

THE LAST OF THE IMPRESSIONISTS

Nicolas Bondenet

"Without his daughter-in-law, Claude Monet would have lived in an isolation that would have killed him; it was she who kept him alive for us, posterity must not forget her."
—René Gimpel, *Journal d'un collectionneur*[1]

The death of Alice Hoschedé in 1911 left Claude Monet alone and despondent and living with his son, Michel Monet, in the great house at Giverny. In 1912, Jean Monet fell gravely ill, and he and Blanche Hoschedé-Monet, married since 1897, hurriedly left Beaumont-le-Roger to return to Giverny and their family. The couple moved into the Villa des Pinsons at the other end of the village; however, on February 9, 1914, Jean succumbed to his illness, taking years of carefree happiness with him. The Belle Époque was now over, and World War I sounded the death knell.

Jean-Pierre Hoschedé left for the front; Michel Monet, exempted from service, enlisted as a volunteer. Marthe Hoschedé, the eldest sister, married her brother-in-law Theodore Earl Butler following Suzanne Hoschedé's death, and fled to the United States with her niece and nephew, Lily and Jim. Blanche, widowed and alone, abandoned her paintbrushes. She moved back into her stepfather and father-in-law's home and assumed the role of steward and head of the household.

In the eyes of many, Blanche Hoschedé-Monet became the "blue angel" that Georges Clemenceau describes in his correspondence[2]—loyal and considerate by the side of the inconsolable old man. During this troubled period, she was the driving force that stimulated the creativity of the master of Impressionism and pulled him out of the slump into which the successive deaths of Suzanne, Alice, and Jean had plunged him. Hoschedé-Monet assisted Monet in his great enterprise—his great masterpiece—the *Water Lilies*, for which he built a vast, new studio (fig. 29). It was a harbor of peace amid a war-torn Europe. She tirelessly supported her stepfather in his final years of creation, sharing his pain and joy until December 5, 1926.

With the death of Claude Monet, an entire world disappeared. The life that had been so abundant had been swept away since the beginning

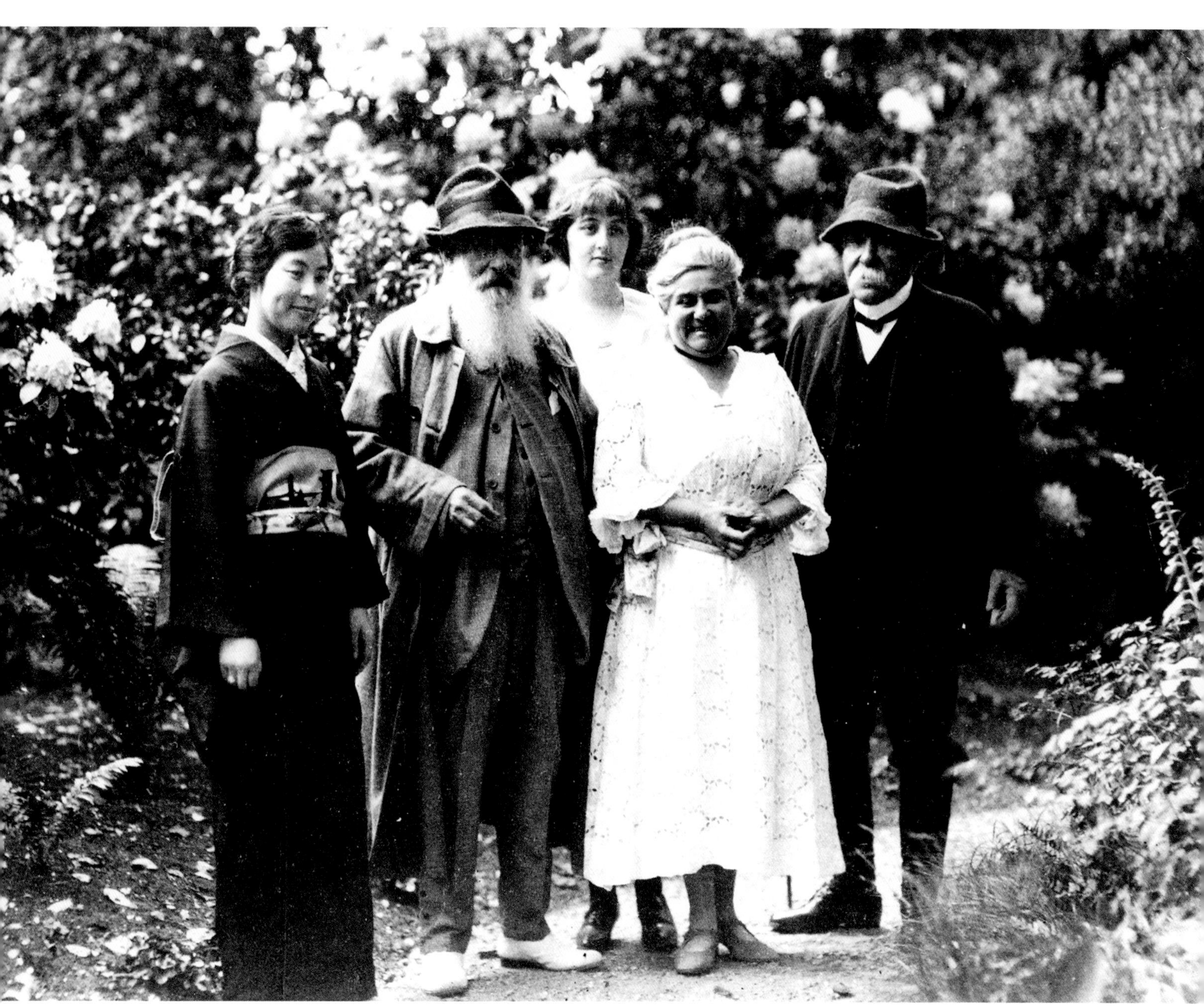

Fig. 9 Blanche Hoschedé-Monet (center) in the company of Claude Monet (left), Georges Clemenceau (right), and Lily Butler (back), June 1921. Collection of Philippe Piguet

of the war. Giverny was left as nothing more than a small village, quiet and empty. Hoschedé-Monet, alone in the great house, was sixty years old. Reputedly, she had not touched her paintbrushes in twelve years.

Hoschedé-Monet, much more than her stepbrother Michel Monet, was the living memory of the master of Giverny. As Monet's only heir, Michel, who lived in Sorel-Moussel near Dreux with his wife, Gabrielle Bonaventure, asked Blanche to stay at the family home in Giverny and look after it until her death. She maintained the house and the flower beds in the state that Claude Monet had left them, caring for the irises, Japanese peonies, and water lilies. In this capacity she also inherited the management of Monet's remaining works, a heavy responsibility that she fulfilled with fervor and determination. She also ensured with attention and vigilance that the large series of *Water Lilies* gifted to the French state in 1922 would be installed at the Musée de l'Orangerie as outlined in Monet's will. "We did all of that according to his wishes, and that is why, as long as we live, we will change nothing as it currently stands; we will ensure that what he wanted remains so. His will is clear."[3]

However, on the occasion of the exhibition *L'Art flamand de van Eyck à Bruegel* at the Orangerie in 1935, tapestries covered the panels of the *Water Lilies*. These were hung in defiance of the terms of Monet's donation, which prohibited the removal of the paintings or the exhibition of other works in their place. Unwilling to respect the wishes of the donation, the museum's administration proposed moving the works to the Musée d'Art Moderne de Paris. Hoschedé-Monet was not at all happy with this, and benefited from the support of Georges Clemenceau, who helped her negotiate with the Orangerie. She also assisted with details for his memoir on Monet, *Claude Monet: Les Nymphéas*, as she had done for Gustave Geffroy for his biography of Claude Monet in 1922.

After so many years without painting and entirely dedicated to running the household and helping her stepfather, Hoschedé-Monet, encouraged by her friend Clemenceau, decided to take up her paints and brushes once again. She was now the painter of the family, the heir of the master. Brushes in hand, Hoschedé-Monet tirelessly reproduced Monet's garden, also painting the house, and of course the pond of water lilies, as if to prevent it all from fading away. She painted to remember her former happiness and to console herself. It seemed she was heeding Clemenceau's advice: "Hold fast to your brushes. . . . They have and will have the virtue of making you forget the void."[4]

Hoschedé-Monet had started living again. She frequently received Monet's friends at the house in Giverny, including Thadée Natanson and the painters André Barbier, Paul Signac, Pierre Bonnard, Édouard Vuillard, and Maximilien Luce, as well as many writers and journalists who had come to learn from her about Claude Monet. Always charming, down-to-earth, and kind, she welcomed visitors on pilgrimage who came to

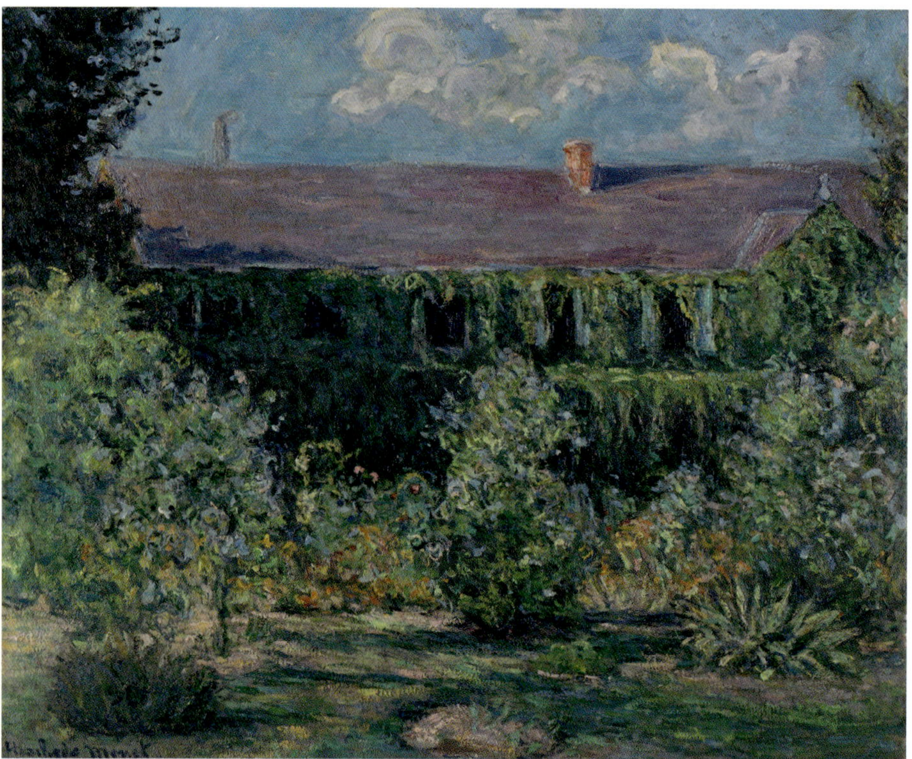

admire the property and gardens. In this way, despite her humble disposition, Hoschedé-Monet was the first to initiate the tourism at Giverny surrounding the garden and water lily pond, which were always well maintained and in bloom.

By this time, the landscapes of Giverny were rarely depicted in Hoschedé-Monet's paintings. She no longer moved about the surrounding countryside as she had before and preferred the shady softness of the garden at home or at her nephews' homes, as well as views of the neighboring farm from her window. In bad weather, always busy, she devoted herself to still lifes, bouquets of flowers, fruits, or vegetables (as in fig. 11).

Often presented as modest in the extreme, Hoschedé-Monet and her work became better known through the help of dealers and gallerists. Beginning in 1926 with the loss of the master of Impressionism, the popularity of Monet's artistic heir increased tenfold. The Galerie Durand-Ruel began to purchase Hoschedé-Monet's paintings for between 1,000 and 3,000 francs, when it had previously bought them for between 100 and 300 francs.[5]

Fig. 10 Blanche Hoschedé-Monet, *The House and Garden of Claude Monet, Giverny* (*La Maison et le jardin de Claude Monet, Giverny*), after 1926. [See pl. 25]

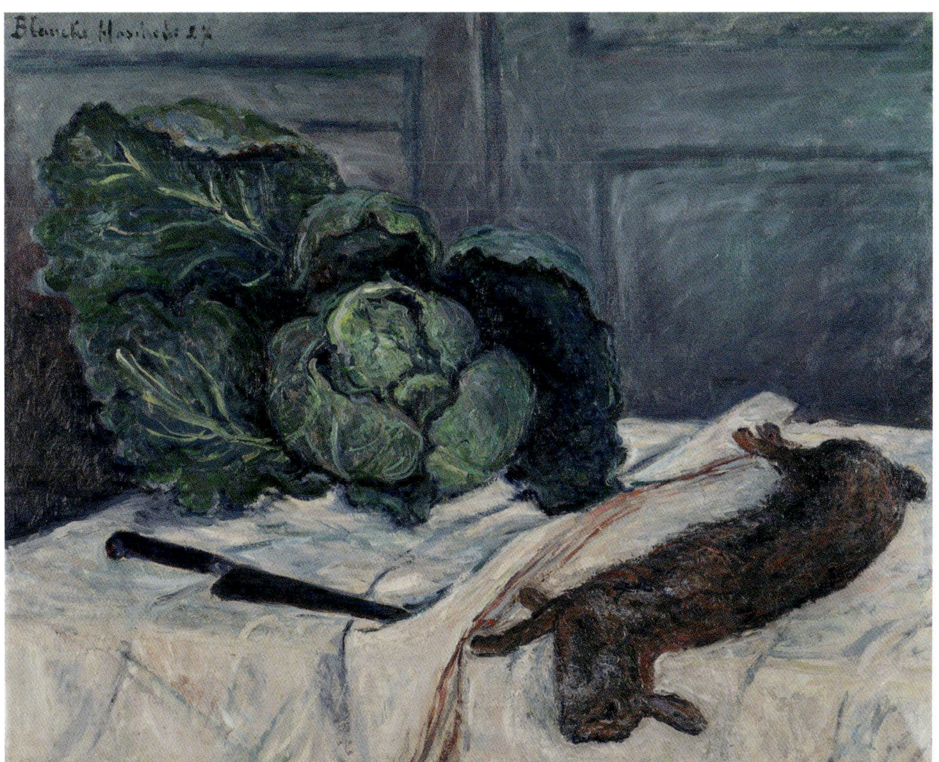

In November 1927, Galerie Bernheim-Jeune offered Hoschedé-Monet her first solo exhibition, followed by a second in 1931. She found her way back to the Salon des Indépendants in Paris from 1929 to 1935 and showed again at the Salon de Vernon in 1929 and 1942, as well as the Salon de la Société des Artistes Rouennais from 1931 to 1935. The critics were captivated. Lucien Rebatet wrote in *Le Petit Parisien* on November 7, 1942: "Madame Blanche Hoschedé did not bore her contemporaries by the publicity of her name. She could however boast of many titles that remain. . . to some specialists . . . unknown. Of course, the influence of Claude Monet is constantly present in these landscapes, these still lifes. But it does not stifle the femininity that appears in her paintings with great freshness."[6]

However, the age of Impressionism was over, and the world had made room for new generations of artists and movements—including the École de Paris, Art Deco and the International Style, and Dadaism and Surrealism—while Hoschedé-Monet loyally painted in the spirit of Monet for her own enjoyment. She nevertheless developed

Fig. 11 Blanche Hoschedé-Monet, *Still Life with Cabbage and Rabbit* (*Nature morte au chou et au lapin*), 1927. [See pl. 23]

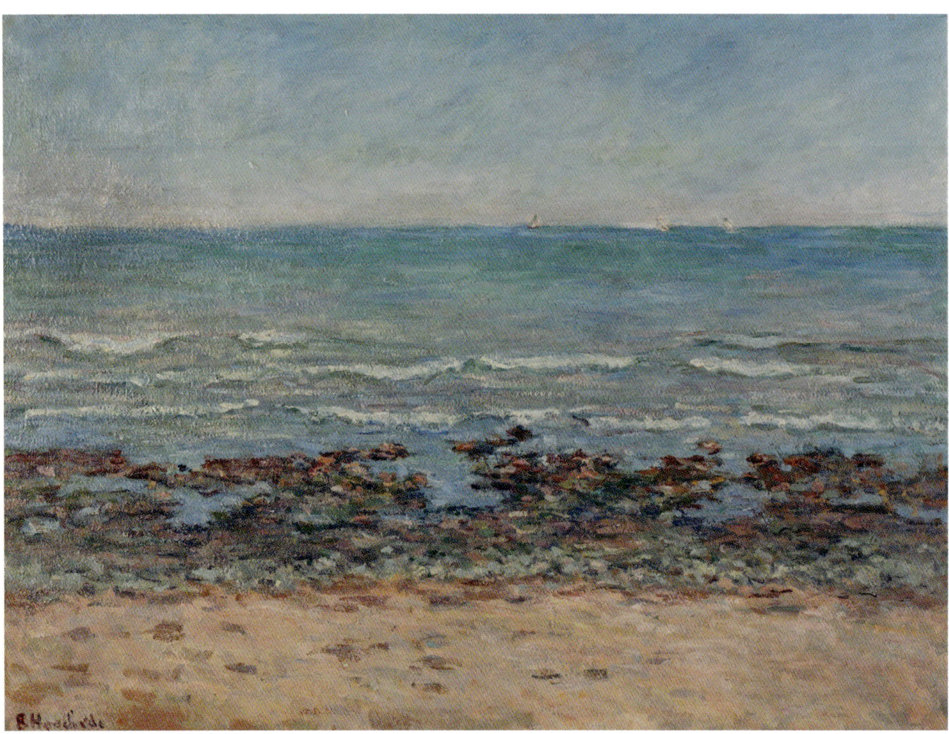

a very personal approach. This new period of
her work is largely marked by an interest in floral
subjects and garden views, which, despite their
varied range of color seem more somber, less bright
and luminous than before. The blunter contrasts
diverge sharply from the softer and more nuanced
tones of her earlier period, and the brushstrokes
are broader and more fluid. One also is struck by
the less dynamic compositions, which are framed
and smothered by vegetation—always present
is the garden.

It was Hoschedé-Monet's many trips traveling
throughout the regions of France and abroad that
gave her work a breath of air, an unprecedented
freshness, renewed lighting and atmosphere, and
new pictorial horizons, as seen in the blue of the
Atlantic Ocean and the English Channel (fig. 12),
the turquoise of Lake Bourget (pl. 32), the light
of the South of France, Venice and Italy, and in
the mountains. Staying at Clemenceau's home on
three separate occasions between 1927 and 1929,
in the former fisherman's cottage at Saint-Vincent-
sur-Jard in Vendée, "she painted the misty sea
and the dancing flowers"[7] and the small house of
Belébat situated on the dune where Clemenceau
had managed to grow a richly flowered garden

Fig. 12 Blanche Hoschedé-Monet, *The
Beach at Diélette (The English Channel)*
(*La Plage de Diélette [Manche]*), ca. 1932–39.
[See pl. 30]

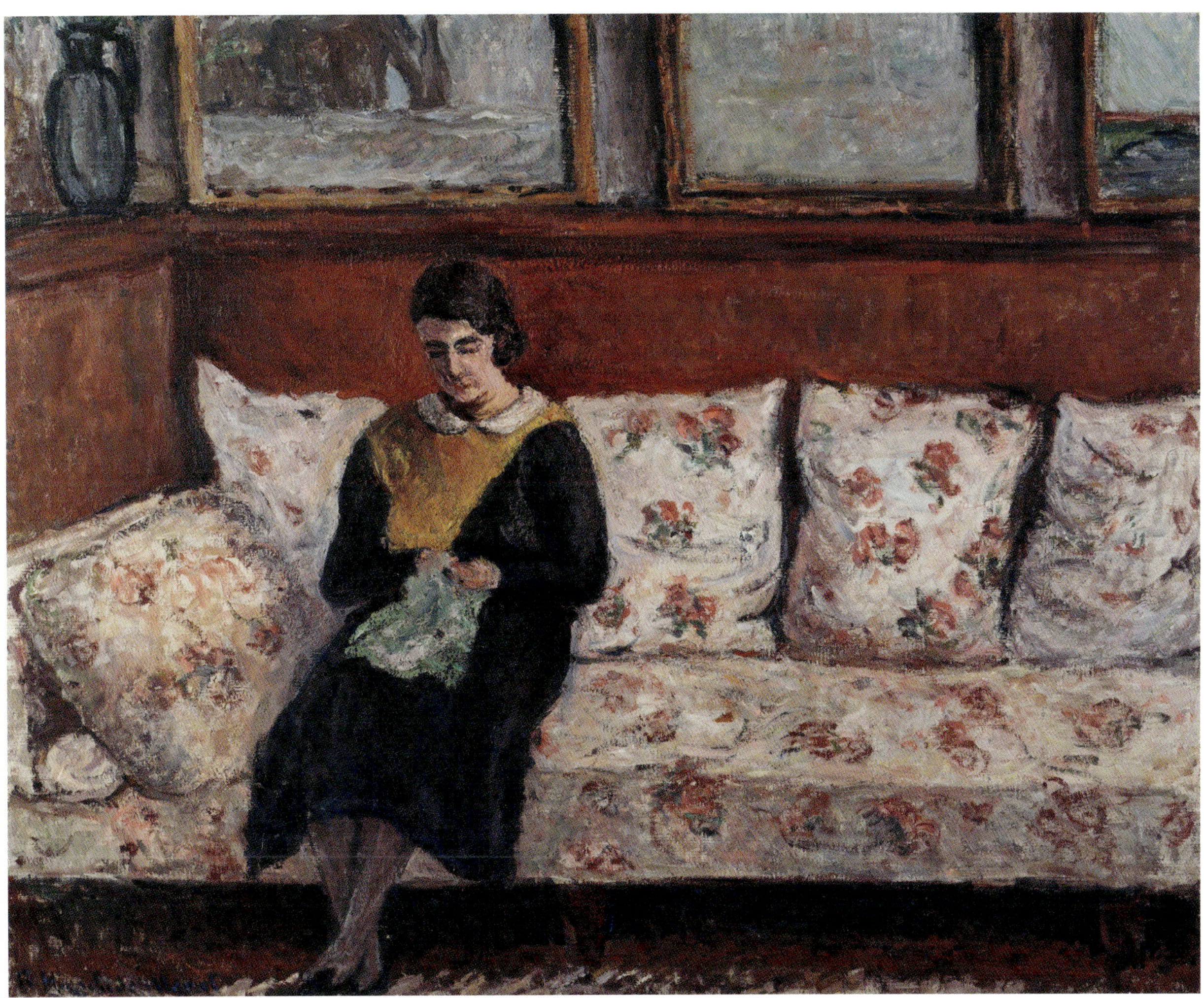

in the sand (pls. 27, 28). Like Monet in his time, Hoschedé-Monet went to Venice in 1930 and then to Bassano del Grappa accompanied by her brother, Jean-Pierre Hoschedé, before stopping over in Saint-Jean-Cap-Ferrat outside of Nice. She also visited Lake Bourget, near Switzerland. Each site possessed its own range of color, from snow-capped peaks at sunrise to sunny beaches on the English Channel. The canvases are bright and colorful in shades of blue and turquoise, with free and spirited brushstrokes, the best of which were recognized at the salons and in the press:

Fig. 13 Blanche Hoschedé-Monet, *Nitia Salerou in the Salon, Giverny (Nitia Salerou à Giverny)*, ca. 1940. Oil on canvas, 25⁹⁄₁₆ × 31⁷⁄₈ in. (65 × 81 cm). Musée Blanche Hoschedé-Monet, Vernon (2006.2.1)

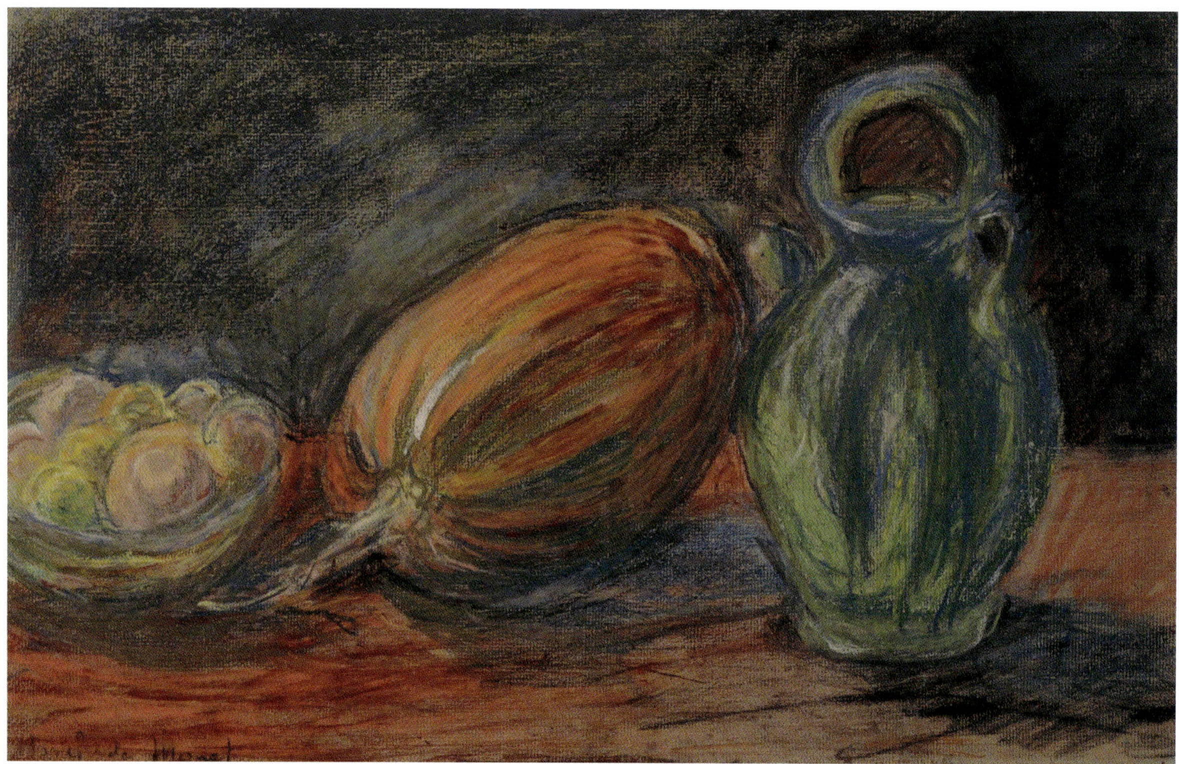

Madame Blanche Hoschedé-Monet is more than the heiress of a great name. Daughter of the most prestigious colorist of the end of the last century, she felt that the example given by her father, Claude Monet, should still be followed, and that the elements he loved were still worthy of being painted.[8] We do not find, therefore, in the works of Madame Blanche Hoschedé-Monet, any trace of this false originality by which so many female painters, eager to make a name for themselves, seek to impress the gallery. You will hardly see any of Madame Blanche Hoschedé-Monet's works except at the Salon without a jury, that of the Indépendants. True talent, nobility of heart and of spirit, are always accompanied by great modesty.[9]

But this newfound happiness was brutally interrupted by a new war. Forced into exile in the summer of 1940 following Germany's invasion of France during World War II, Hoschedé-Monet

Fig. 14   Blanche Hoschedé-Monet, *Still Life with Squash and Blue Pitcher* (*Nature morte à la courge et au pichet bleu*), ca. 1942. Pastel on blue-grey Michallon paper, 11 ⅝ × 18 ¹¹⁄₁₆ in. (29.5 × 47.5 cm). Musée Blanche Hoschedé-Monet, Vernon (99.15.1)

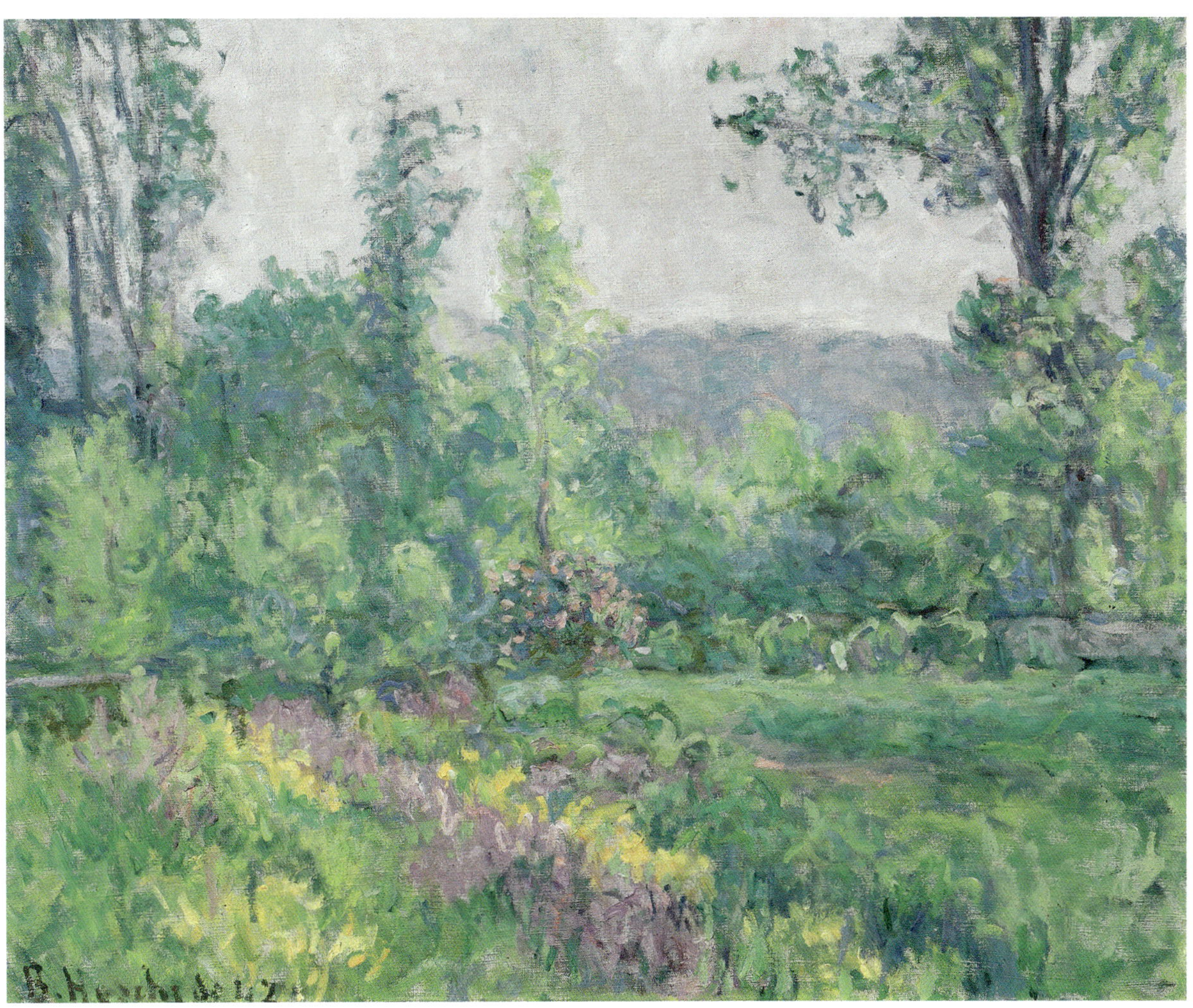

had to leave the house, garden, and many of her stepfather's works behind in Giverny. The entire family found refuge in Gipcy near Moulins in the Allier region, and then in Aix-en-Provence. Upon her return in autumn, noting some thefts but little damage, she decided to remain in Giverny with her youngest sister, Germaine, and her niece, Nitia Salerou (fig. 13).

With the assistance of her brother-in-law, Albert Salerou, mayor of Giverny, Hoschedé-Monet requested help from the director of the Musées Nationaux to prevent the house in Giverny from

Fig. 15 Blanche Hoschedé-Monet, *A Corner of Claude Monet's Garden at Giverny (Coin du jardin de Claude Monet à Giverny)*, 1947. Oil on canvas, 19¾ × 24⅟₁₆ in. (50.1 × 61.1 cm). Private collection (Bonhams, London, October 19, 2023, lot 29)

being requisitioned by the German army. Despite assurance from the commission for the preservation of works of art in France, headed by Count Franz Wolff-Metternich, Hoschedé-Monet had to repeat the request for protection and obtained an order from the German authorities that forbade access to the property by any occupant. The bombings in Vernon sadly did not spare Giverny. The great studio lost its glass roof, and shards of glass pierced some of the canvases from Monet's collection. Blanche, staying in the cellar, remained unshaken. With incredible composure, she also sheltered numerous Giverny locals.

The handwritten notebooks of Louise Damasse, a painter and drawing teacher from Vernon, tell us that during a visit to Giverny in September 1941, Hoschedé-Monet confessed that while Monet's paintings had not suffered too much, "the gardens are seriously damaged, especially by the harsh winters."[10] Times were difficult, and maintaining the gardens was no longer a priority. A group of local artists attempted to continue holding the annual Salon de Vernon exhibition, but Hoschedé-Monet did not participate, except in 1942, when she showed a "still life with blue pitcher" for a charity sale benefiting prisoners of war. This rare pastel drawing is preserved today in the Musée Blanche Hoschedé-Monet (fig. 14). In autumn of the same year, she was granted a third solo exhibition, at the Galerie Alfred Daber in Paris.

Hoschedé-Monet, now over seventy-five years old, barely left Giverny and only chose to set up

her easel in the garden or in her home. She mainly painted her flowers in the garden or arranged in vases, with landscapes and various still lifes exhibited for the last time during her lifetime in the spring of 1947 at the Galerie d'Art Drouot Provence in Paris. One of her last paintings—a spring view of Giverny dated to 1947 that sold at Bonhams in 2023 (fig. 15)—brings together all the virtuosity of an accomplished artist who dedicated her entire life to painting and to the Impressionist movement. The hardships and grief she endured never managed to extinguish her ardent desire to live and paint the beauty of nature.

In late autumn 1947, Hoschedé-Monet fell seriously ill. December had been fatal to Claude Monet, so she fled the harsh Normandy winter for the south of France. Staying in Nice with one of her nieces, she painted a view of Mont Chauve from her window, as well as a bouquet of pink cyclamens (fig. 33). Hoschedé-Monet died suddenly on December 8, 1947, at the age of eighty-two. Buried on December 20, 1947, in the Giverny cemetery, she now rests in the family tomb alongside her parents, Ernest and Alice Hoschedé; her husband, Jean Monet; and her stepfather, Claude Monet.

Following Hoschedé-Monet's death, her brother Jean-Pierre Hoschedé ensured that his sister's memory would be preserved and her legacy nurtured. In 1949, he donated *The Water Lily Pond, Giverny* (*Le Bassin aux nymphéas, Giverny*) to the Musée Municipal de Vernon (fig. 16). This would be the first work by Hoschedé-Monet to enter the

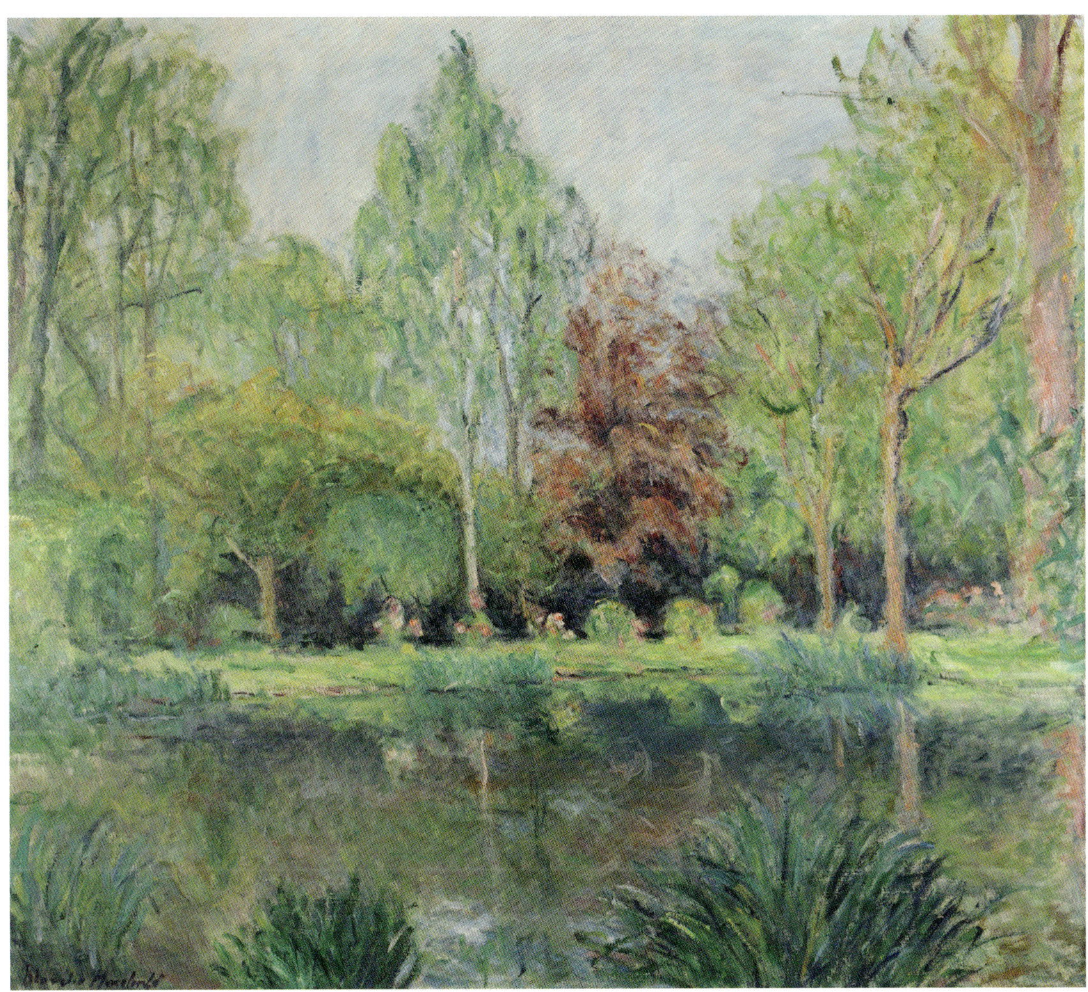

collection of the museum that would eventually come to bear her name. He also organized a solo exhibition of his sister's work at Vernon's Salle des Fêtes in 1957 and wrote a first biographical essay about her in 1961. Further biographical work has been conducted by Philippe Piguet, the great-grandson of Alice Hoschedé, who is currently writing the catalogue raisonné of Hoschedé-Monet's oeuvre.

Since her death, many exhibitions have brought Hoschedé-Monet's work to light and to the attention of the public. These include the show at

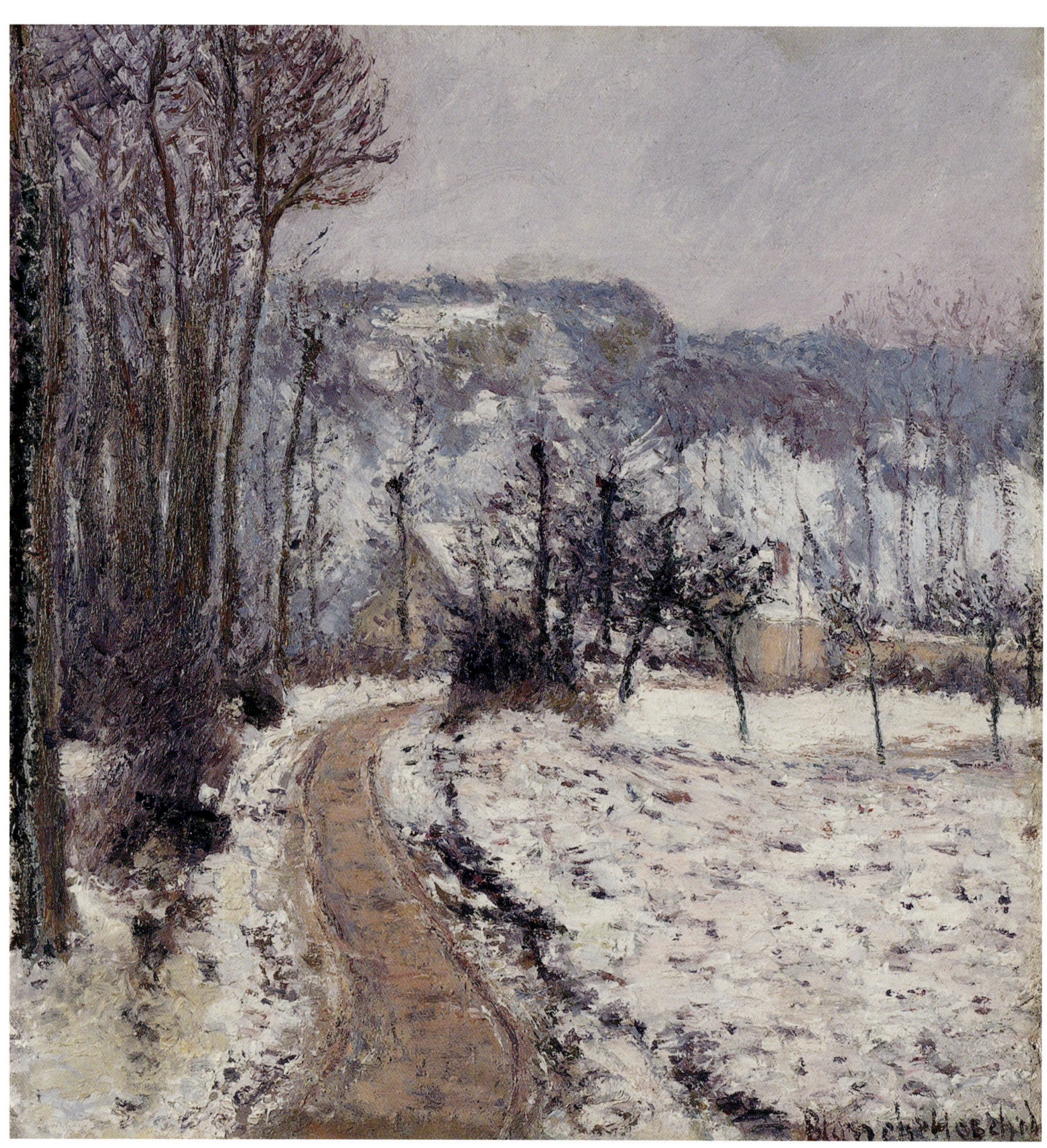

Fig. 17 Blanche Hoschedé-Monet, *Snowy landscape, Valley of the Seine, Normandy* (*Paysage enneigé, val de Seine normand*), before 1914. Oil on canvas, 16⅛ × 16⅛ in. (41 × 41 cm). Musée Blanche Hoschedé-Monet, Vernon (2024.1.1)

the Galerie Zak in Paris (1954), at Rouen's Musée des Beaux-Arts (1959), and at the Charles E. Slatkin Galleries in New York (1960). Titled *Claude Monet and the Giverny Artists*, this exhibition presented twelve paintings by Hoschedé-Monet. In 1966, the Galerie Durand-Ruel brought together paintings by Hoschedé-Monet, Jeanne Baudot, and Paule Gobillard under the title *Dame et Demoiselles,* and finally the Galerie Robert Tuffier in Les Andelys exhibited nearly thirty-five paintings by Hoschedé-Monet in 1971. The city of Vernon and its museum have honored the memory of this major artist from the region on two occasions, in 1991 and in 2017 on the seventieth anniversary of her death. And the exhibition in 2010 at the Musée de Louviers, *Blanche Hoschedé-Monet: Un destin impressionniste*, included a catalogue that constitutes the first attempt at a complete survey of her work.

Hoschedé-Monet had bequeathed two works to the Musées Nationaux, which are now on long-term loan to the Musée des Beaux-Arts de Rouen (pls. 33, 41), and gifted multiple paintings to the Musée Clemenceau, Paris (including pls. 24, 27, 28), as well as one painting to the Musée des Beaux-Arts, La Cohue, Vannes. The bequest of Michel Monet left three works to the Musée Marmottan Monet, Paris (including pl. 26), and the Piguet family has donated paintings to various museums in France (Musée Toulouse-Lautrec, Albi and Musée des Augustins, Toulouse). But today, it is the Musée Municipal de Vernon that holds the largest public collection of works by the artist, with eight paintings and one pastel. It is a collection that will continue to be enriched in the years to come. To commemorate the 150th anniversary of Impressionism in 2024, the Musée Municipal de Vernon was renamed the Musée Blanche Hoschedé-Monet, in homage to the figure who was at once a daughter of the region; an accomplished artist; legitimate and worthy heir of Claude Monet and keeper of his memory, painted work, and garden; and finally, one of the last Impressionists.

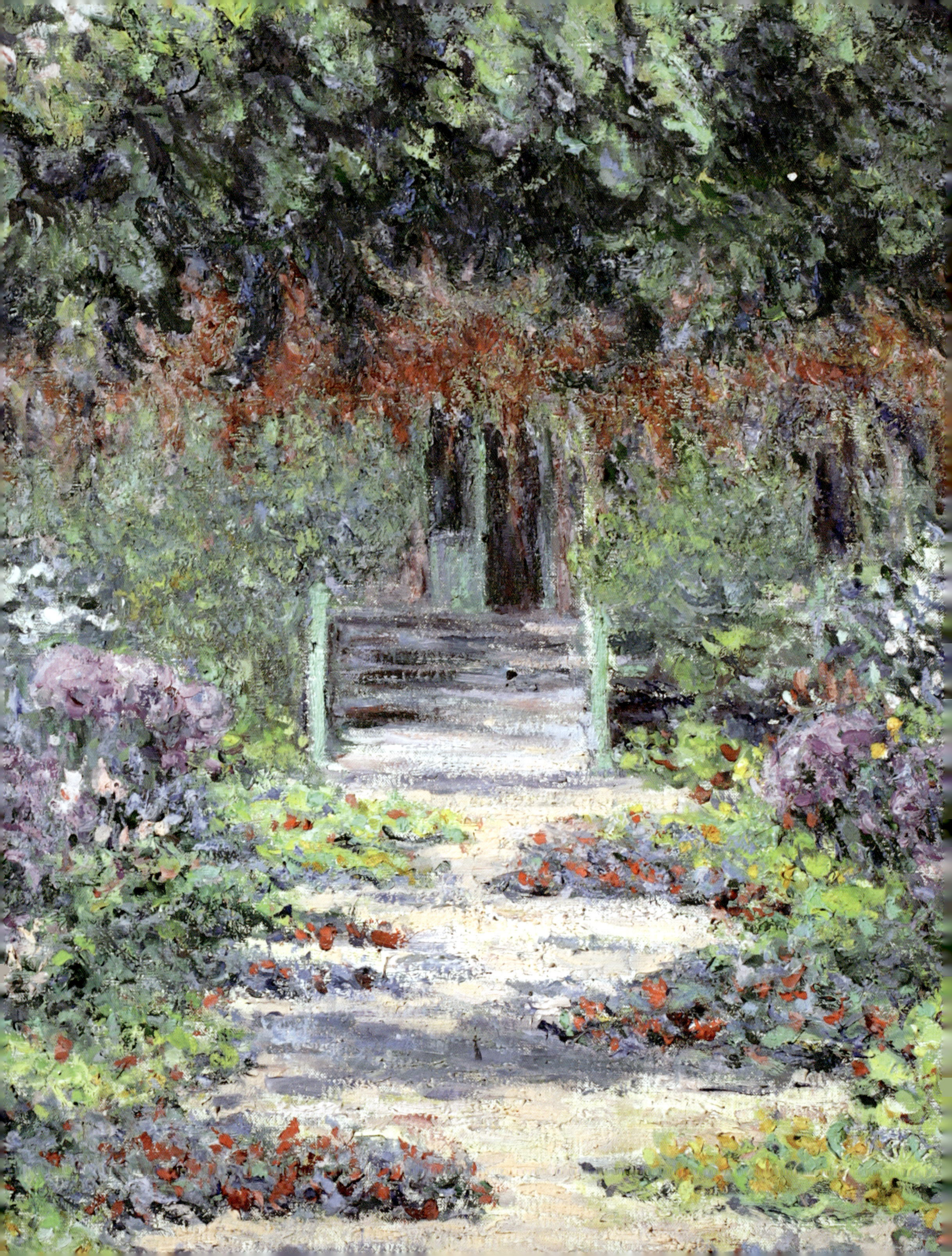

THE PAINTER HITS PAUSE

EXAMINING BLANCHE HOSCHEDÉ-MONET'S HIATUS, 1912–1926

Nancy Mowll Mathews

Paradoxically, Blanche Hoschedé-Monet is more often remembered in art historical literature for the lengthy hiatus in her artistic career—when she became the primary caretaker of Claude Monet, his house, gardens, and art—than for her own body of work. That she would have paused her painting to oversee Monet's is surprising since she worked in the context of such strong, dedicated women artists in Giverny, both French and American. To understand this hiatus, it is important to see the larger context of the other surviving Impressionist artists, Renoir, Degas, and Cassatt, who also tapped younger relatives and caretakers to help them continue to paint and manage the legendary status they had achieved in their old age. And finally, we will explore how two artists, Monet and Hoschedé-Monet, who had benefited and enjoyed working side by side for decades, might have found alternative ways of continuing their long collegiality during this period.

We start with Monet's color lithograph of Blanche Hoschedé-Monet (fig. 18) dated to 1894.[1] Based on the oil portrait *Blanche Hoschedé Painting* (*Blanche Hoschedé peignant*, ca. 1892),[2] it is one of the series of twenty lithographs that comprises a "virtual" retrospective exhibition of Monet's work from the 1870s and '80s.[3] Of the three Monet/Hoschedé women in the lithographic series (Camille, Germaine, and Blanche), the one of Blanche identifies her first and foremost as a painter. While the original oil portrait commemorates a social episode in 1888 among the Hoschedé sisters and their American artist-friends, John Leslie Breck and Theodore Butler,[4] the drawing Monet made for the lithograph was completed a few years later, in the early 1890s. It coincides with the prominence of women artists in Giverny at this time.

Many international female artists and art students took the train out to Giverny from Paris in the 1880s when the colony was just getting known.[5] Soon they achieved success among the artists there as well as in their home countries. For example, Lilla Cabot Perry, who had multiple Giverny residences over a twenty-year period, made a strong impact on the artistic community, becoming close friends with both

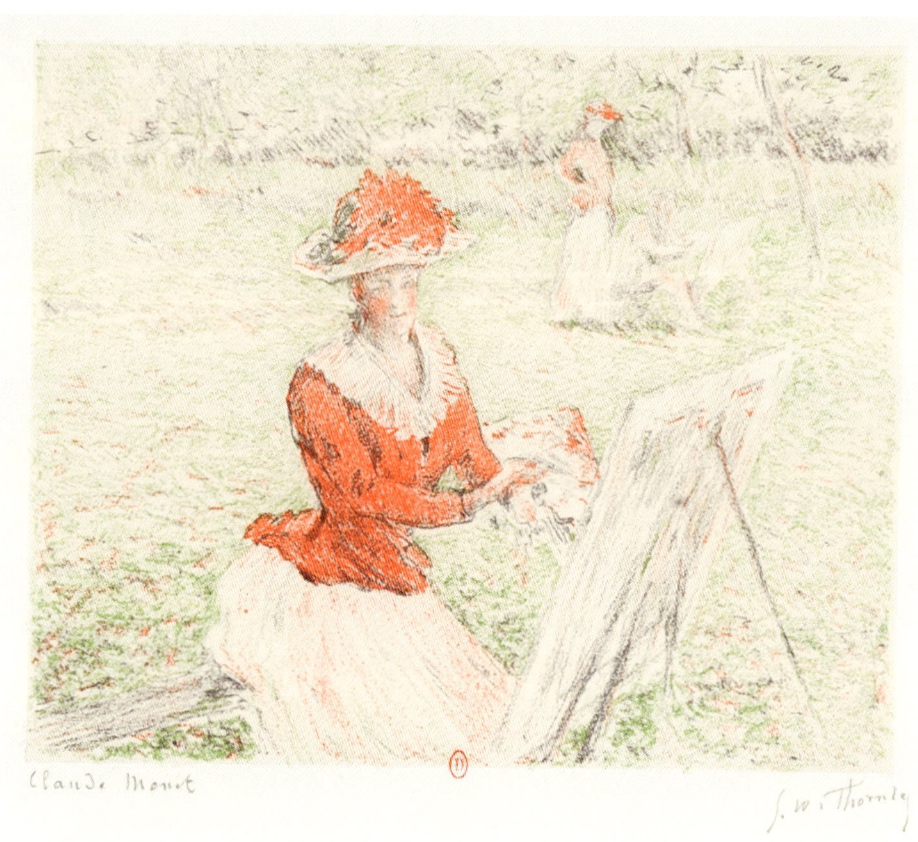

Theodore Robinson and Claude Monet during her first stay from 1889 to 1891. But perhaps even more impressive to Hoschedé-Monet were the visits of Berthe Morisot, old friend of Claude and Alice Monet,[6] who, although she is not known to have set up her easel in Giverny, was actively working and exhibiting in Paris. Hoschedé-Monet also continued to have a relationship with Morisot's daughter, Julie Manet Rouart, and Camille Pissarro's daughter-in-law, Esther Pissarro, both artists themselves.

In 1892, women artists were in the spotlight thanks to the upcoming World's Columbian Exposition, or Chicago World's Fair, of 1893, which was to have a major pavilion devoted to the achievements of women. For the American arts community, it was an important event since, in addition to the exhibits, the Woman's Building itself was designed by a female architect and all the painted and sculptural decorations were commissioned from women artists. The president of

Fig. 18 William Thornley, after Claude Monet, *Blanche Hoschedé Painting* (*Blanche Hoschedé Peignant*), ca. 1894. Transfer lithograph printed in gray-black, green, and red on off-white chine appliqué, 6⁵⁄₁₆ × 7⁷⁄₈ in. (16 × 20 cm). Bibliothèque de l'Institut National d'Histoire de l'Art, Paris, Collections Jacques Doucet (NUM FOL EST 83)

the board of the Woman's Building, Bertha Honoré Palmer, visited Giverny on her trip to Europe that year to meet the American women working in France who were involved in the project. Among them were Mary Cassatt, who was in Giverny in the fall of 1892, and Mary Fairchild MacMonnies, who came with her husband in 1890, 1893, and steadily after 1895.[7] The encouragement offered by this community of active and successful women was not wasted on Hoschedé-Monet, who began her own *carnet des comptes* listing works for sale and exhibition in 1890.[8] It was an added compliment that Bertha Palmer and her husband acquired one of her works during their visit to Giverny in 1892.[9] Within the context of these successes, it is noteworthy that Monet chose *Blanche Hoschedé Painting* for his lithographic "exhibition" to honor her and the many women artists who had been his colleagues.

Giverny continued to be a draw for the next two decades, especially for American artists. In 1907, Mary Colman Wheeler started a women's art school in which the major artists of Giverny taught, including Frederick Frieseke and Richard Miller.[10] Throughout the 1890s until the First World War, many artist-couples were in residence. The most prominent were Mary and Frederick MacMonnies, who bought a house in 1901, divorced in 1909, and each then married other artists in Giverny. Although primarily a sculptor, Frederick MacMonnies took on many women students in sculpture and oil painting, including Alice Jones, who would become

his second wife in 1910. Others include the artist-couple Guy (painter) and Ethel (illustrator) Rose, who bought a house in 1904. And Philip Hale often came with his wife, Lilian Westcott Hale, and sister, Ellen Day Hale, both artists. While most of the Americans retreated to the United States when war threatened, the MacMonnies moved to Paris but kept their house in Giverny, which was then used as a field hospital under the auspices of Dr. William Johnston, an American doctor and artist. Alice Jones MacMonnies also started a knitting factory in the house for clothing for the troops.[11]

With all these high-powered women around her, it is a little surprising to compare the Hoschedé-Monet of the early 1890s—a modern woman and emerging professional—to the Hoschedé-Monet of this famous 1915 photograph of Blanche leaning over to watch Claude paint (fig. 19). The photograph establishes the image we have of her helping the aging Impressionist achieve his last great works of art by sacrificing her own well-established career. Her brother, Jean-Pierre Hoschedé, was very clear about this, writing simply "She stopped painting."[12] Monet's distinguished friends like Gustave Geffroy and Georges Clemenceau lauded her sacrifice, calling her his "angel."[13] And from the evidence we have,[14] there is no question that the *Water Lilies* cycle, given to the French state for display in the Musée de l'Orangerie, would not have been realized without the personal and professional intervention of this woman standing in the plain white dress.

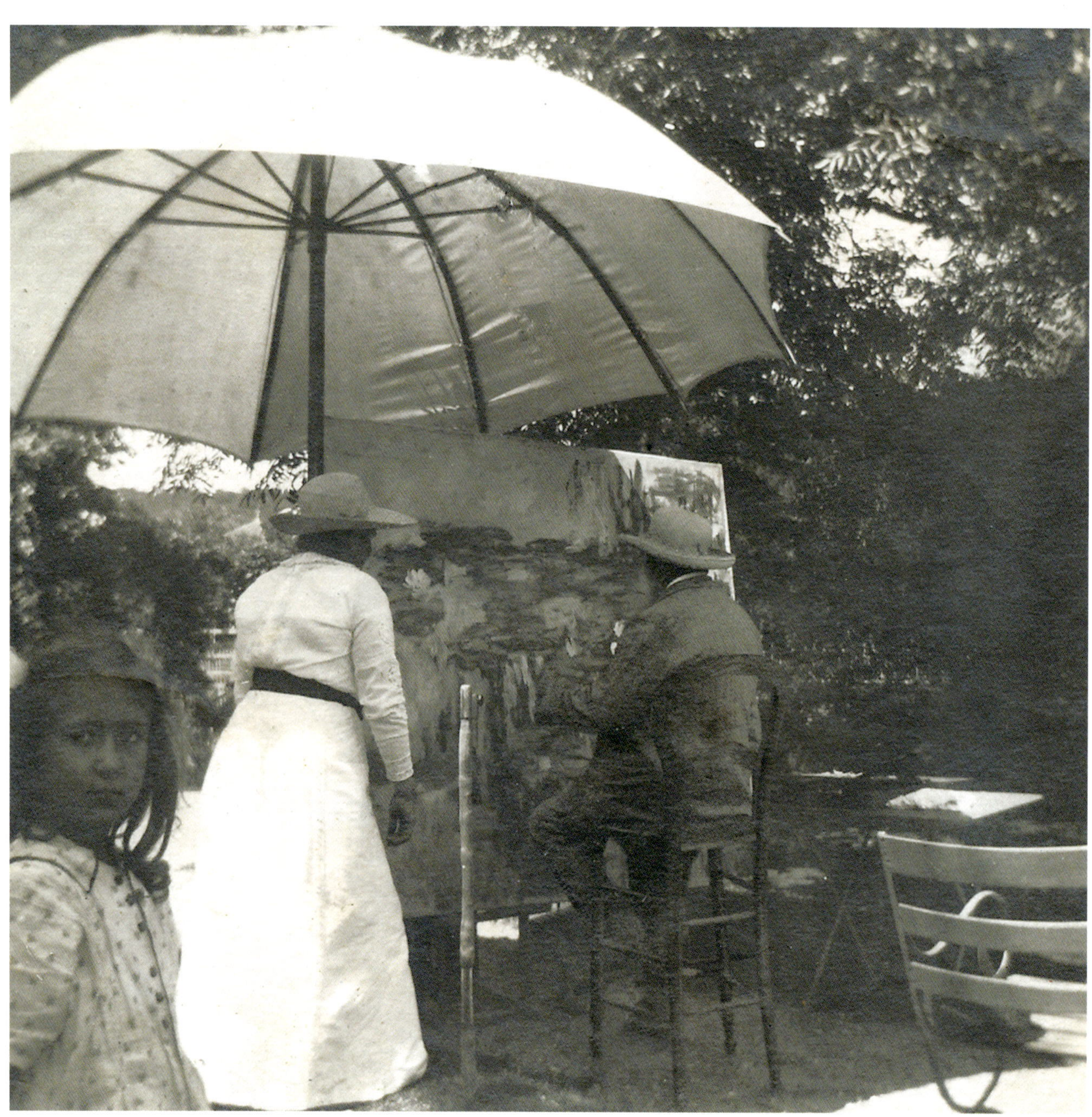

Fig. 19   Claude Monet painting by the lily pond, watched over by Blanche Hoschedé-Monet and Nitia Salerou, Germaine Hoschedé's daughter, July 18, 1915. Collection of Philippe Piguet

But she was not the only one put into this position in the mid-1910s. Hoschedé-Monet joined a select group of caretakers of the last surviving Impressionist artists—Monet, Renoir, Degas, and Cassatt—who helped them as they struggled to continue working and to deal effectively with the demands of their growing international fame. The caretakers were a combination of younger relatives and long-time household managers, each one taking on the elevated tasks of communicating with dealers, collectors, journalists, and artistic pilgrims while at the same time being responsible for the physical wellbeing of an aging artist. And as if this task (which none of the caretakers expected or were prepared for), wasn't monumental enough, they had to carry out their responsibilities during World War I. In each case, the caretakers had an impact on the final reputation and legacy of the artists we revere today.

The photograph of Hoschedé-Monet and Monet also includes Hoschedé-Monet's niece, Nitia Salerou, and if not taken by her mother, Germaine Hoschedé Salerou, or father, Albert Salerou, their presence is implied by Nitia's glance. This photograph bears a strong resemblance to the view of Monet painting in the Sacha Guitry film, *Ceux de chez nous*, which was also shot in the summer of 1915.[15] But it shows the family context for Monet's painting in a way that the Guitry film and other photographs of Monet with palette in hand do not—and suggests how many people it took simply to get the artist to sit at his easel by the pond.

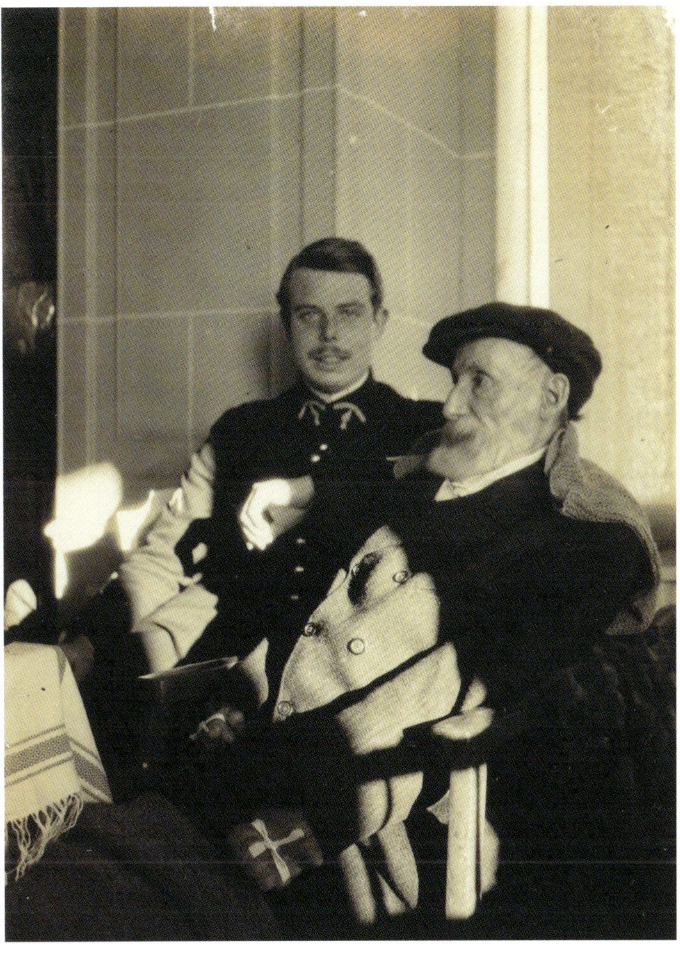

This was true for all the aging Impressionist artists, but especially for Auguste Renoir, Monet's old colleague and frequent visitor to Giverny, who had himself bought a country home with extensive gardens called Les Collettes in Cagnes-sur-Mer in 1908. His rheumatoid arthritis grew progressively debilitating, affecting not only his mobility but

Fig. 20 Auguste Renoir with his son Jean Renoir, photograph by Pierre Bonnard, ca. 1916. Musée d'Orsay, Paris (PHO 19873162)

also his ability to hold a brush. Nevertheless, he actively designed his gardens and continued to paint as Monet did. This was possible, of course, because like Monet he could afford a large household and grounds staff, and because his wife Aline Charigot and her cousin Gabrielle Renard took on the management of the estate and his professional activities.

Renoir's three sons also played a part in the care of their father in the last years of his life, but particularly Jean Renoir (fig. 20), who returned home to Les Collettes after the Armistice brought an end to his military service. For a year Jean shared in his father's physical care but also enabled him to achieve his last paintings, learning how the artist liked to set up his palette and how the canvases were rolled on a wood contraption to allow him to reach all parts of a large painting.[16] Like Hoschedé-Monet's role in Monet's *Water Lilies*, Jean Renoir helped his father while he created his last major painting, *The Bathers* (1918–19; Musée d'Orsay, Paris), and oversaw the donation of it to the French state after his father's death.[17] Only twenty-five at the time, Jean would use this experience with his father's art to become an artist himself—as a ceramicist and filmmaker. And he would go on to write *Renoir, My Father* in 1958, allowing future generations to glimpse the intimate life of a great artist especially in his last days.

Jean Renoir may have been inspired to write about his father by the 1949 book *Mon oncle Degas* by Edgar Degas's niece and final caretaker, Jeanne Fevre.[18] Like the Monet and Renoir families, the Degas family was complicated. Because Degas was unmarried and always lived in Parisian apartments, there was no house and garden full of children, relatives, and employees ready to help him in his old age as in the case of Monet, Renoir, and even Cassatt. But Degas indeed had a large family—four siblings and many aunts and uncles, nieces, and nephews spread out around France, Italy, and the Americas. When Degas's health began to fail, it was his friend Mary Cassatt who suggested in 1913 that he invite his niece Jeanne Fevre, who was living in the South of France, to come to Paris and oversee his living conditions and professional affairs as Hoschedé-Monet was doing for Monet.[19]

When Sacha Guitry arrived at Degas's door in 1915 hoping to include him with Monet, Renoir, Rodin, and others in *Ceux de chez nous*, the artist dismissed him quickly. But Guitry nevertheless went out with his film crew to catch Degas walking his usual route and was able to add him to his tribute to the artistic geniuses of France.[20] The film also shows a female companion keeping in step with the older man (fig. 21). This woman has been identified as Jeanne Fevre, who was at the apartment when Guitry called and, although seemingly surprised in the film to see Guitry disobey Degas's refusal, keeps Degas from noticing and allows the moment to be recorded for posterity.[21] At Degas's death, it was Fevre who oversaw the dispersal of his collection and directed the casting of his fragile wax sculptures into

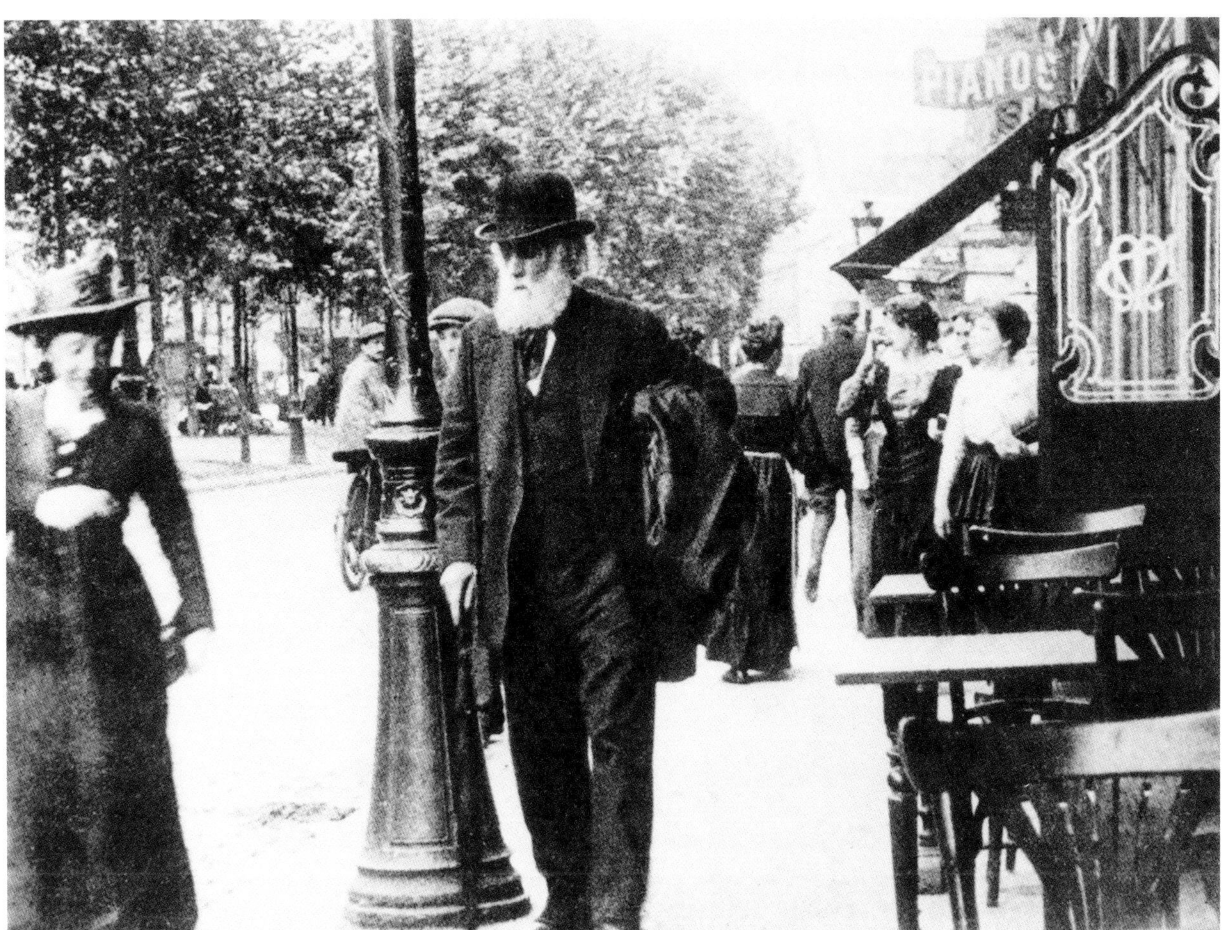

bronze, including *The Little Dancer Aged Fourteen*, now probably one of Degas's most famous and beloved works.[22]

Like Hoschedé-Monet and Jean Renoir in their fulfillment of familial responsibilities, Fevre was in Degas's family. But it is important not to overlook the role of Degas's household manager of some thirty years, Zoé Clozier (fig. 22), who worked closely with Fevre to manage the thousands of works of art that had been moved into Degas's final apartment in 1912. Clozier not only made Degas's life comfortable and pleasant for those many years, but she was also an intellectual companion in the sense that Degas's compromised eyesight required that he have someone else read to him.[23] Her importance is made clear by her appearance

Fig. 21 Sacha Guitry, *Degas on Boulevard de Clichy*, 1915. Film still from *Ceux de chez nous*. Yale University Library, New Haven, Visual Resources Collection (109089)

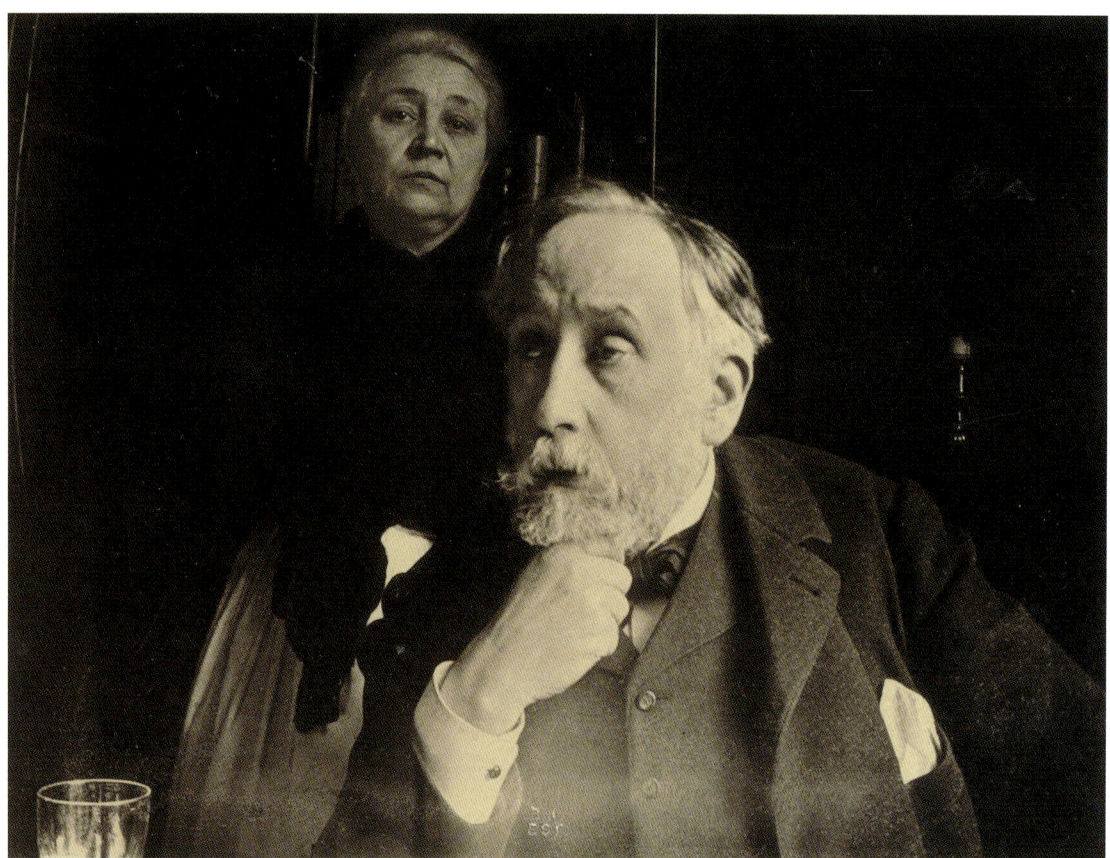

in one of Degas's own photographs from the
1890s, a series of images taken in his apartment
that feature his closest friends, such as Renoir and
Stéphane Mallarmé.

Finally, Mary Cassatt, the youngest of the
four surviving Impressionists, was having her own
struggles with ill health and deteriorating eyesight.
In 1910, at age sixty-six (fig. 23), she was in excellent
health—a lifelong horsewoman, walker, and

gardener—but, after a trip with her family to Egypt
in 1911, she began to lose strength and suffer from
cataracts that couldn't be corrected.[24] Like Monet
and Renoir, she delighted in her country house and
gardens, called Beaufresne, where she would work
in the summers and entertain art world friends and
family.[25] Interestingly, although she was adamant
that Degas have one of his family members come
to care for him, Cassatt herself never looked in that

Fig. 22 *Self-Portrait of Edgar Degas with Zoé
Clozier*, photograph by Edgar Degas, ca. 1895.
Bibliothèque Nationale de France,
Département Estampes et Photographie,
Paris (EO-53-PET FOL)

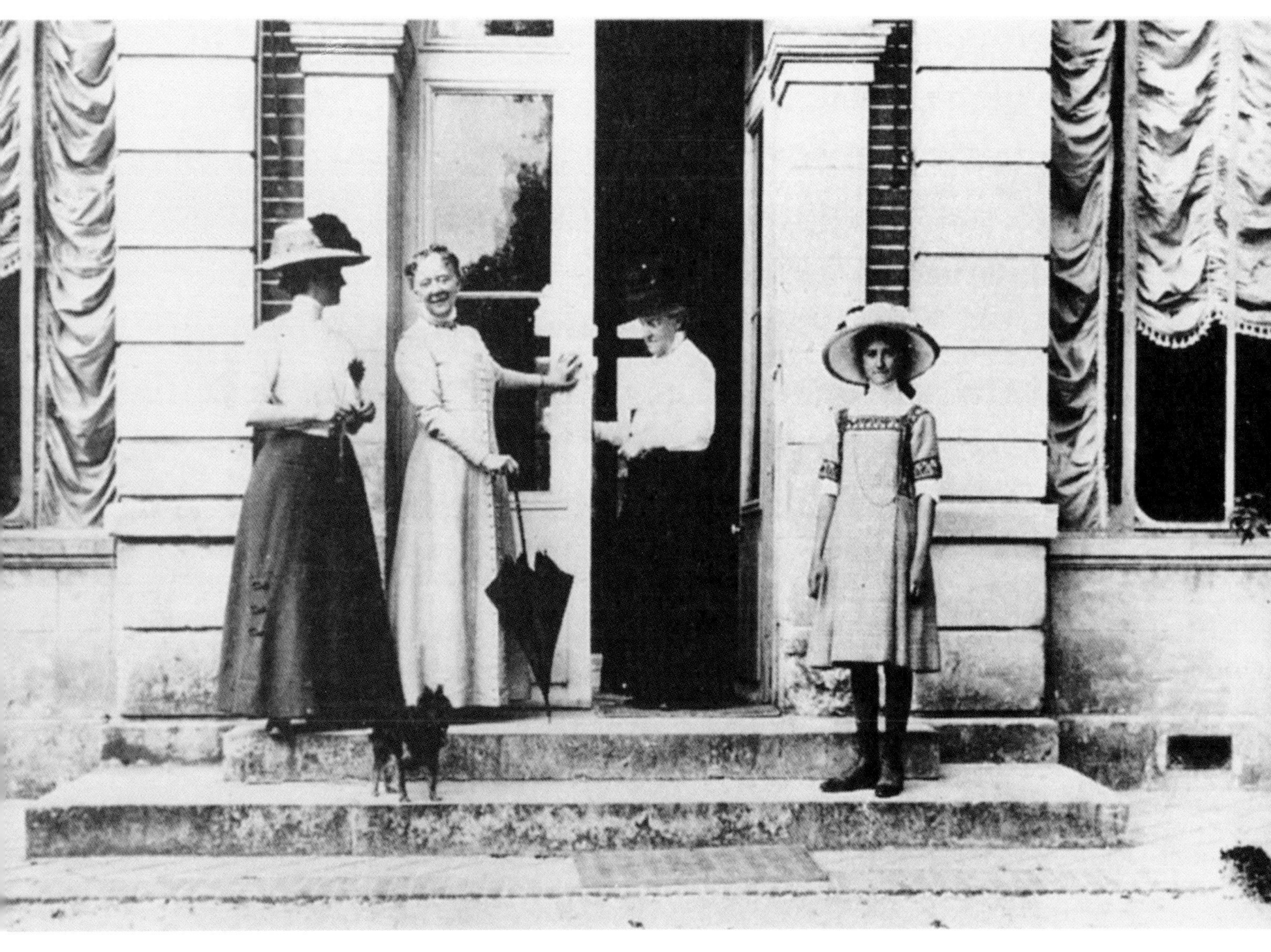

Fig. 23   Mary Cassatt at Beaufresne, 1910. Pictured from left: Madame Joseph Durand-Ruel, Cassatt, unidentified woman, and Marie-Louise Durand-Ruel. Durand-Ruel Archives, Paris

direction for the care that she needed. Instead, she relied primarily on her longtime household manager, Mathilde Valet (fig. 24). Valet was on the upper rung of household employees. As well as reading and writing in several languages, she could oversee all the other employees while still serving as personal assistant to the lady of the house. In the photograph of Valet, presumed to be for an identity card or passport, she is dressed in a rich but no-nonsense suit with a feathered hat and elaborately decorated collar.

As Cassatt grew more infirm and no longer able to see well enough to paint, she and Valet focused on the proper distribution and exhibition of the works still in her possession. In 1915, Cassatt worked with her best friend, the collector Louisine Havemeyer, to mount an exhibition in New York for the benefit of women's suffrage. Like Monet and Renoir, Cassatt was horrified by the outbreak of war and sought ways of using her art to benefit society so that such a war would not happen again.[26] Taking on the duties of a museum registrar, Valet, like Hoschedé-Monet, typically made exhibitions happen by overseeing the packing, shipping, and insurance of works still in the artist's possession.[27]

Seeing how the other aging Impressionists were supported in the last phase of their artistic lives clarifies for us the evolution of Blanche Hoschedé-Monet's career. In this context, it is easier to understand the change in her image from the fashionable *plein air* painter of the late nineteenth century to the attentive assistant helping the older

Monet to paint his large canvases of water lilies. In the case of the other artists, their caretakers worked full time to allow the artist to keep painting (Renoir) or to help them manage the property and works of art in their possession (Degas, Cassatt). For Hoschedé-Monet, the job was both—it should not be surprising that her own painting had to be put aside, at least for a while.

It is also important to note that Hoschedé-Monet did not just sacrifice her career to help Monet's. She had already been forced to pause her painting because of her husband, Jean Monet's illness.[28] No works can be dated to the last two years of Jean's severe decline and death in February of 1914.[29] In addition, the death of her mother in 1911 had already left a vacuum in the management of the estate which Michel Monet and the other Hoschedé children in Giverny had helped to fill. But the departure of her brothers—Jean-Pierre Hoschedé and Michel Monet—to military service at the outbreak of the war, the departure of her sisters—Marthe Hoschedé Butler and her family to the United States in 1914, and the planned departure of Germaine Hoschedé Salerou and her family to the South of France—left her quite alone soon after the 1915 photograph (fig. 19) was taken.

For many studying the output of this artist, however, there is the hope that perhaps Hoschedé-Monet resumed creating art after her initial pause. Certainly, she can claim some second-hand credit for the Monet paintings of that last decade, including the "grandes décorations," or large-scale series of *Water Lilies*. As a painter herself, she was more helpful than Jean Renoir with his father in setting up Monet's art supplies, large canvases, and selection of subjects, as they worked together placing the easel and umbrellas in the gardens. Some art historians have gone so far as to suggest that Hoschedé-Monet's hand might be discernable under the layers of Monet's paint.[30] This shared creation of his late paintings, whether she put brush to his canvas or not, was a version of the collaboration they had enjoyed in years past.

While Hoschedé-Monet may have enjoyed this role, it was not the same as painting herself. If her brother was correct, that she sacrificed her own painting until Monet's death, it would amount to a hiatus of fourteen years.[31] The fact that she had enough paintings to show in a 1927 exhibition in Paris, less than a year after Monet's death, certainly suggests that the hiatus was not that long.[32] And when we compare Hoschedé-Monet's known works to Monet's around 1920, particularly of the garden and Japanese bridge, such as her *Garden of Giverny (The Path under the Rose Arches)* (*Le Jardin de Giverny [L'Allée des rosiers]*) (pl. 24) versus his *Path under the Rose Arches, Giverny* (*L'Allée des rosiers, Giverny*) (fig. 25), we see the kind of side-by-side interpretation of motifs that had been so striking in the early days of their artistic collaboration. The "twinning" of their canvases was most noticeable in the 1890s, and a good example is the relationship between Hoschedé-Monet's *Morning on the Seine (Matinée sur la Seine)* (fig. 37, pl. 13) and Monet's

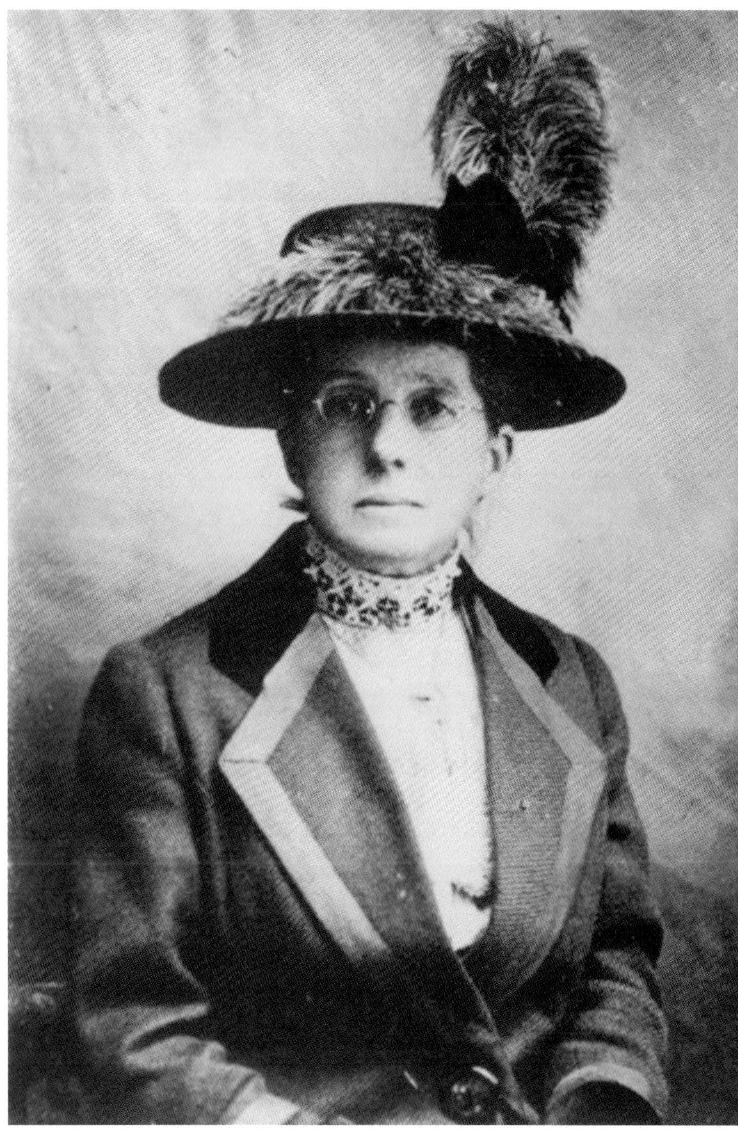

Fig. 24 Mathilde Valet, ca. 1914. Smithsonian Institution, Washington, DC, Archives of American Art, Frederick Arnold Sweet research materials on Mary Cassatt

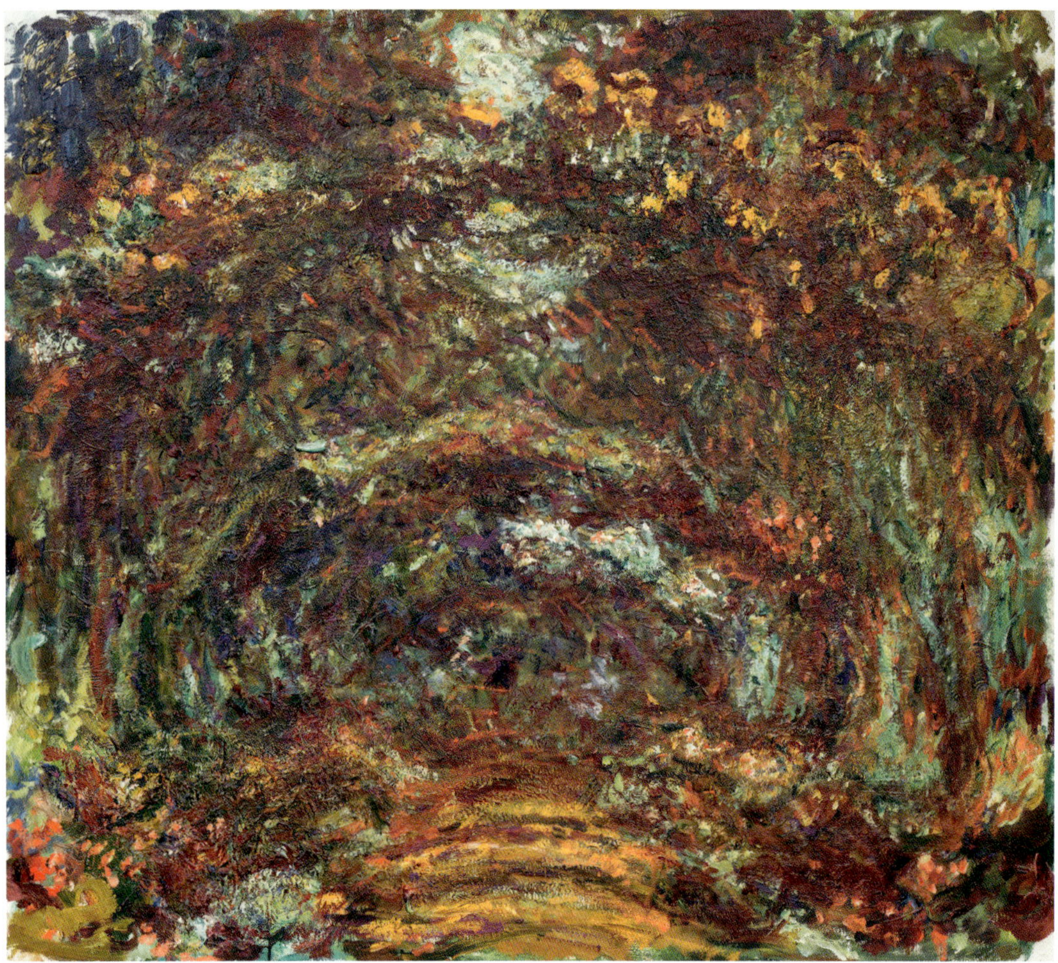

Morning on the Seine, near Giverny (fig. 38), which shows them exploring the same theme and suggests a virtual, if not actual, day of painting. As Theodore Robinson said in 1892, "they both like to work together."[33]

After Hoschedé-Monet helped Monet establish his latest project of the large *Water Lilies* with a new studio and a new painting routine for the wall-size canvases, it would not be surprising that she itched to have a brush in her own hand once again. When the Armistice was declared at the end of 1918, life gradually returned to normal as the Monet family and support group came home to Giverny. Although Blanche continued to manage the Monet

Fig. 25   Claude Monet, *The Path under the Rose Arches, Giverny* (*L'Allée des rosiers, Giverny*), ca. 1920–22. Oil on canvas, 35 1/16 × 39 3/8 in. (89 × 100 cm). Musée Marmottan Monet, Paris, legs Michel Monet, 1966 (inv. 5089)

estate, the day-to-day care of the elderly artist could be shared with her brothers, sisters, brothers-in-law, and nieces and nephews as well as the reassembled household staff. Her sister Suzanne's children, Lily and Jimmy, both followed their father and grandfather to become artists themselves and attracted other young artists, both men and women, to the family group after 1921.[34] Although American artists never returned in force to Giverny, many women came again to paint in the summers, with the passage of the 1920 Women's Suffrage amendment in the United States giving fresh impetus to their quest to assert their own identities.

A date in the early 1920s for Hoschedé-Monet's *Garden of Giverny (The Path under the Rose Arches)* (pl. 24),[35] like that given to Monet's *Path under the Rose Arches*, might indicate Hoschedé-Monet at work again during her supposed break from painting. The many paintings Hoschedé-Monet also did of the pond and Japanese bridge, both front and side views, show the wisteria having grown lush at the top of the trellis but not yet on the uprights, indicating a date before 1926 as documented in photographs of the changing profile of the wisteria on the trellis over the bridge.[36] Certainly, her stepbrother, Michel Monet, believed that a similar painting by Hoschedé-Monet, *The Garden and Home of Monet in Giverny (Le Jardin et la maison de Monet à Giverny)*,[37] was painted in Monet's lifetime, before 1924, as noted in the donation records of the Musée des Augustins.[38] The painterliness of the Hoschedé-Monet canvases of the pond and garden, while not as abstract as Monet's, suggest an artist who once again can revel in her paint and brushes and is a tribute to the longstanding father-and-daughter collaborative practice.

While Hoschedé-Monet did not publish a memoir about Monet, as Jeanne Fevre did for Degas and Jean Renoir did for his father, she had apparently intended to. Her writings about their stepfather were published by her brother, Jean-Pierre Hoschedé, in his remarkable *Claude Monet, ce mal connu* in 1960, giving us an intimate glimpse of what both artists accomplished, especially in Monet's last years, and is appropriately dedicated to "ma sœur Blanche." Whether or not Hoschedé-Monet and Monet had returned to painting side by side in the last years before Monet's death, their bond was strengthened during Hoschedé-Monet's hiatus from painting and lives on in their shared artistic legacies.

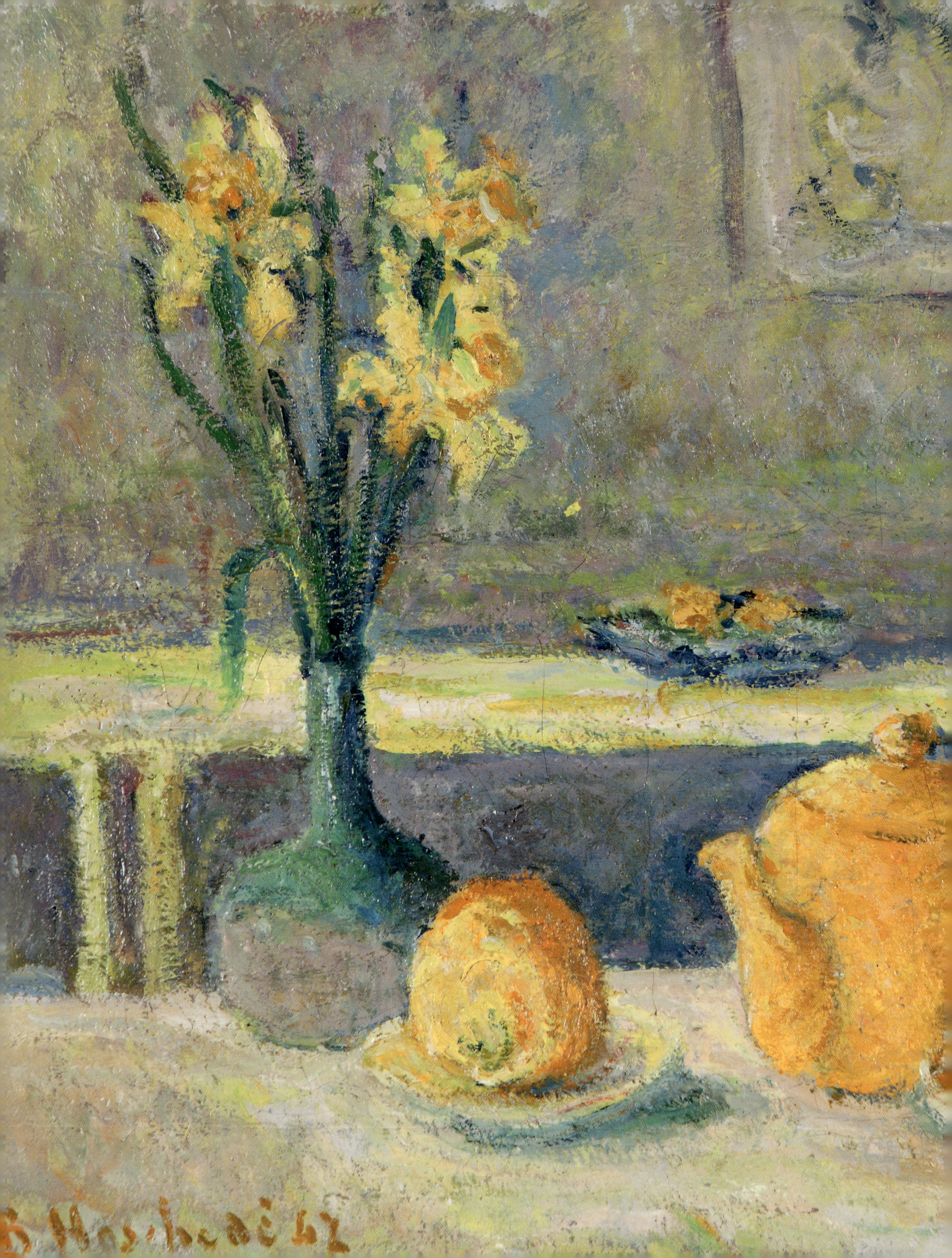

IN THE LIGHT OF CLAUDE MONET

Philippe Piguet

"To my sister Blanche,
in recognition of what she was to Monet,
of what she did for his memory."
—Jean-Pierre Hoschedé, *Claude Monet, ce mal connu*[1]

The dedication that Jean-Pierre Hoschedé included at the beginning of *Claude Monet, ce mal connu* says in just a few words who Blanche Hoschedé-Monet was—but only partially. She was at once Monet's stepdaughter and daughter-in-law, his helper, and his partner. She ensured that her stepfather's home and gardens, not to mention his oeuvre, would stand the test of time. Motivated by total admiration for the great artist that Monet was, Hoschedé-Monet demonstrated an absolute devotion to helping him bring his radical dream of painting to fruition. In this respect, Georges Clemenceau's words describing her as the painter's "blue angel" are as close as possible to a reality that was her daily life.[2] But Blanche was an artist as well: an "Impressionist painter. Not in the shadow, but in the light of Claude Monet," as expressed by Jean-Pierre Hoschedé, her brother and first biographer, in the opus that he dedicated to her before he died.[3]

"It was in 1876 that I saw Monet for the first time. I was just eleven years old but I remember his arrival at my parents' house in Montgeron. He was introduced to me as a great artist, and he had long hair. That struck me, and I immediately had sympathy for him because we could tell he was fond of children."[4] Taken from the notes that Hoschedé-Monet had made with the intention of writing a book on Monet, which was instead completed by her brother, this anecdote of the first time she met the artist speaks volumes about how she felt even at a young age. This "sympathy" was to find expression over time, especially in the sharing of a common passion for painting. Raised in a family whose head, Ernest Hoschedé, was a great connoisseur of art, Hoschedé-Monet spent her childhood surrounded by paintings, her eye shaped—perhaps without realizing it—by the example of Corot, Courbet, and other painters of the Fontainebleau school, as well as the Impressionists who adorned the family walls.

The Hoschedé and Monet family's subsequent move to Giverny, and the everyday life shared with the artist, would only contribute to developing Hoschedé-Monet's interest in painting to the point of wanting to do it herself, especially since Monet never failed to encourage her.[5] In his biography on Monet, Jean-Pierre Hoschedé recounts how, in her early days, "Blanche always accompanied Monet to his painting locations, carrying his canvases, his supplies and hers as well," specifying that "she worked in his vicinity" but "without ever painting the same subject as him."[6] Finally, he adds that once the two artists returned home, "Monet would look at what she had painted, give her compliments, or more often, point out what he thought to be bad, poorly constructed, but I never heard him tell her how it should be done."[7] In fact, Monet did not make Hoschedé-Monet his student—Monet never gave a lesson—but a sort of ally, a confidante in painting.

Although absolutely a painter, Blanche Hoschedé-Monet never sought to make her art a career. While she participated in salons and in various group exhibitions, she didn't have her first solo exhibition until after the death of her mentor. What was holding her back then? Not that she wasn't sure of herself, but she was discretion and humility personified. Hoschedé-Monet's devotion to Monet had made her set down her brushes and forego her art when, widowed in February 1914,

she decided to take her place beside him so that he wouldn't have to worry about anything other than painting. It was undoubtedly by way of paying homage to Monet that she agreed to her first solo exhibition after the master had passed. The fact that she only had three others in the twenty years before her own death in 1947 clearly shows that painting was not a job for her, but a way of being. Her work was another means of continuing in the world, beyond space and time.

Throughout the trials and tribulations of life, the familial and pictorial relationship between Hoschedé-Monet and Monet never faltered. Whether they lived in the same household or apart, whether they worked in close proximity or on their own, Blanche Hoschedé-Monet created a body of work that, if it shows obvious kinship, is not motivated by any mimetic intention. It is defined simply by the markers of an aesthetic unique to a movement—Impressionism—with which it was intimately linked.

Born in 1865 and raised amid her father's passion for art, then in Giverny from the age of eighteen in a blended family led by Monet, Hoschedé-Monet belonged to the generation that witnessed the advent and development of Impressionism. When she began to paint in the early 1880s, having never received any artistic education, she drew from the examples of her own life—not the least of which was Monet. While Monet contributed to her learning, she would gradually forge her own aesthetic identity and distinguish herself from the

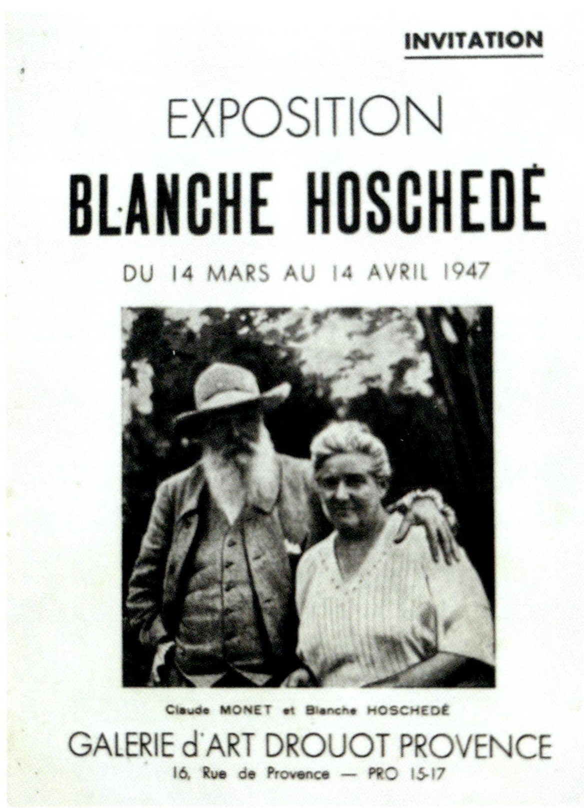

painter of Giverny by developing a more personal style through her way of apprehending and treating her motif. Hoschedé-Monet's painting called for a denser and less fluid subject matter.

Moreover, even when she chose subjects that Monet had painted in multiple iterations, she never adopted the systematic principle of the *series* as he did. She preferred instead the *sequence*—while the latter considers the same subject from different points of view, the former seizes the motif in order to produce several versions and study it in depth.

While Monet, as a meteorologist of the soul, passed from one canvas to another to capture all the subtle variations that light and atmosphere imposed on his chosen subject, Hoschedé-Monet preferred to depict a single moment, seeking to account for the weight of its presence. In a view of Impressionism where the two major paths are the fluid and the solid, if Claude Monet is a follower of the first, then the art of Blanche Hoschedé-Monet is better described by the second. The works of the Impressionist painter translate the world into the transparency of air; those of Hoschedé-Monet offer a view of raw reality in direct relationship with nature, with the earth. She did not seek sublimation, but applied herself to rendering the depth of her vision.

Illustrated on the invitation for her exhibition at the Galerie d'Art Drouot Provence in 1947, the photograph showing Hoschedé-Monet alongside Monet (fig. 26) is touching in more ways than one. Wearing a hat and tweed suit, the painter of Giverny puts a protective arm around his stepdaughter, his hand resting on her shoulder; modestly dressed in a white blouse, she seems almost embarrassed to pose in this way beside him. Both fix their gaze on the photographer, like two old friends who have known each other forever, but they each appear independent, shown on equal footing in a sort of total mutual respect. To be sure, Blanche Hoschedé-Monet's daughterly love for her stepfather and father-in-law, and the admiration that she had for the painter, matched the esteem that Claude Monet held for her as an artist.

Fig. 26 Claude Monet and Blanche Hoschedé-Monet on the invitation for the exhibition *Blanche Hoschedé*, Galerie d'Art Drouot Provence, Paris, 1947. Collection of Philippe Piguet

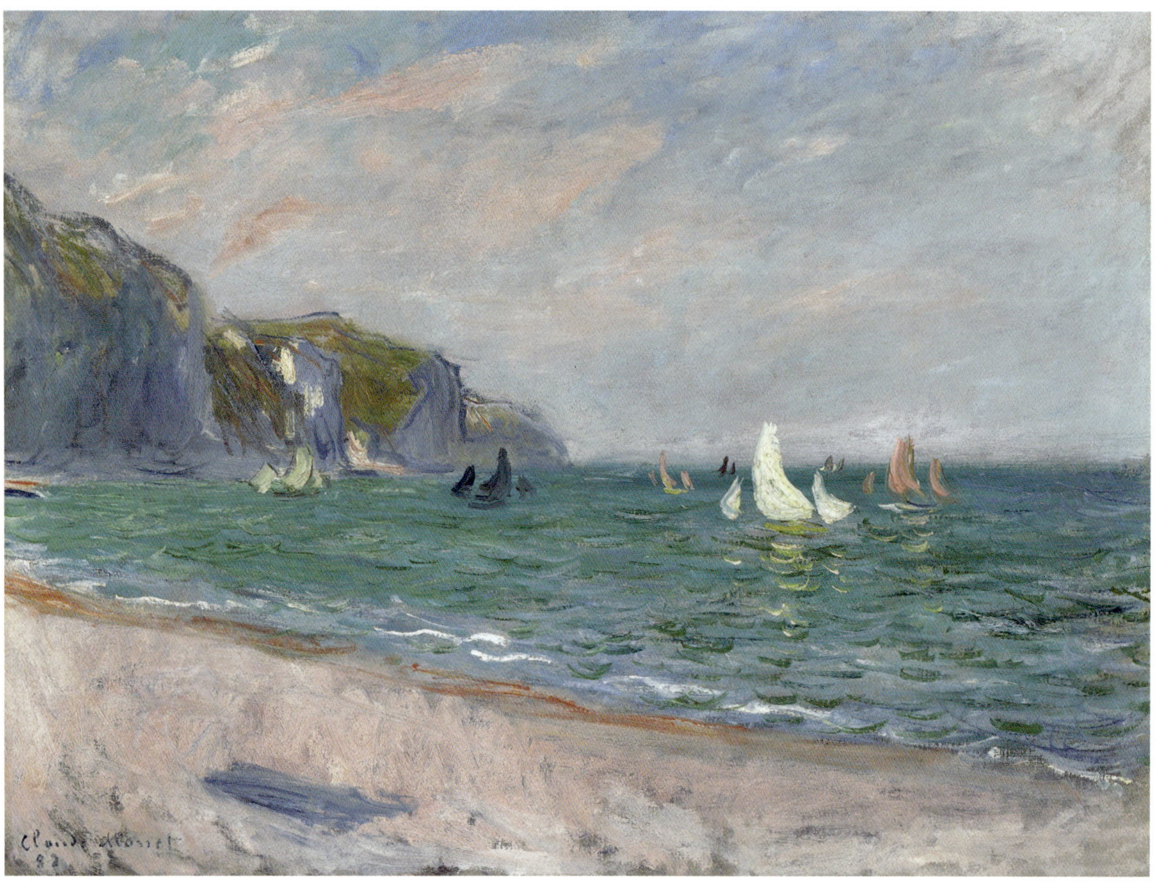

There are many letters that attest both to Monet's encouragement of Hoschedé-Monet to develop her artistic eye by attending exhibitions, as well as to the attention that he paid to her work, curious about the progress that she was making. In 1891, Monet wrote to Gustave Geffroy on Hoschedé-Monet's behalf for a pass to the Salon du Champ-de-Mars (Salon of the Société Nationale des Beaux-Arts): "Mademoiselle Blanche Hoschedé, obliged to come to Paris the day after tomorrow, May 13th, would like to make the most of her stay by visiting the Champ de Mars. I promise to take her there and will ask you to obtain a means of entry."[8] The following October, Monet brought his stepdaughter to England to visit her brother Jacques Hoschedé, who lived in Lymington as a ship broker. While passing through London, they met James McNeill Whistler, dined at his home,

Fig. 27   Claude Monet, *Boats in front of the Cliffs of Pourville* (*Bateaux devant les falaises de Pourville*), 1882. Oil on canvas, 23⅝ × 31⅞ in. (60 × 81 cm). Private collection

and went to see the famous Peacock Room that he had created for Frederick Leyland.[9] Later, during the trip that Monet took to Norway in 1895, away from his family for two months, he wrote to his wife Alice (Blanche's mother) about her work: "I can't wait to see what she has done in my absence, especially from what you tell me."[10]

If these few examples bear witness among many others to the bond that connected Blanche Hoschedé-Monet and Claude Monet, the former's paintings are an even more striking form of its expression, especially her early works, created when she was still learning from him. For example, in her sketchbook, we find a view of the cliffs of Pourville (pl. 1), dated October 3, 1882, which is similar to Monet's painting from the same period (fig. 27).[11] Hoschedé-Monet—who was not yet seventeen—was already accompanying Monet to his painting sites, but often sketched the subject in her own way. A few years later, not long after the Hoschedé-Monet family had settled in Giverny, Blanche took up her brushes and painted her first canvases alongside Monet: here, a view of the bank of the Epte river; there, another showing a meadow with haystacks (pls. 4 and 5). The young artist often chose a different point of view distinct from Monet's; her touch is more emphatic, out of concern for capturing what she saw on her canvas rather than what she felt. This is evident especially in the way she depicted the trees at the edge of the Epte, as in *Poplars at the Water's Edge* (*Peupliers au bord de l'eau*) (fig. 28). She gave them large trunks,

using a muted brown palette, and contrasted their silhouettes from the surrounding landscape rather than blending them into it.

In her early years, if Hoschedé-Monet drew upon subjects found in Monet's work, she quickly distinguished herself from him in several ways. When Monet painted a morning landscape, he faded it into the fog, always taking care to transcribe the quivering of the air on his canvas. Hoschedé-Monet's compositions are more built-up, with a dynamic that is regulated by an interplay of marked lines, sometimes vertical, sometimes diagonal, which provide the whole its supporting structure. These lines seem to give the sense of being present, before the motif, which the artist strived to reproduce through her sensitivity to the subject. Hoschedé-Monet reveals herself to be more drawn to wooded landscapes than to the water of the river or even the Seine, climbing hills in search of her own subject matter (as in pl. 11) and favoring clusters of trees that loom in space, as if to highlight them (like pl. 7).[12]

If she took up snowy landscapes, like Monet and his *Giverny in the Snow* (*Effet de neige à Giverny*, 1893),[13] Hoschedé-Monet painted with a thicker brushstroke, creating a surface which reveals a subject that is more pictorially dense. This can be seen in *Ice Floes at Vernon* (*Les Glaçons à Vernon*) (pl. 8), and in *Balustrade and Fir Trees in the Snow* (*Balustrade et sapins sous la neige*) (pl. 37). If she shared with Monet the same aesthetic preoccupation with color, she was less radical,

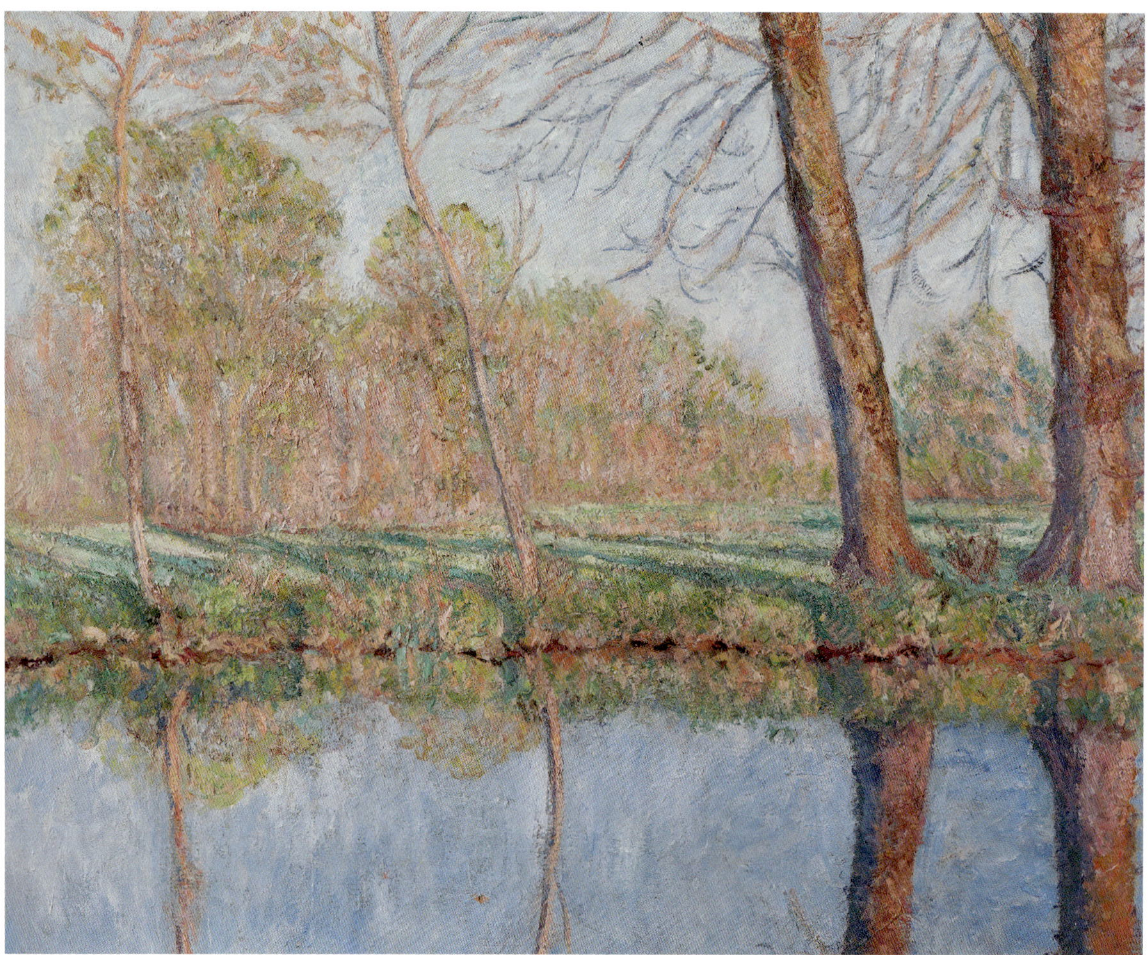

careful to let the subject show through while Monet would fully absorb it in pure pigment.

Following her marriage in 1897 to Jean Monet, Claude Monet's eldest son, Blanche began a new life in Rouen that would drive her to break free from her earlier models, without straying too far from them. Having been Monet's stepdaughter, she now became his daughter-in-law, and no longer lived in daily proximity to the artist. This change was important, especially in addition to the fact that, living in the city, Hoschedé-Monet was further from the nature that had constituted the native soil of her painting. She would nevertheless remain faithful to both the methods she learned and to an iconography

Fig. 28 Blanche Hoschedé-Monet, *Poplars at the Water's Edge* (*Peupliers au bord de l'eau*), ca. 1893. Oil on canvas, 26 × 31⅞ in. (66 × 81 cm). Musée des Beaux-Arts, Rouen (1909.1.17)

essentially comprised of landscapes, now including views of the Seine in Rouen, the port, and the surrounding areas: Croisset, Eauplet, Canteleu, etc.

View of Rouen (*Vue générale de Rouen*) (pl. 14), which Hoschedé-Monet likely painted from a window in her home, speaks volumes about the advice she had received and retained. It's not so much the city itself that the artist seems to have wanted to feature, but something of a more general atmosphere that enveloped and characterized it. Her approach doesn't lie in the attention to detail but in the representation of the elements of her view which are immediately visible: the spire and towers of the cathedral contrasted against the blurred background of hills, the discreet silhouettes of Saint-Maclou church and two factory chimneys and, in the foreground, the combined effect of the roofs of different buildings. Everything here is treated in a simpler manner that does not aim to describe, but to evoke. With the surface strictly divided into two equal planes opposite in weight between sky and ground, the horizon line passing exactly through the middle of the painting, the composition joins the aerial and the urban into one with great sensitivity.

Quite different in style, the smaller *View of the Port of Rouen* (*Vue du port de Rouen*) (pl. 15) that Hoschedé-Monet probably painted a few years later is more in line with a local aesthetic, that of the École de Rouen. The dominant blue-gray palette, the focus brought to the detail of the port, the truncated view of the ferry bridge, the significance accorded to the Seine, and the activity of the boats all seem to come from a more narrative vision than the earlier painting. While we still find the imposing silhouette of the cathedral, which helps to immediately locate the subject, it is represented less vividly. In lieu of a straightforward landscape, the unique composition and developed treatment of an urban atmosphere and motif is evidence of a greater pictorial maturity on the part of the artist.

As for the paintings of the banks of the Seine at Croisset (pls. 17 and 18), rather than considering them as a series, but instead as several atmospheric and luminous variations of the same view day by day, these works again acknowledge Hoschedé-Monet's attention to capturing a given moment—a sort of freeze frame that holds the subject suspended in time. If Monet strived to translate trees blowing in the wind and the rippling surface of water in shimmering light, thus emphasizing the passage of time, Hoschedé-Monet was more attentive to transcribing onto her canvas the depth of a lived moment. While she placed herself more in the position of an observer in relation to the idea of time, of a suspended, condensed moment in nature, Monet accentuated the transience of man's relationship to the world, of his fleeting and constantly renewed experience of it.

Widowed in February 1914, having come to live with her stepfather in Giverny who himself had been widowed for three years, Blanche Hoschedé-Monet abruptly stopped painting to dedicate herself fully to the daily life of the household which required much attention. The decision was

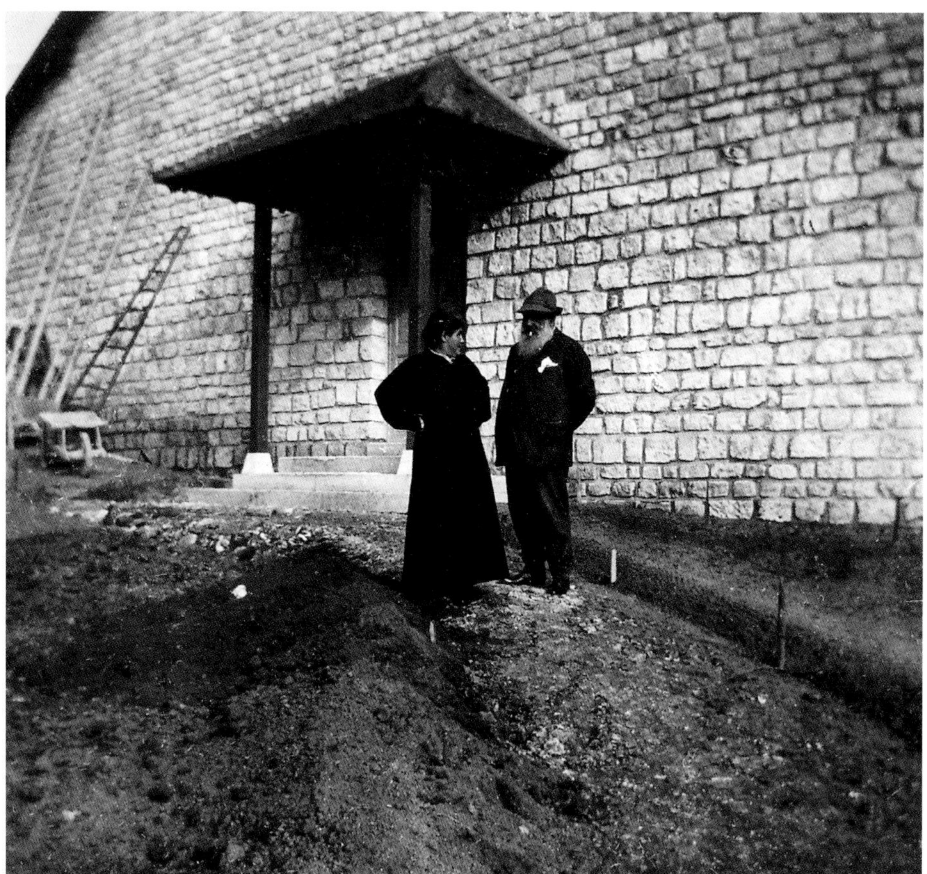

a perfectly natural sacrifice for the person she was most fond of, and whom she knew had a greater work to accomplish, that of the large-scale series of *Water Lilies* he would refer to as his "grandes décorations" (fig. 29). It was an adventure that she would experience anew with Monet and a substitute of sorts for the fact that she was no longer painting herself. In short, it was a decision that imposed itself upon her, and that she obviously accepted.

From the moment that she moved back in with her stepfather, "you could say that Monet found the courage to survive and to live, and the strength to work, through the presence of the woman who became his devoted daughter, keeping his home intact, encouraging him to take up his painting tools again, receiving his friends as her mother had once done," wrote Jean-Pierre Hoschedé.[14] In this way, Hoschedé-Monet knew how to calm the

Fig. 29 Blanche Hoschedé-Monet and Claude Monet standing before the newly constructed studio built for Monet's large-scale *Water Lilies*, Giverny, spring 1915. Collection of Philippe Piguet

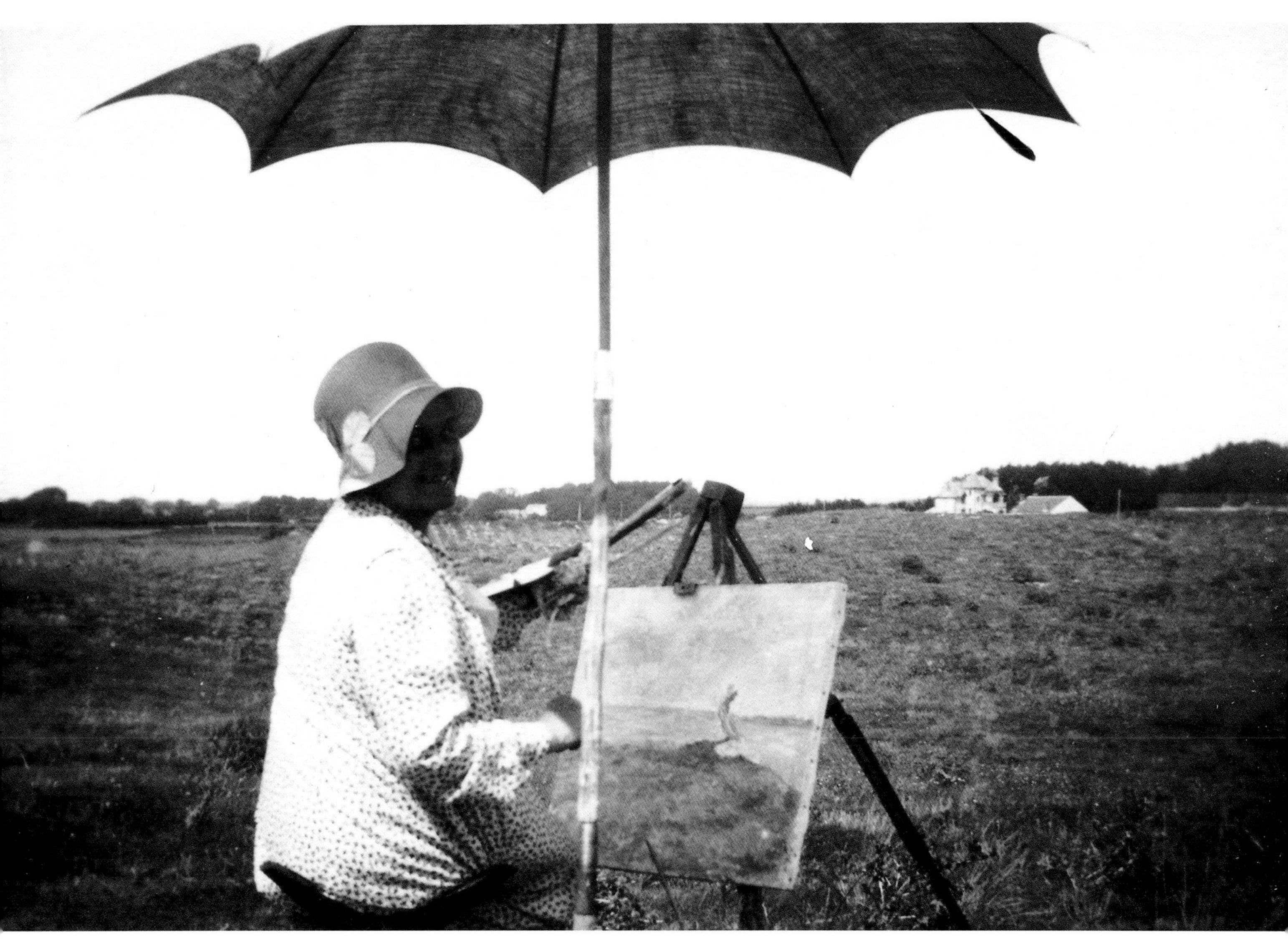

Fig. 30   Blanche Hoschedé-Monet painting
en plein air, ca. 1927–29. Collection of
Philippe Piguet

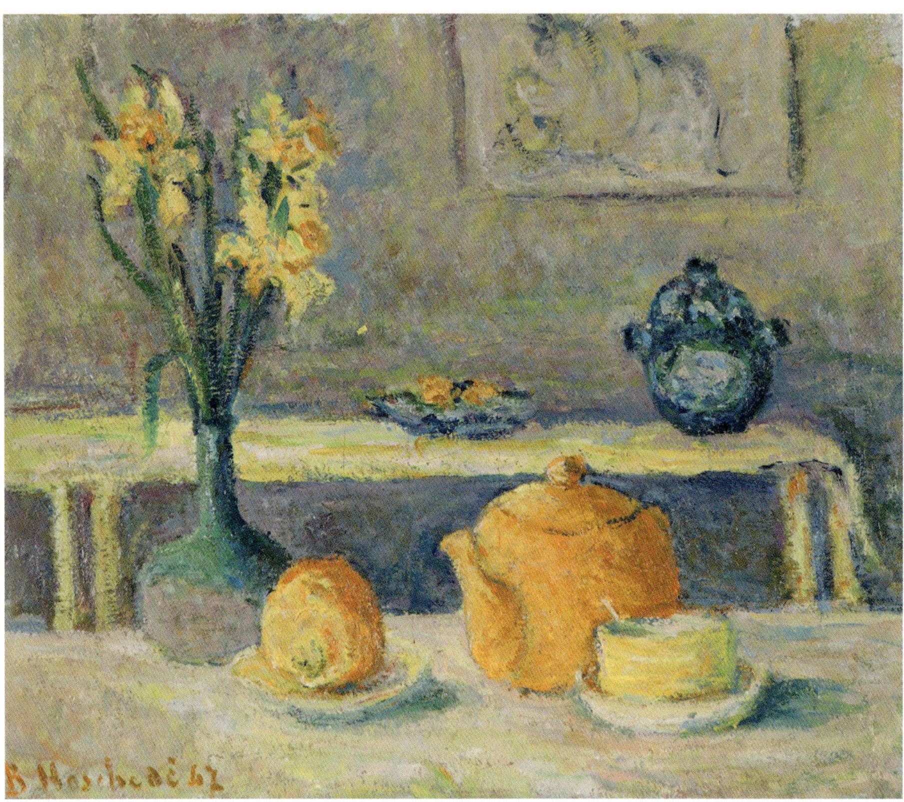

anxiety of the painter, who at times believed his vision had been lost due to his cataracts and was "by her presence alone, the most devoted healer of his morale, the most committed that is possible to imagine."[15]

Soon after Monet's death on December 5, 1926, it was a surprise for many to see Hoschedé-Monet pick up her brushes once again (fig. 30). Invited to remain at the family home in Giverny by her stepbrother Michel, the painter's only heir, to look after the property and to honor its memory,

Hoschedé-Monet found herself as mistress of the house. She immediately applied herself to organizing the installation of the *Water Lilies* at the Musée de l'Orangerie, which were unveiled on May 17, 1927. From then on, she was able to devote herself fully to painting, and had her first solo exhibition in November 1927 at the Galerie Bernheim-Jeune, less than a year following Monet's death and just five days before her sixty-second birthday.

This final period, which would end with her death twenty years later in December 1947,

Fig. 31 Blanche Hoschedé-Monet, *Monet's Dining Room in Giverny* (*La Salle à manger de Monet à Giverny* [*Le Thé*]), 1947. Oil on canvas, 14 ¹⁵⁄₁₆ × 18 ⅛ in. (38 × 46 cm). Collection of Philippe Piguet, on long-term loan to the Musée des Impressionnismes Giverny (MDIG D 2012.1.2)

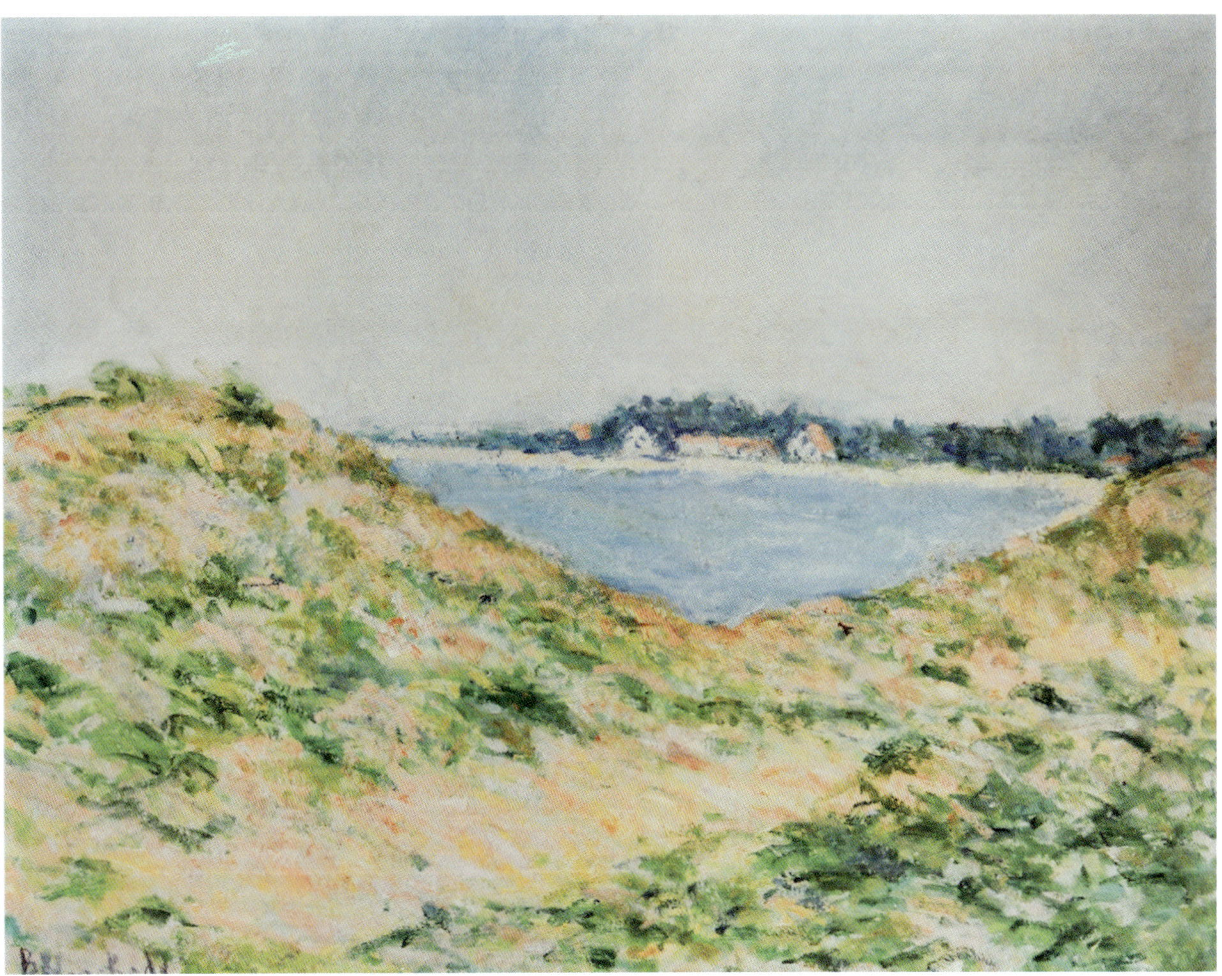

corresponds to a certain change in the way Hoschedé-Monet resumed her creative journey. Her return to painting was solely to satisfy a passion that moved her deeply—far from any career objective—in fervent homage to the man who had encouraged her. Although she would only have three other solo exhibitions in her lifetime, she regularly participated in various salons in Normandy and in Paris. With more free time than before, the artist now had the opportunity to travel with family or visit friends.

Settled in her stepfather's home, Hoschedé-Monet chose subjects that were within her reach but that she had not previously tackled: Monet's

Fig. 32 Blanche Hoschedé-Monet, *Kervoyal-Damgan: The Sea (Morbihan, Brittany)* (*Kervoyal-Damgan: la mer [Morbihan, Bretagne]*), 1937. Oil on cardboard, 14 15/16 × 18 1/8 in. (38 × 46 cm). Private collection

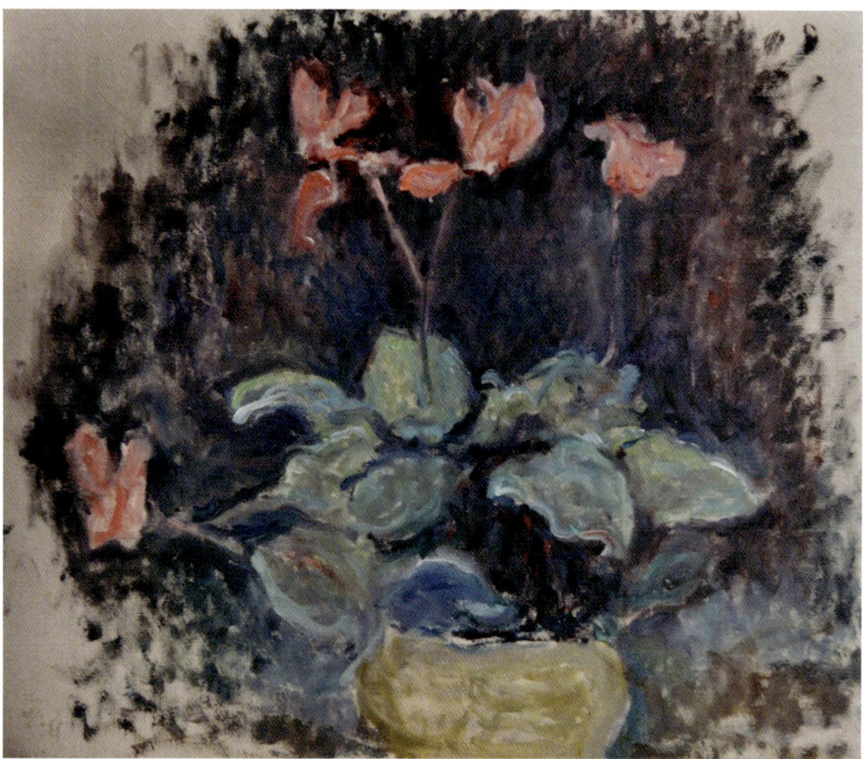

house, his garden, and the pond of water lilies. Of these motifs, she highlighted the lushness and chromatic diversity of the vegetation in particular. She framed the house by drowning it in a profusion of flowers, focusing her gaze on the central path, and based her composition on the ascending perspective and interplay of flowered arches (pl. 24); she captured different points of view of the garden to depict its abundantly floral appearance (pls. 24–25, 33–35), or even close-ups of certain species (pls. 40–43). She created a few paintings inside the home as well, mostly still lifes,

which reveal one aspect or another, like the living room and studio (fig. 13), or the yellow dining room (fig. 31). Finally, Hoschedé-Monet produced a group of very distinct views of the pond (like pl. 38), positioning herself on one bank to paint the opposite in a composition that often included the surface of the water, the border of flowers, trees, and a piece of sky, as if she sought to express a concrete whole, rather than the ephemeral effects that Monet captured in the reflections of the pond.

This was her way of experiencing and preserving—at the most profound level of her

Fig. 33 Blanche Hoschedé-Monet, *Cyclamens*, 1947. Oil on canvas, 18⅛ × 21⅝ in. (46 × 55 cm). Collection of Marc and Nicole Piguet

emotional memory—the world of her family's property for which she was now responsible, while drawing from it the inspiration for her paintings that was equal to what Monet's presence had provided her. Hoschedé-Monet could not part with the memory of their exchanges, even when they may have been unspoken or differed in opinion, as when she adeptly defended Delacroix against Corot, especially considering Monet's esteem for the latter.[16]

The trips that she took later in life were an opportunity for her to broaden the scope of her iconography and work in different light, so that her paintings became distinguished in certain ways from those of Giverny and its surroundings, or even from the work she made in Normandy. In Brittany, as in Vendée, Hoschedé-Monet painted several coastal scenes, often paying more attention to the shore than to the sea itself—as in *The Beach at Belébat* (*Plage de Belébat*)[17] or *Kervoyal-Damgan: The Sea (Morbihan, Brittany)* (*Kervoyal-Damgan: la mer [Morbihan, Bretagne]*) (fig. 32); on the other hand, *Sunrise* (*Soleil levant*), painted in 1936,[18] is strongly inspired by Monet, especially his *Impression, Sunrise* (*Impression, Soleil levant*, 1872; Musée Marmottan Monet, Paris). In the 1930s and early 1940s, during the various trips she made to southeast France, the landscapes that she brought back from Lake Bourget, the Alps of Provence, Hérault, Antibes, and from the Côte d'Azur underscore the care that she took to convey a frank, more individualized look. It was the same for her still lifes, always very

frontal and direct. Her work recorded the experience she acquired over time, as the impact of Monet's painting gradually dissipated. However, if Monet's influence still finds expression in her final painting, *Cyclamens* (fig. 33), dated 1947, it is because it was not yet finished and can therefore be seen in an early state, closer to the Impressionism defined by Monet's style. But, in reality, the art of Blanche Hoschedé-Monet appeals far more to the expression of a temporality that is not ephemeral, but lasting. This is her mark, what characterizes her.

Blanche Hoschedé-Monet produced relatively few works: no more than three hundred pieces in total. They nevertheless constitute a singular and coherent whole, aligned with an Impressionist aesthetic, especially since nearly four-fifths of her paintings were completed in Normandy, the birthplace of the movement. She was entirely native to Impressionism, as much in her connection to its artists and characteristic motifs as to its evident influence in her work. Hoschedé-Monet lived in Normandy for sixty-four years: in Giverny (1883–97 and 1913–47), in Rouen (1897–1910), and in Beaumont-le-Roger (1910–13). She explored the region's internal landscapes as well as the banks of the Seine and the cliff-lined coast. The artist nourished her work with the variety of its topography, whether flat or hilly, always endeavoring to give us an image as it was, in its most direct representation. To quote Jean Pierre-Hoschedé one last time, she was "not in the shadow, but in the light of Claude Monet."[19]

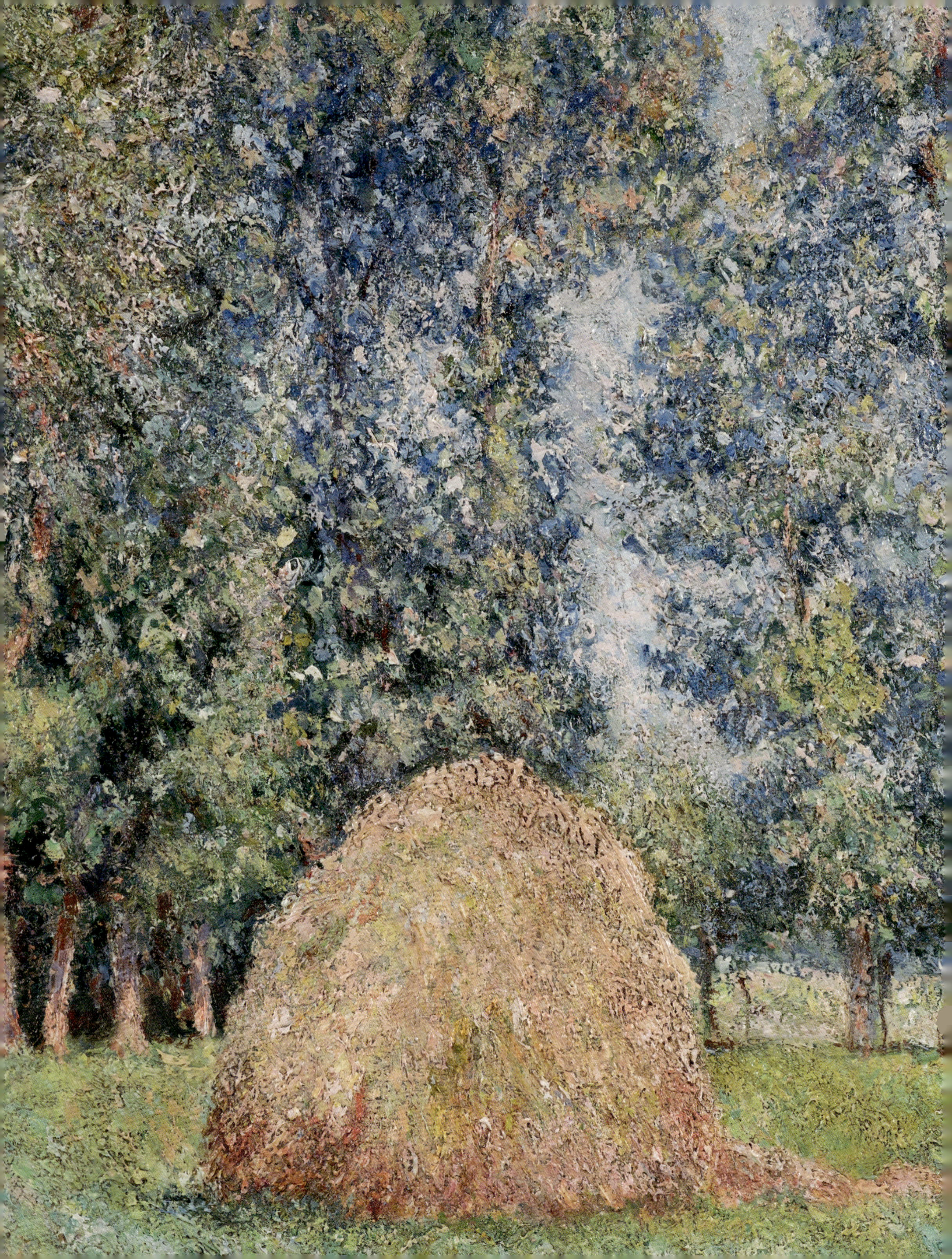

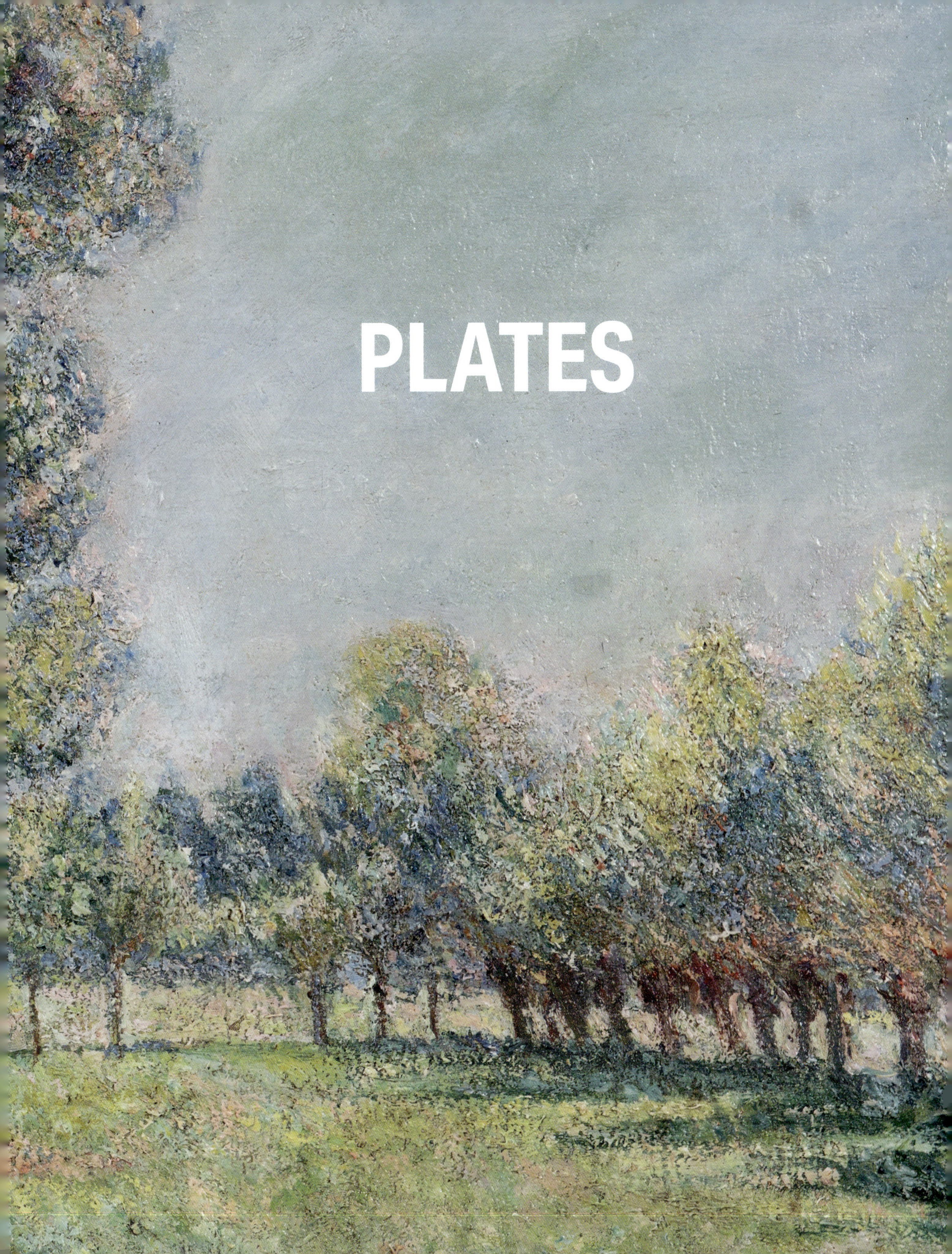

PLATES

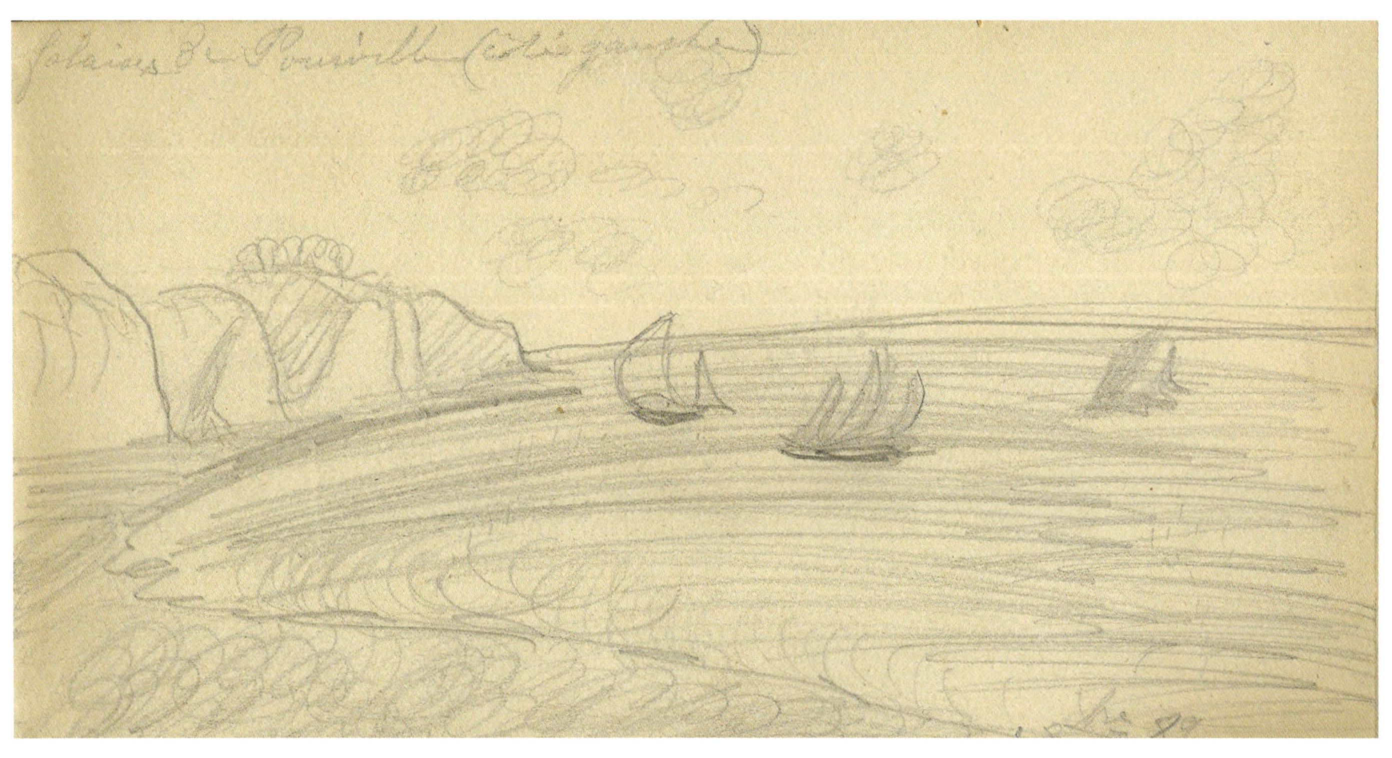

Pl. 1

BLANCHE HOSCHEDÉ-MONET
Sketchbook
1882–84
4 ½ × 7 ⅞ × ¹³⁄₁₆ in. (11.5 × 20 × 2 cm)
Collection of Philippe Piguet, on long-term
loan to the Musée des Impressionnismes
Giverny (MDIG D 2009.1.1)

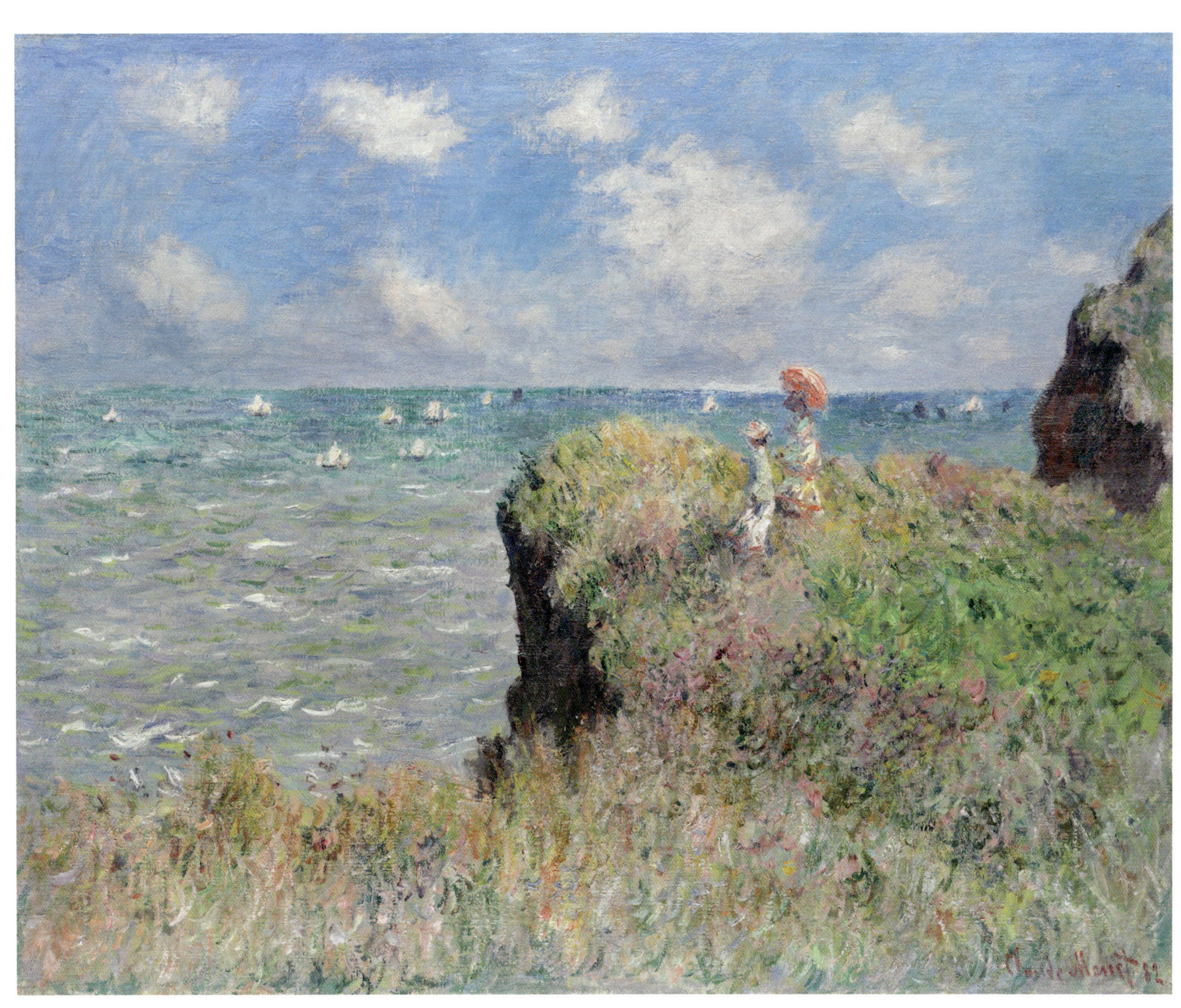

Pl. 2

CLAUDE MONET
Cliff Walk at Pourville
(*Promenade sur la falaise, Pourville*)
1882
Oil on canvas
26⅛ × 32⁷⁄₁₆ in. (66.5 × 82.3 cm)
Art Institute of Chicago, Mr. and Mrs. Lewis
Larned Coburn Memorial Collection
(1933.443)

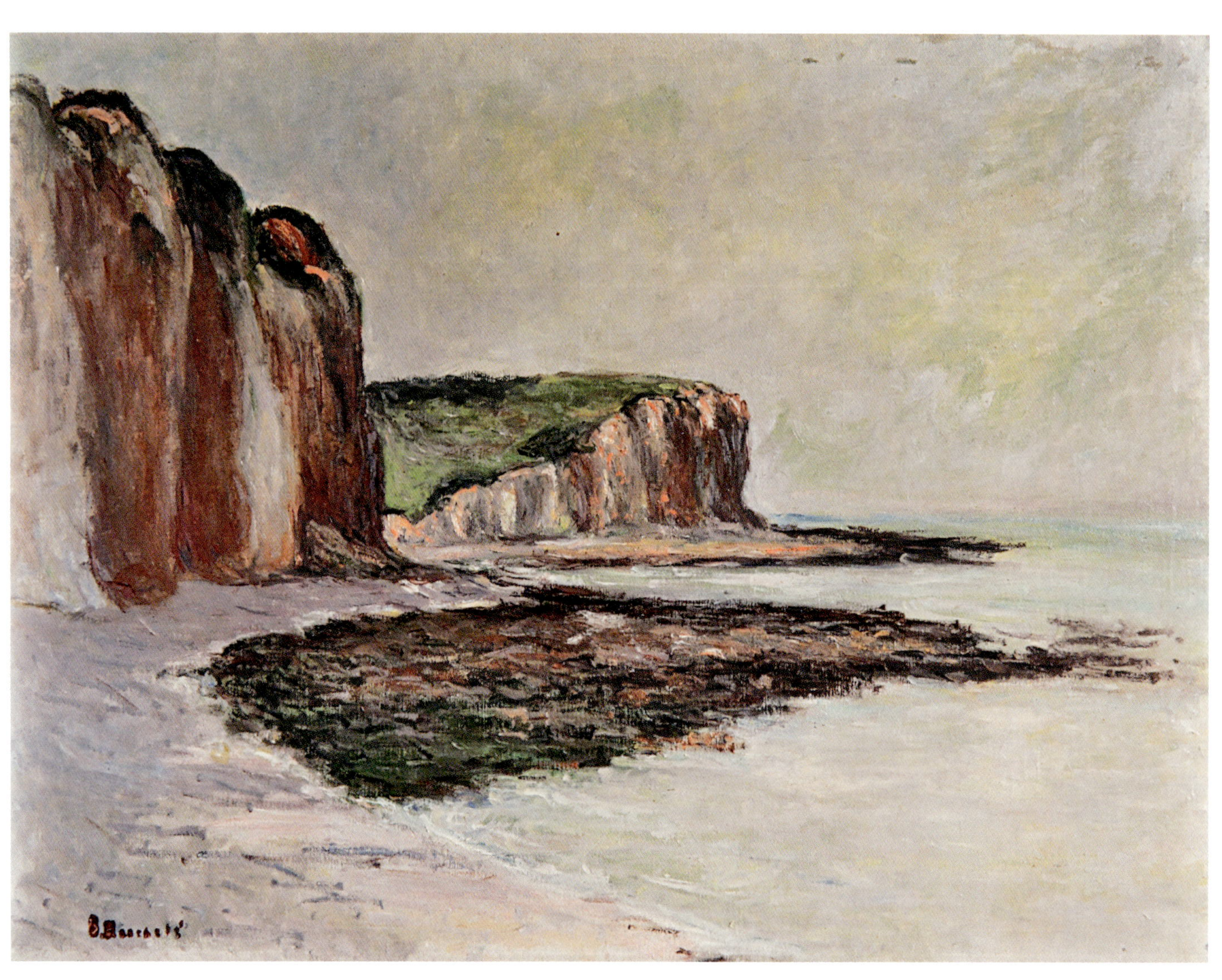

BLANCHE HOSCHEDÉ-MONET
Les Petites-Dalles
ca. 1884–85
Oil on canvas
23⅝ × 31⅞ in. (60 × 81 cm)
Private collection

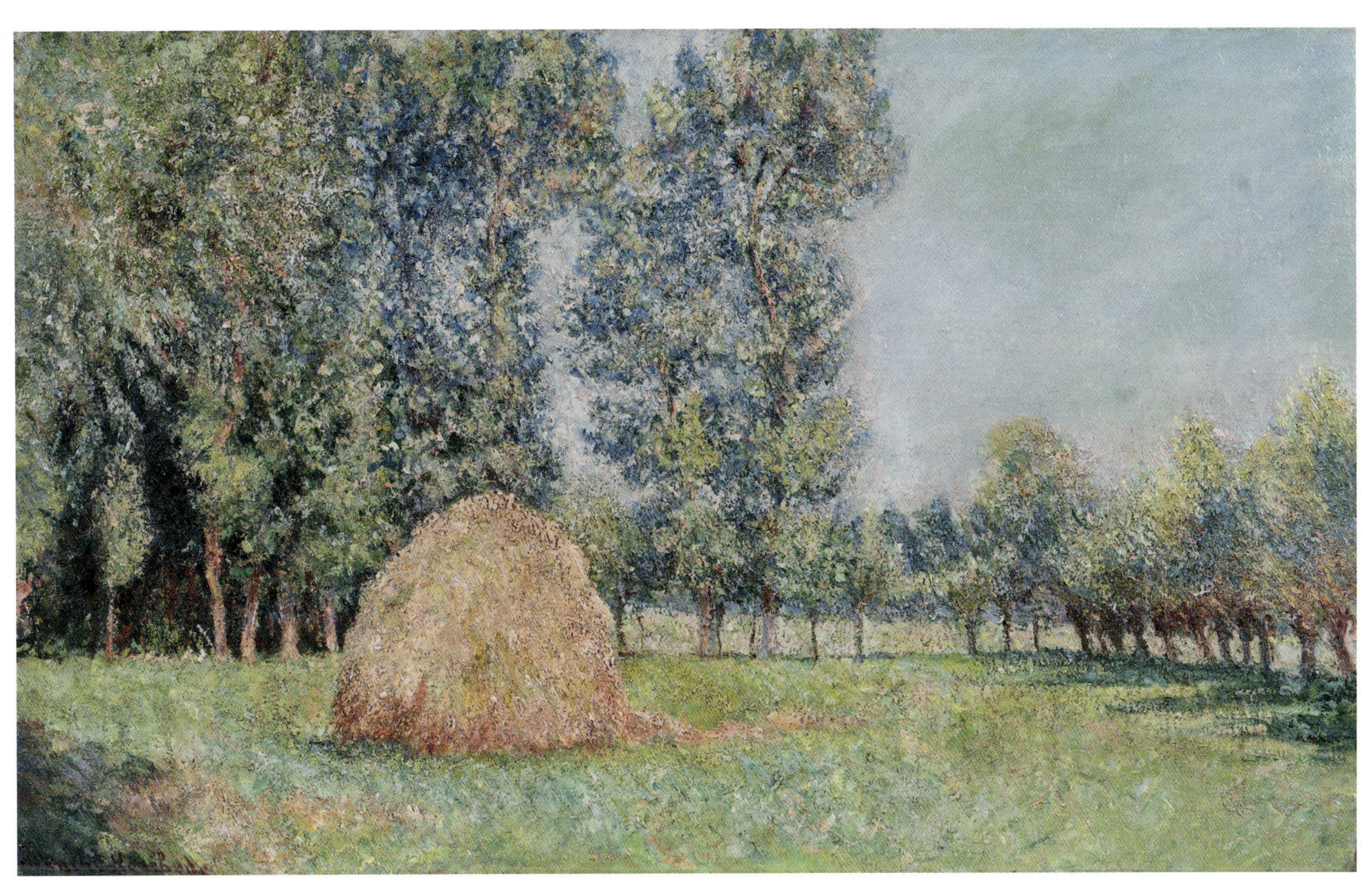

BLANCHE HOSCHEDÉ-MONET
Haystack at Giverny (*Meule à Giverny*)
ca. 1893
Oil on canvas
19 ⅞ × 32 ½ in. (50.5 × 82.6 cm)
Collection of Alice and Rick Johnson

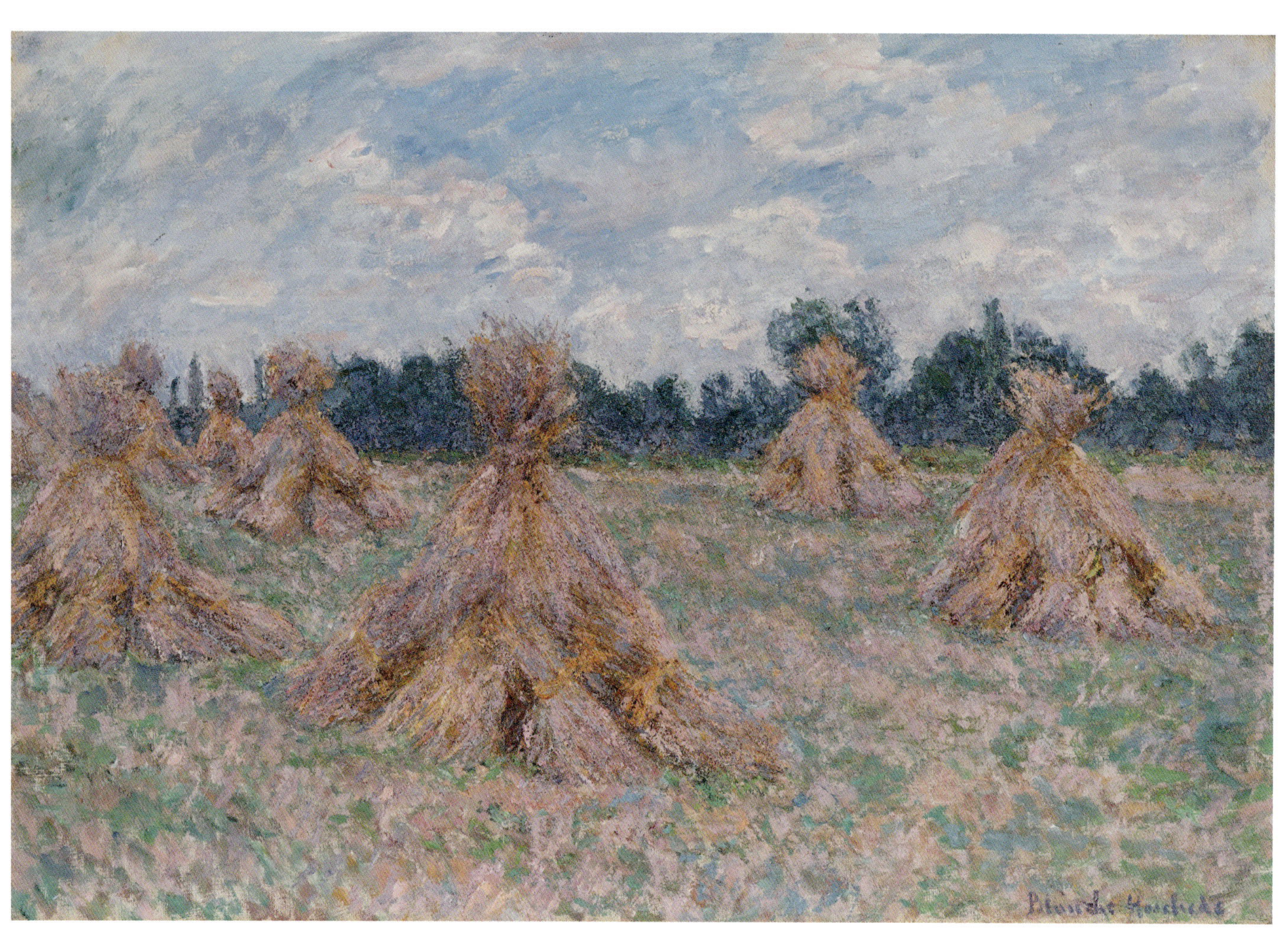

Pl. 5

BLANCHE HOSCHEDÉ-MONET
The Small Grainstacks (*Les Moyettes*)
ca. 1894
Oil on canvas
18 1/8 × 22 1/16 in. (46 × 56 cm)
Collection of Alice and Rick Johnson

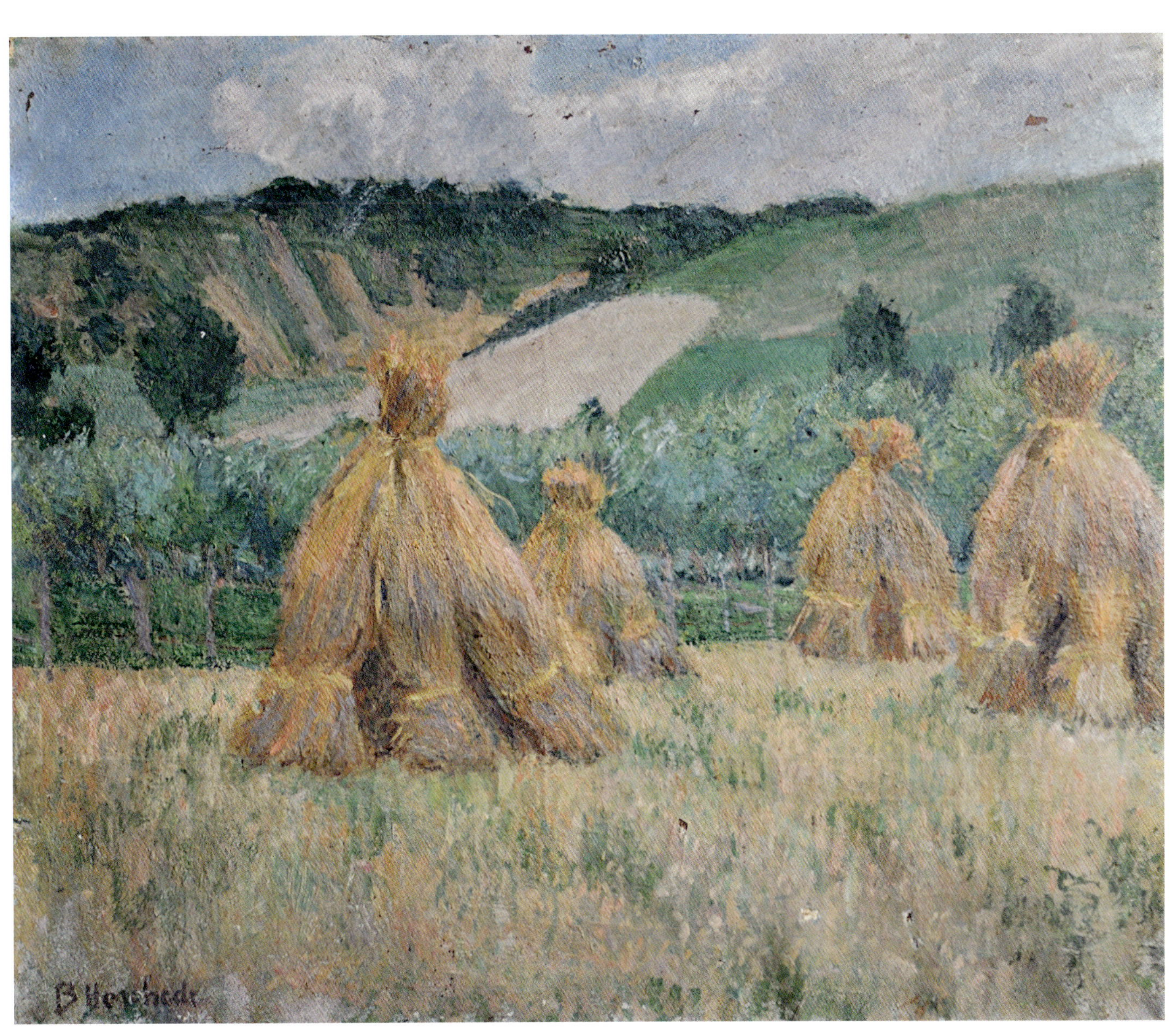

BLANCHE HOSCHEDÉ-MONET
The Small Grainstacks (*Les Moyettes*)
n.d.
Oil on canvas
18⅛ × 22¹⁄₁₆ in. (46 × 56 cm)
Private collection

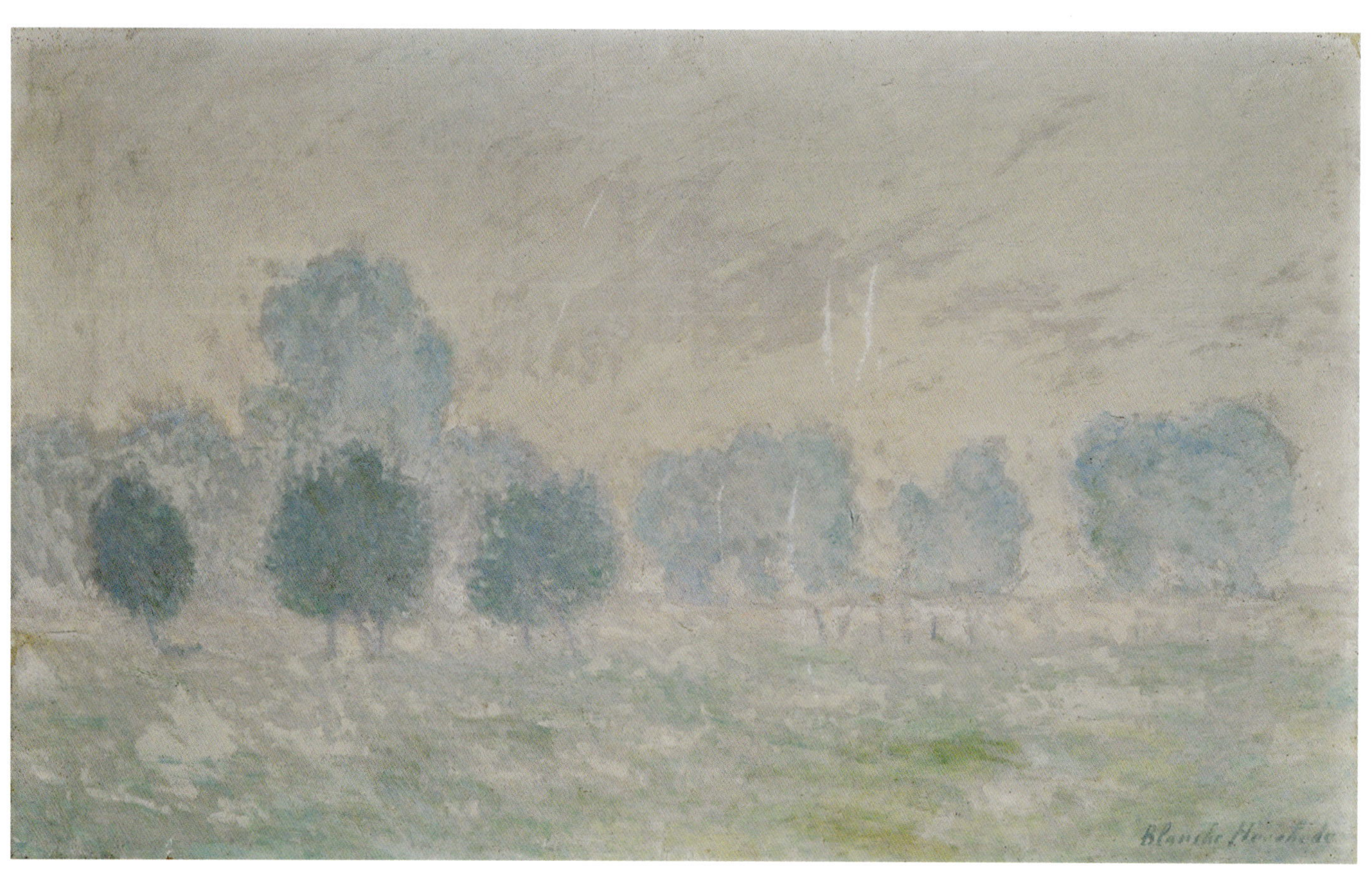

Pl. 7

BLANCHE HOSCHEDÉ-MONET
Trees in the Fog
(*Arbres dans le brouillard*)
ca. 1888
Oil on canvas
20 1/16 × 32 11/16 in. (51 × 83 cm)
Private collection

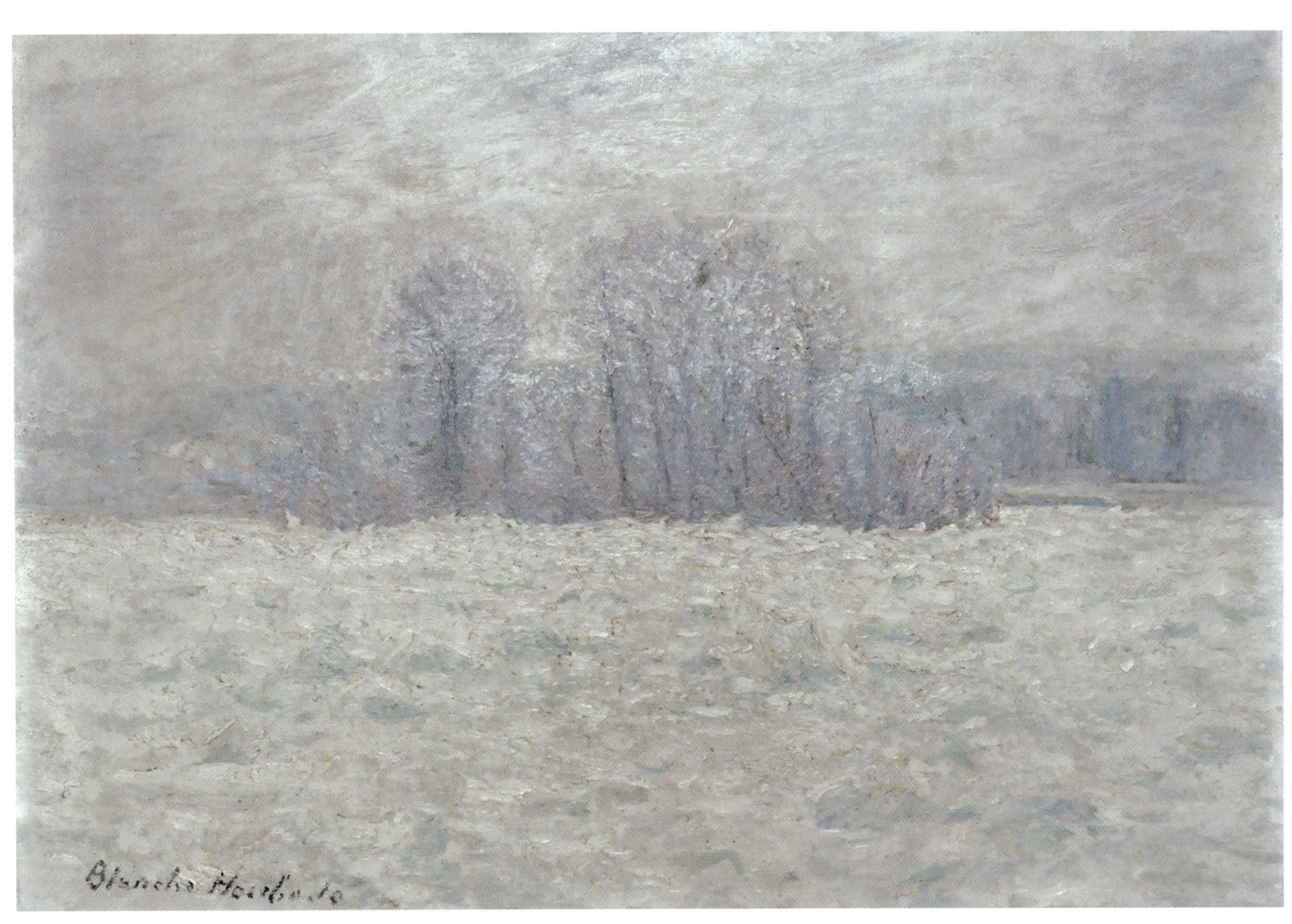

BLANCHE HOSCHEDÉ-MONET
The Ice Floes at Vernon
(*Les Glaçons à Vernon*)
ca. 1893
Oil on canvas
19 11/16 × 28 3/4 in. (50 × 73 cm)
Collection of Marc and Nicole Piguet

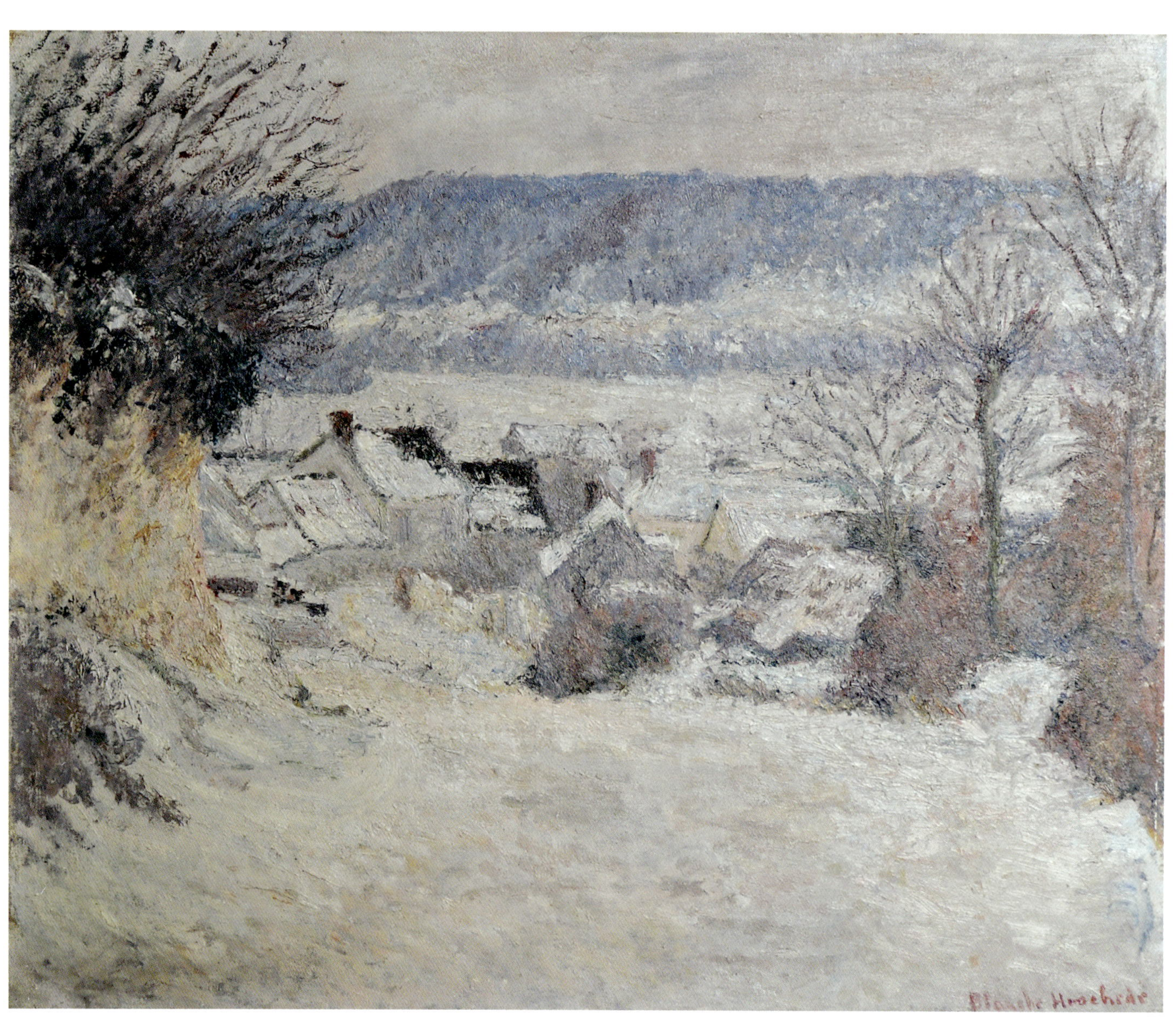

Pl. 9

BLANCHE HOSCHEDÉ-MONET
Giverny in the Snow
(*Giverny sous la neige*)
n.d.
Oil on canvas
23 7/16 × 28 3/4 in. (59.5 × 73 cm)
Collection of Jean-Loup Piguet

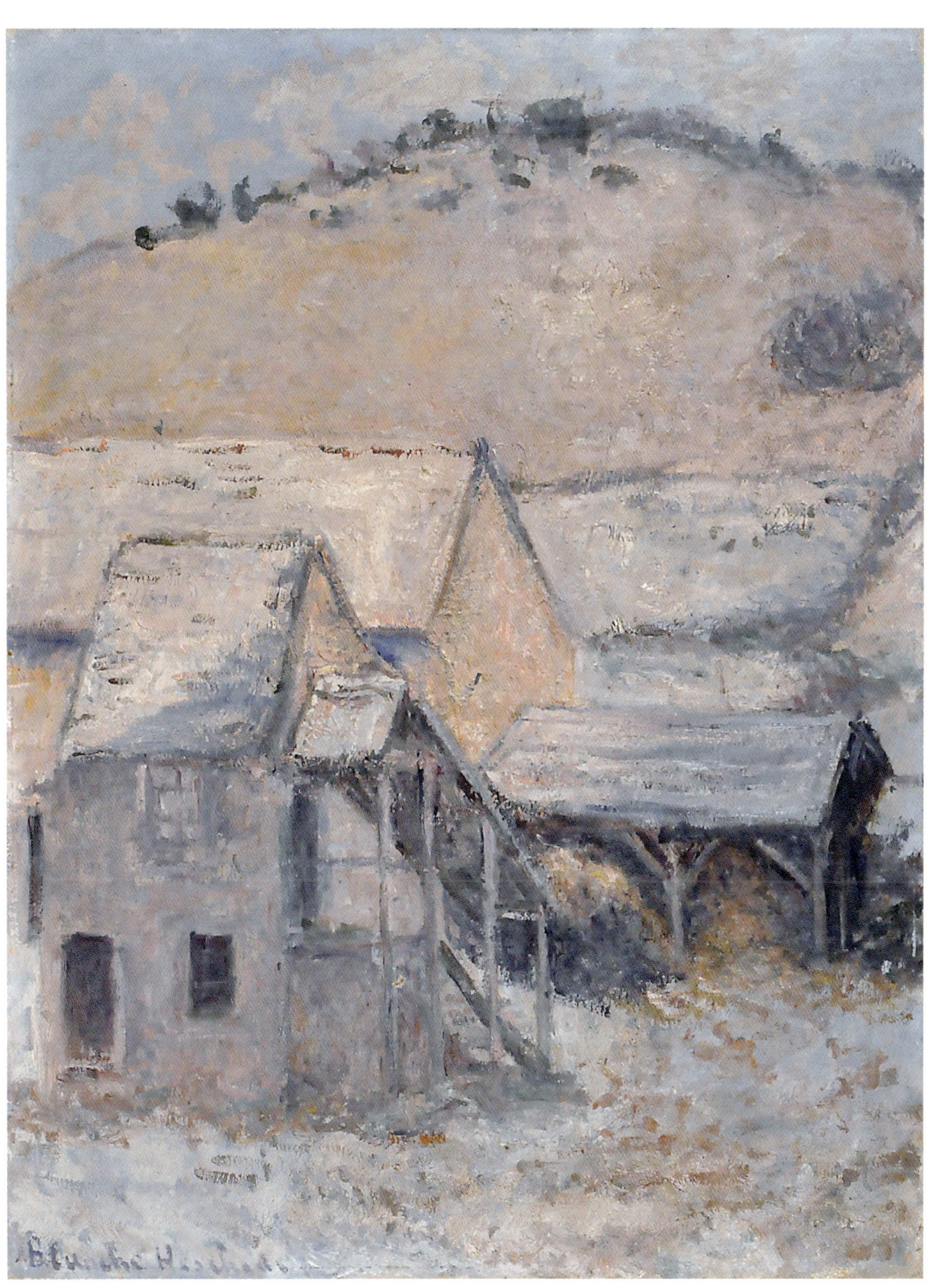

Pl. 10

BLANCHE HOSCHEDÉ-MONET
The Duboc Farm, Giverny
(*La Ferme Duboc, Giverny*)
n.d.
Oil on canvas
28 ¾ × 21 ⁷⁄₁₆ in. (73 × 54.5 cm)
Collection of Philippe Piguet

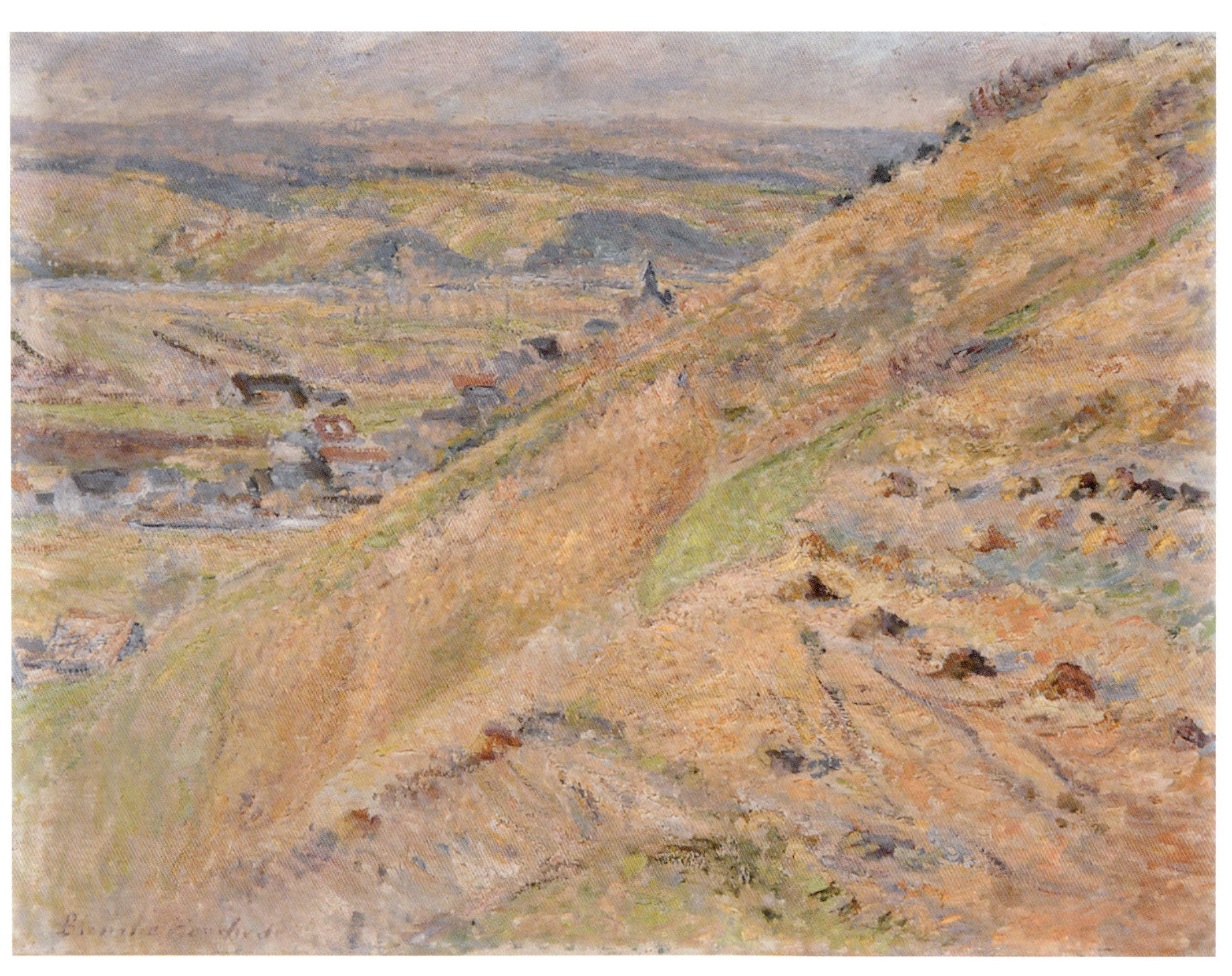

Pl. 11

BLANCHE HOSCHEDÉ-MONET
The Hill, Giverny (*La Côte à Giverny*)
n.d.
Oil on canvas
21⁷⁄₁₆ × 28¾ in. (54.5 × 73 cm)
Private collection

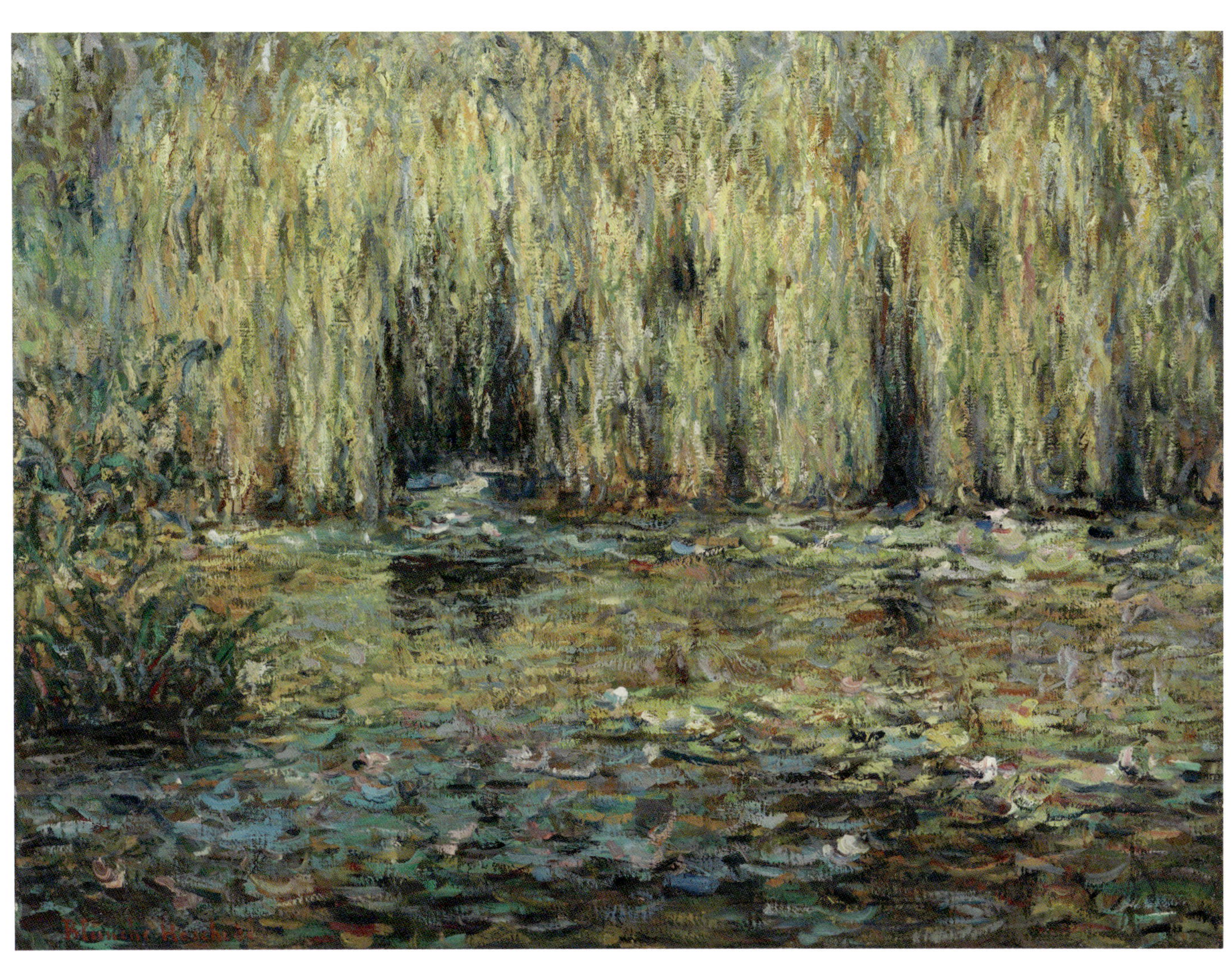

Pl. 12

BLANCHE HOSCHEDÉ-MONET
The Weeping Willows on the Lily Pond at Giverny
(*Les Saules sur l'étang de Giverny*)
ca. 1893–97
Oil on canvas
23¾ × 32 in. (60.3 × 81.3 cm)
Columbus Museum of Art, Columbus, Ohio,
Museum Purchase, through exchange (2013.051)

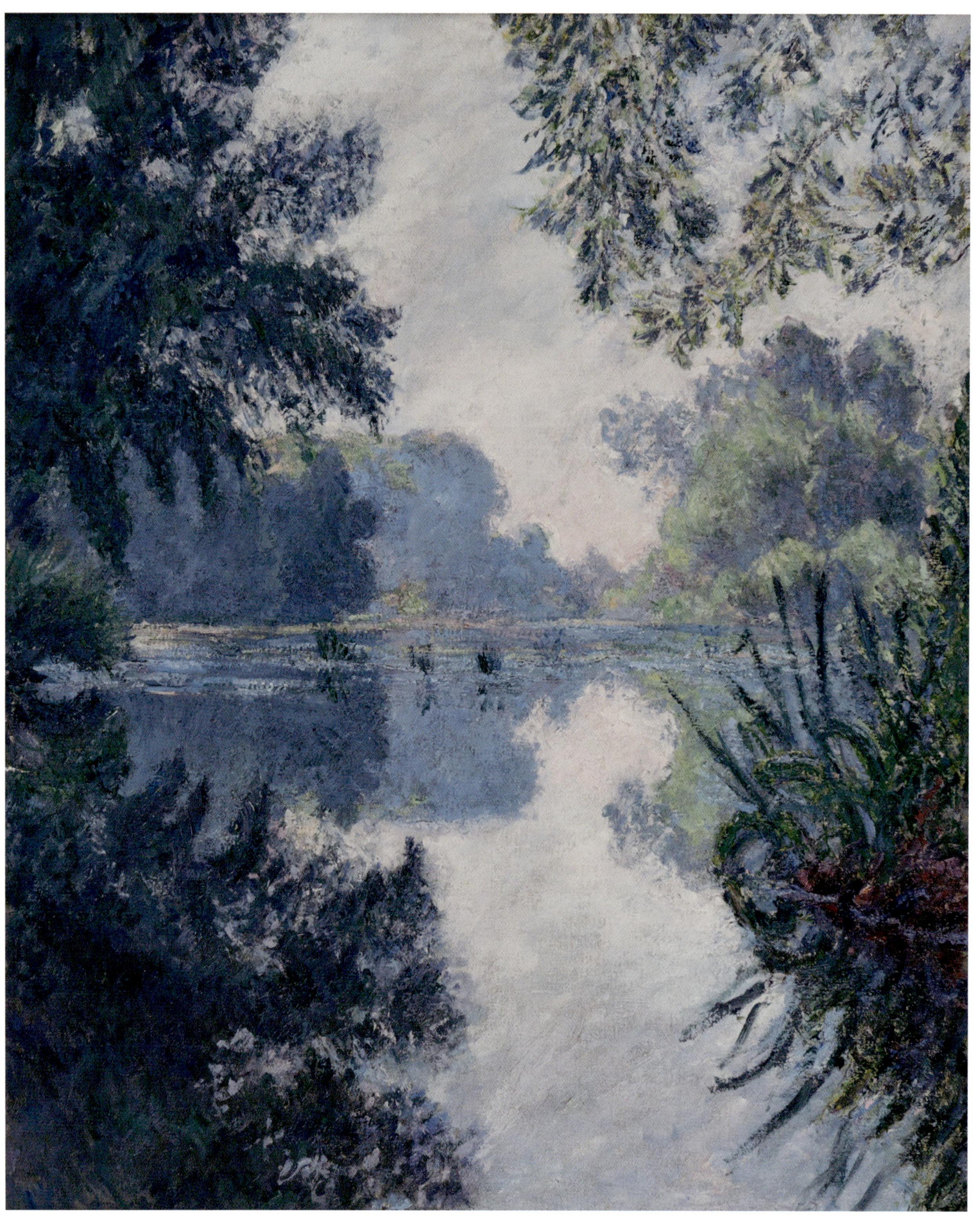

BLANCHE HOSCHEDÉ-MONET
Morning on the Seine
(Matinée sur la Seine)
ca. 1896
Oil on canvas
28 ¾ × 23 ¹³⁄₁₆ in. (73 × 60.5 cm)
Collection of Alice and Rick Johnson

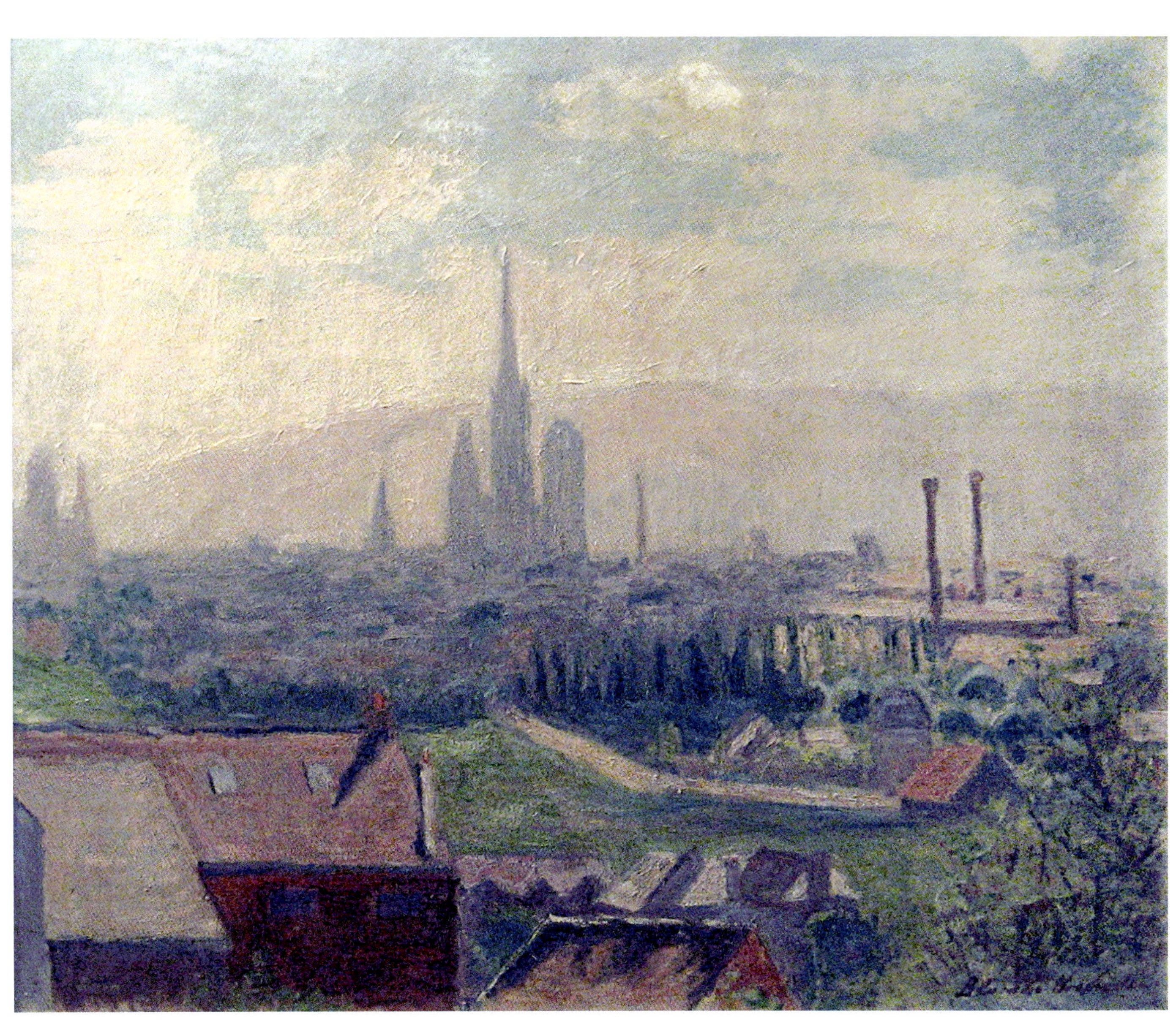

Pl. 14

BLANCHE HOSCHEDÉ-MONET
View of Rouen
(*Vue générale de Rouen*)
ca. 1900
Oil on canvas
23⅝ × 28¾ in. (60 × 73 cm)
Private collection

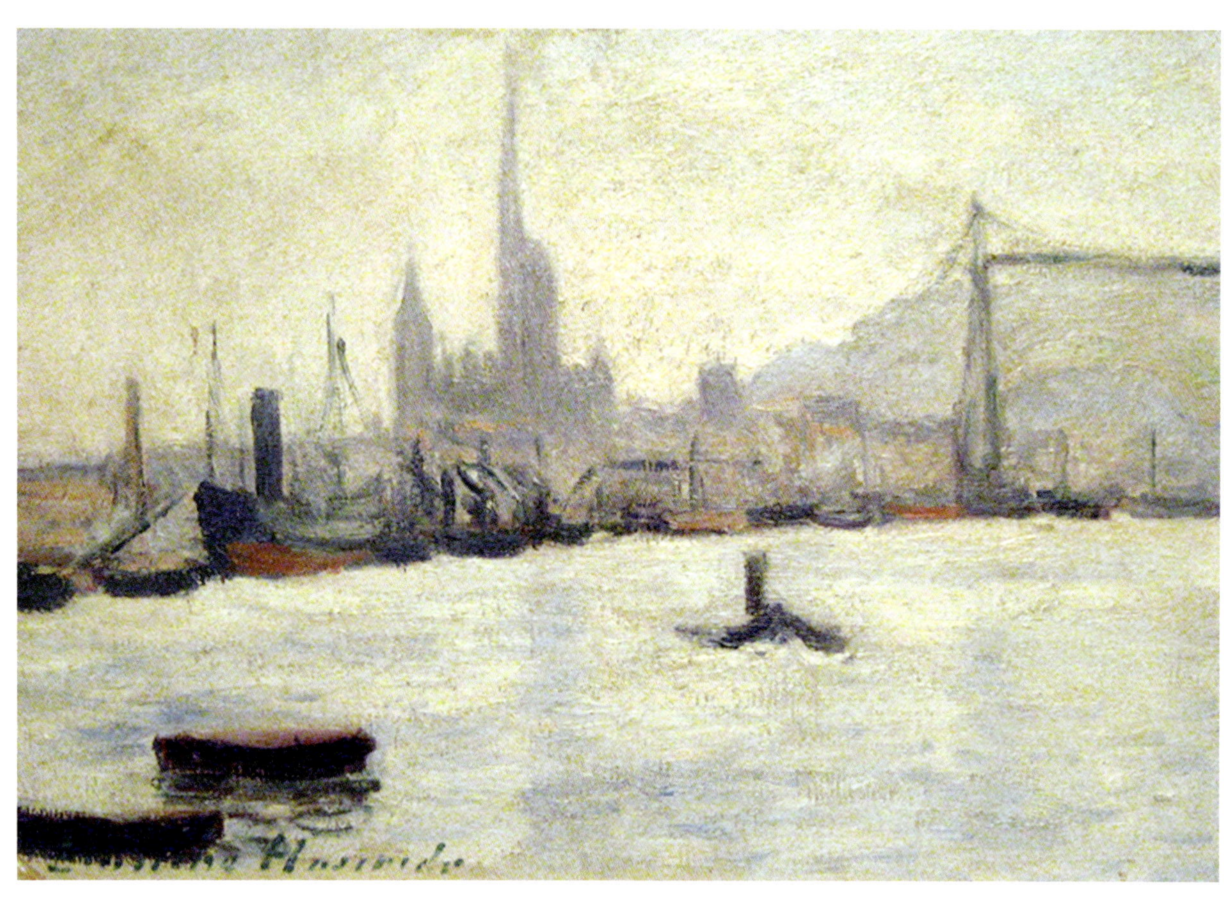

Pl. 15

BLANCHE HOSCHEDÉ-MONET
*View of the Port of Rouen
(The Ferry Bridge)* (*Vue du port de Rouen
[Le pont transbordeur]*)
ca. 1900
Oil on cardboard
9 7/16 × 13 3/4 in. (24 × 35 cm)
Collection of Philippe Piguet

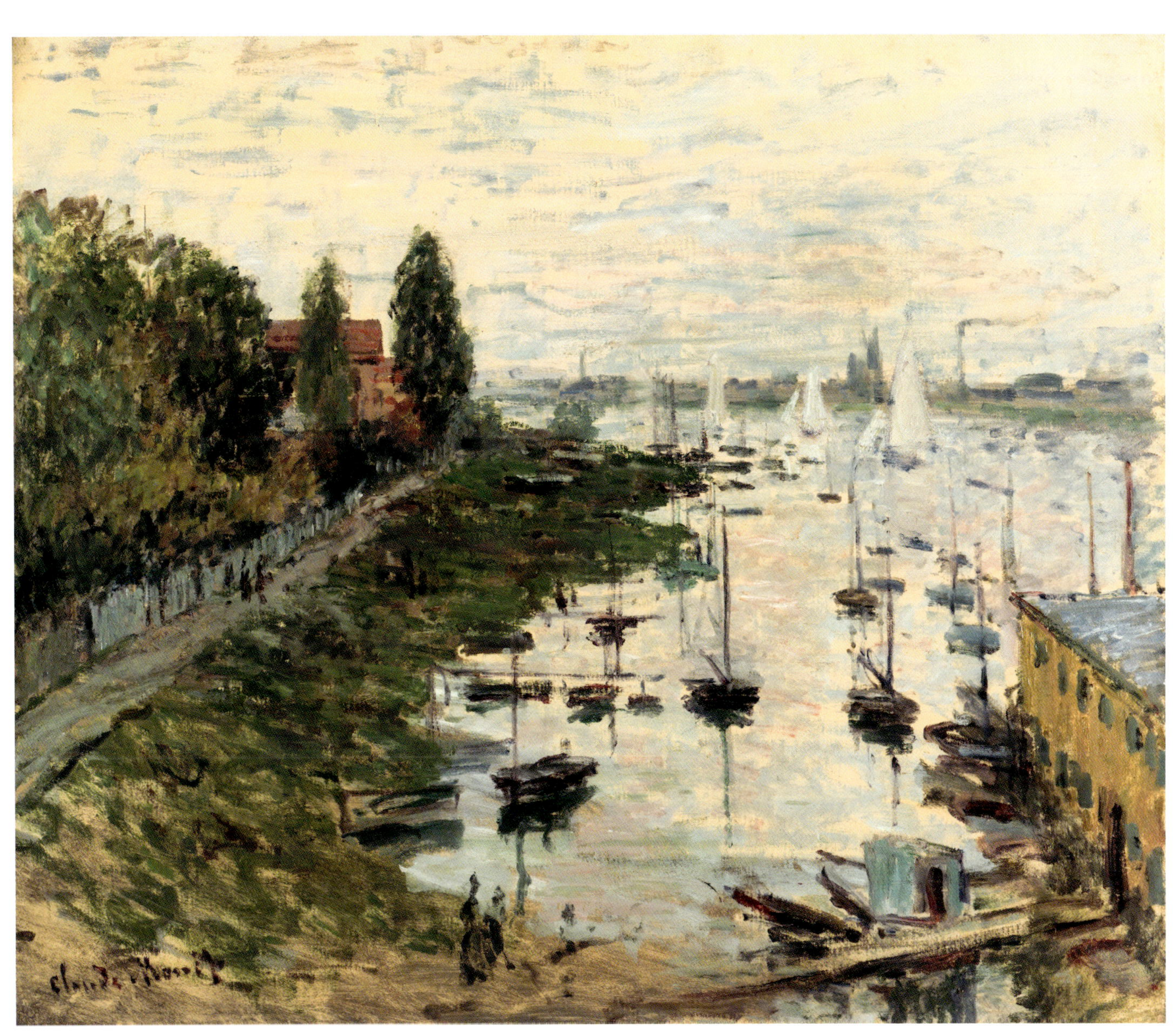

Pl. 16

CLAUDE MONET
The Port of Argenteuil
(*Le Bassin d'Argenteuil*)
1874
Oil on canvas
21¾ × 25⅞ in. (55.2 × 65.7 cm)
Eskenazi Museum of Art, Indiana
University (76.15)

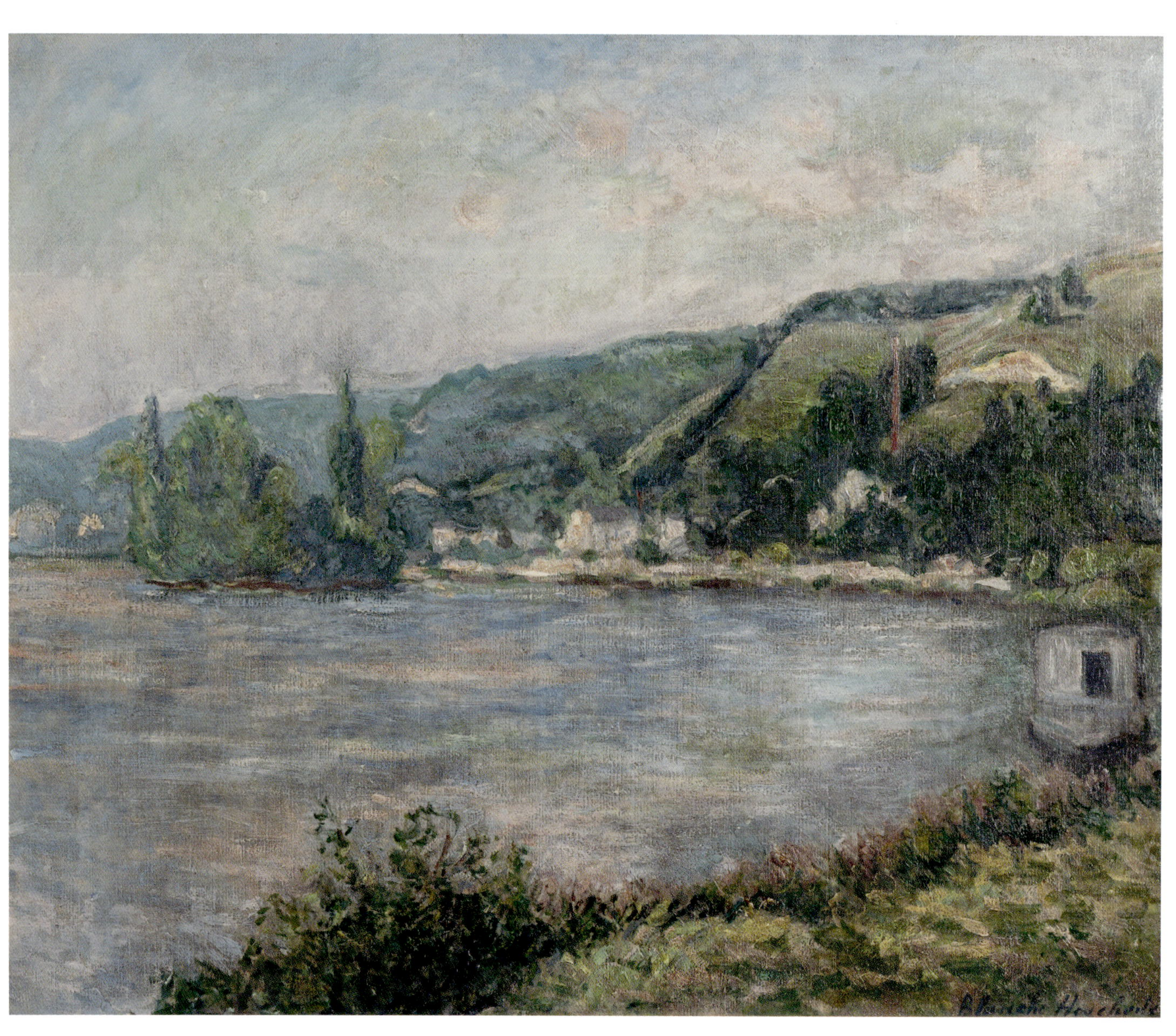

Pl. 17

BLANCHE HOSCHEDÉ-MONET
The Bank of the Seine
(*Bord de la Seine*)
ca. 1897–1910
Oil on canvas
23¾ × 29 in. (60.3 × 73.7 cm)
Collection of Gary Z. and Kathy J. Anderson

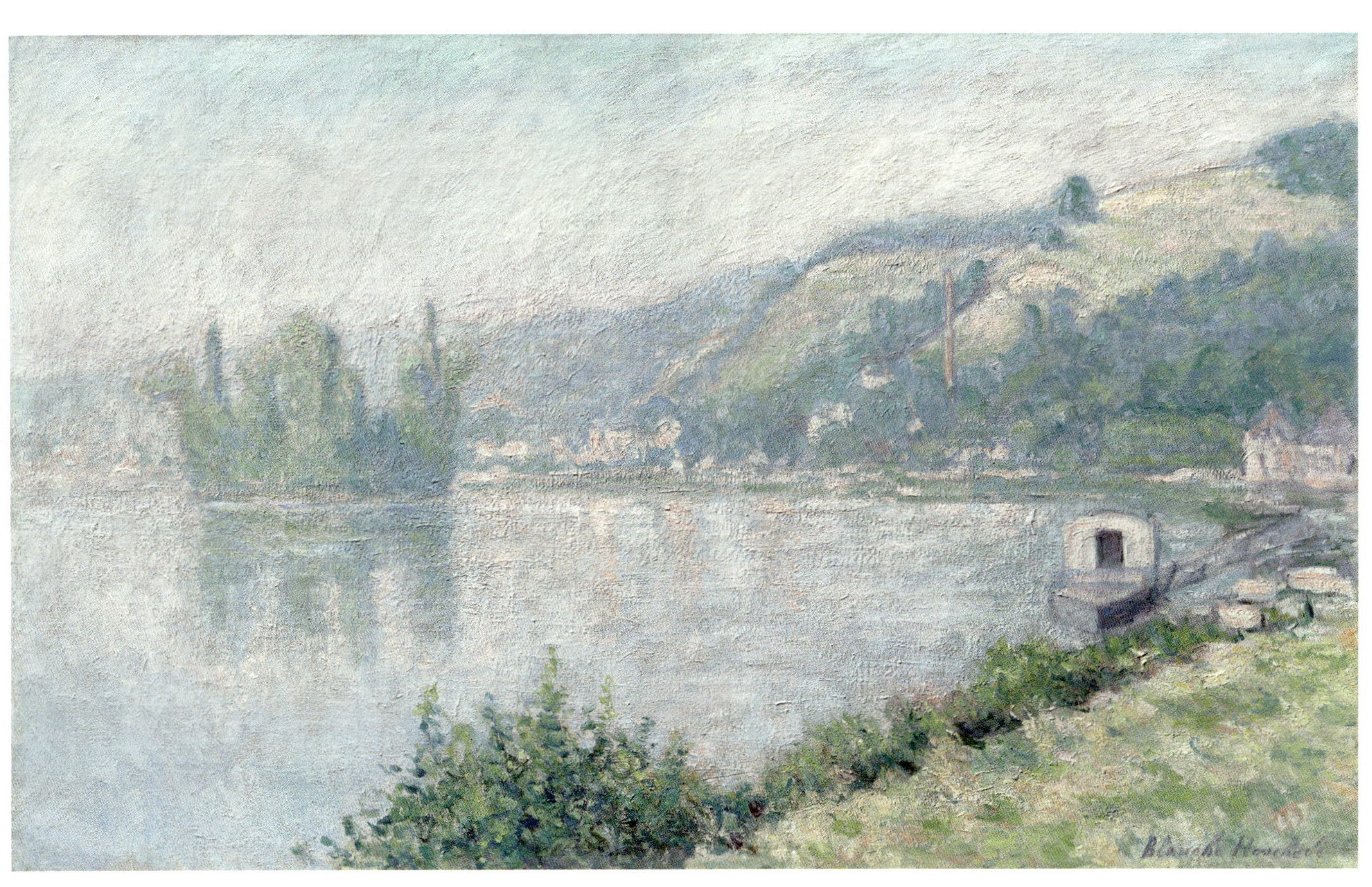

Pl. 18

BLANCHE HOSCHEDÉ-MONET
The Seine at Croisset
(*La Seine à Croisset*)
ca. 1897–1910
Oil on canvas
19 11/16 × 32 5/16 in. (50 × 82.7 cm)
Private collection

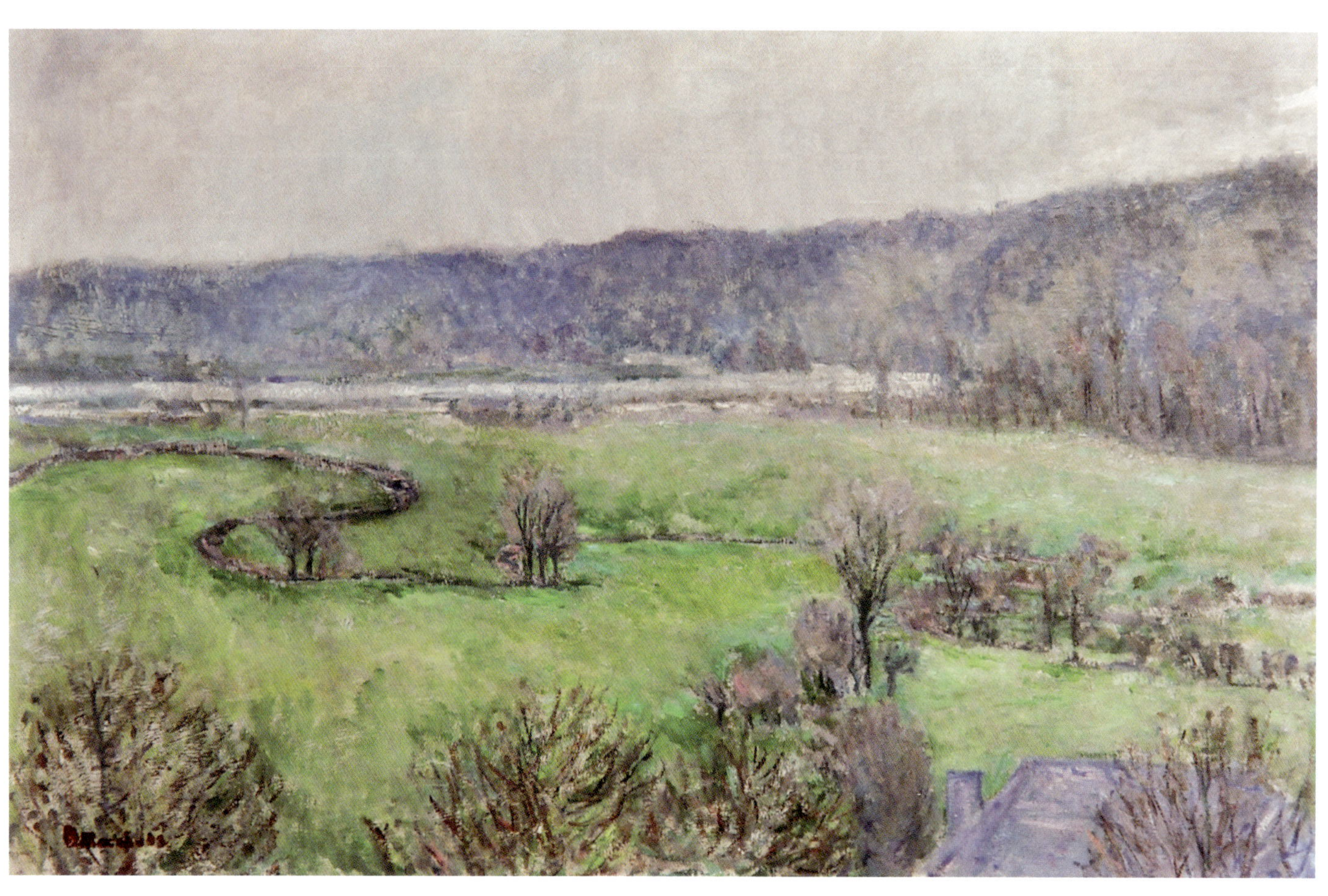

Pl. 19

BLANCHE HOSCHEDÉ-MONET
Meadows downstream from Rouen
(*Prés en aval de Rouen*)
n.d.
Oil on canvas
20 7/8 × 30 5/16 in. (53 × 77 cm)
Collection of Jean-Loup Piguet

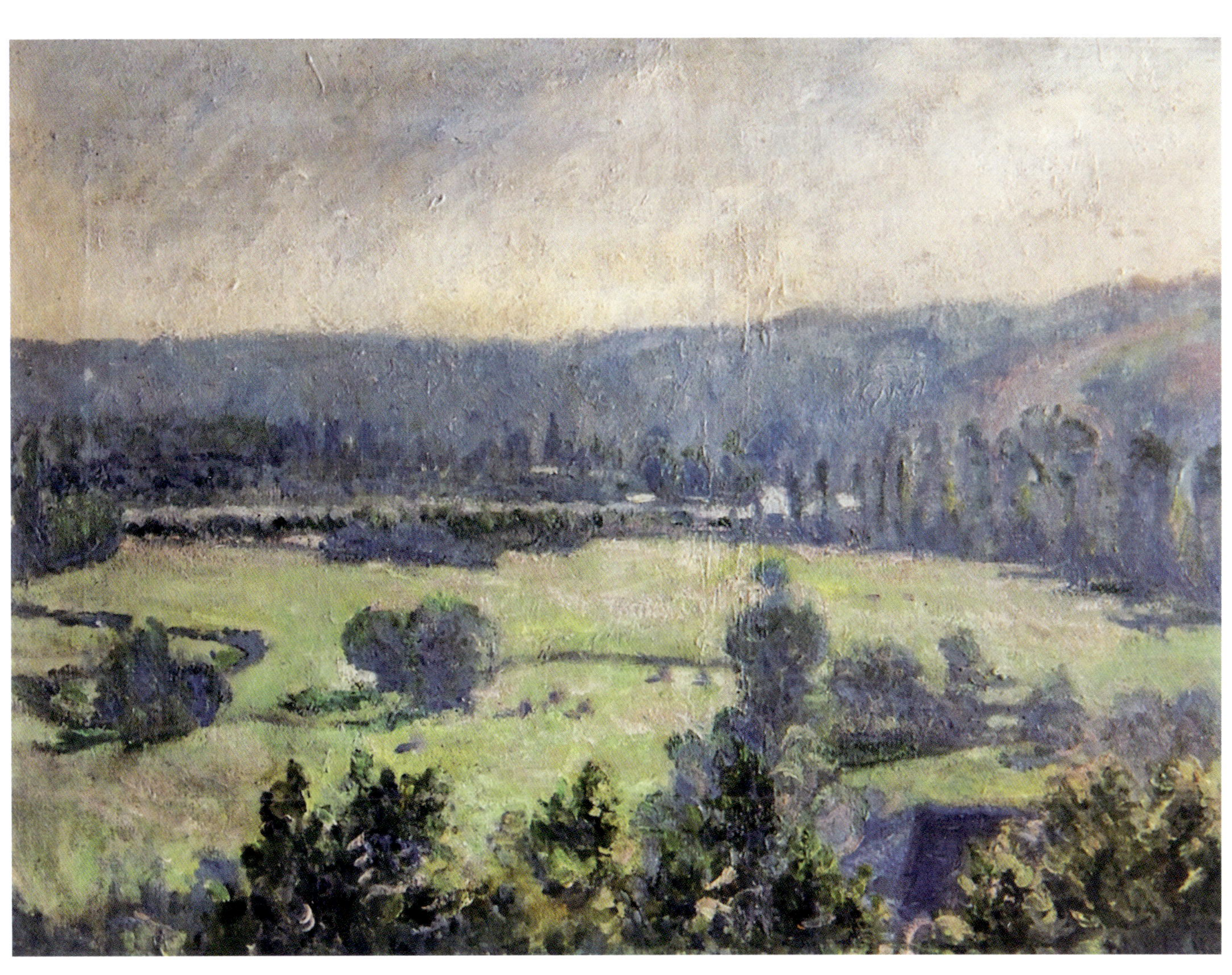

BLANCHE HOSCHEDÉ-MONET
Meadows downstream from Rouen
(*Prés en aval de Rouen*)
n.d.
Oil on canvas
19 11/16 × 28 15/16 in. (50 × 73.5 cm)
Private collection

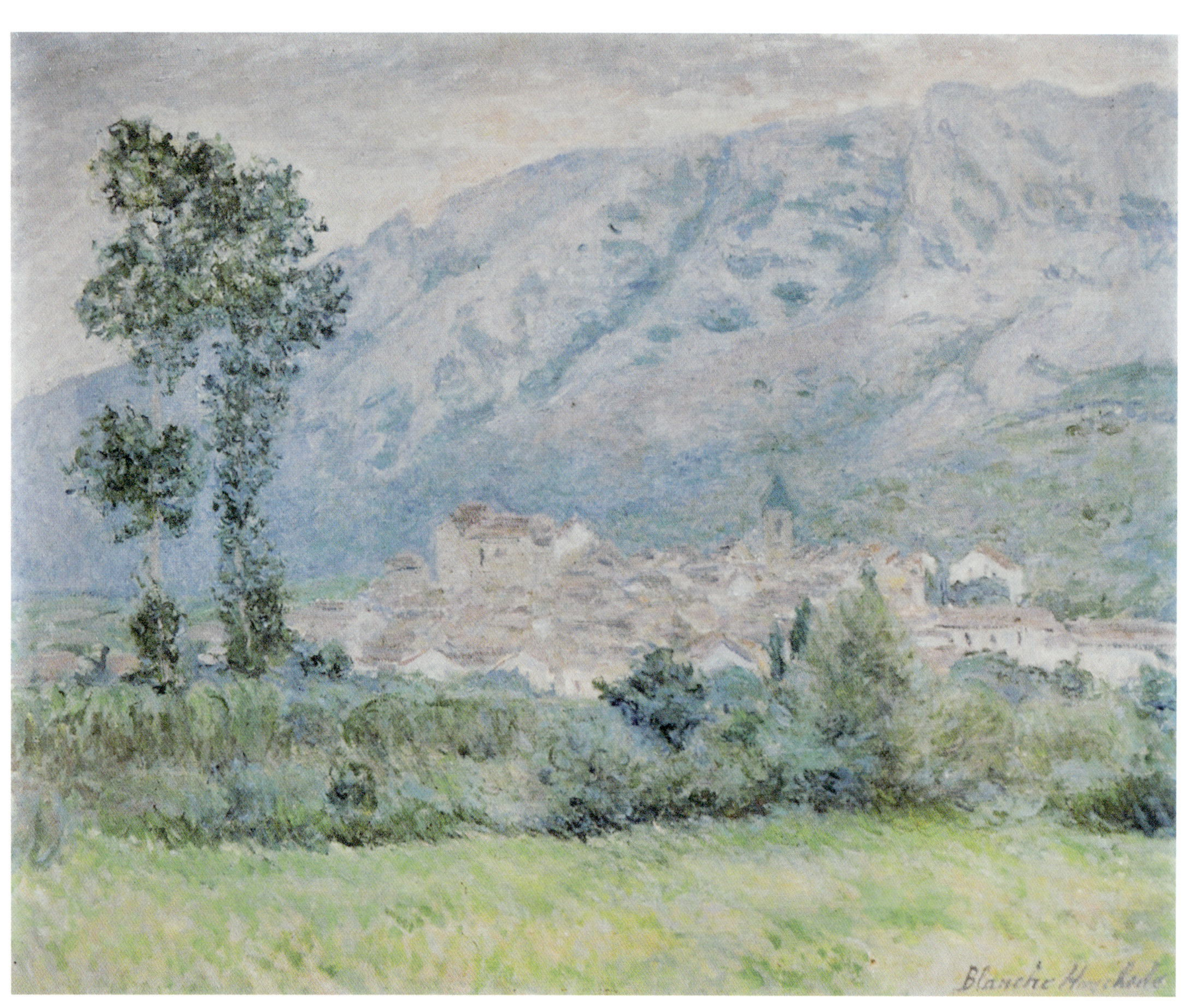

Pl. 21

BLANCHE HOSCHEDÉ-MONET
Le Poujol, Hérault – Evening
(*Le Poujol, Hérault – le soir*)
ca. 1907–11
Oil on canvas
23⅝ × 28¾ in. (60 × 73 cm)
Collection of Jean-Loup Piguet

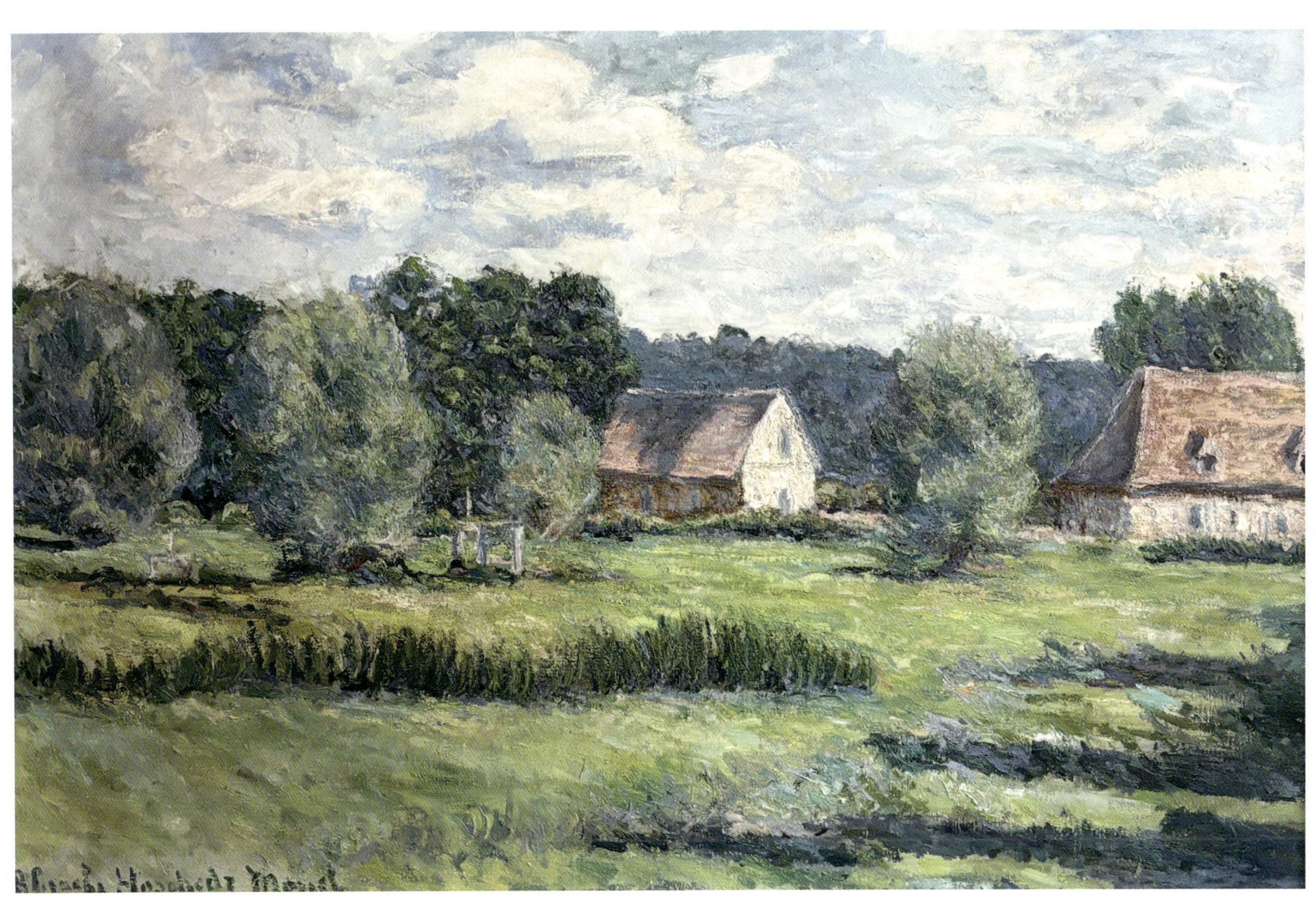

Pl. 22

BLANCHE HOSCHEDÉ-MONET
Normandy Landscape, Beaumont-le-Roger
(*Paysage normand, Beaumont-le-Roger*)
ca. 1910–13
Oil on canvas
19⅛ × 28¾ in. (48.5 × 73 cm)
Collection of Mrs. Catherine Fernandez Herry

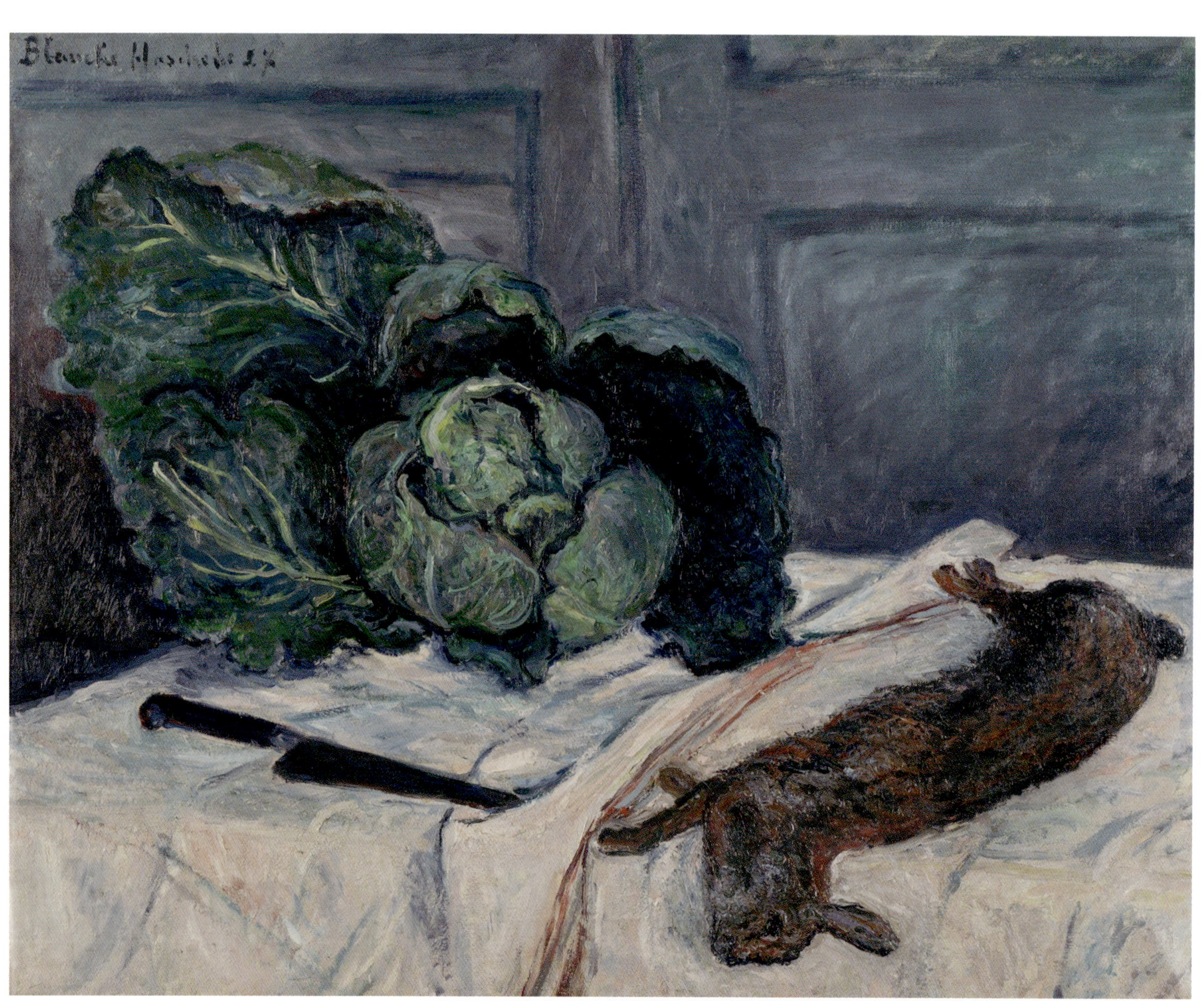

Pl. 23

BLANCHE HOSCHEDÉ-MONET
Still Life with Cabbage and Rabbit
(Nature morte au chou et au lapin)
1927
Oil on canvas
25 9/16 × 31 7/8 (65 × 81 cm)
Musée Blanche Hoschedé-Monet,
Vernon (85.4.1)

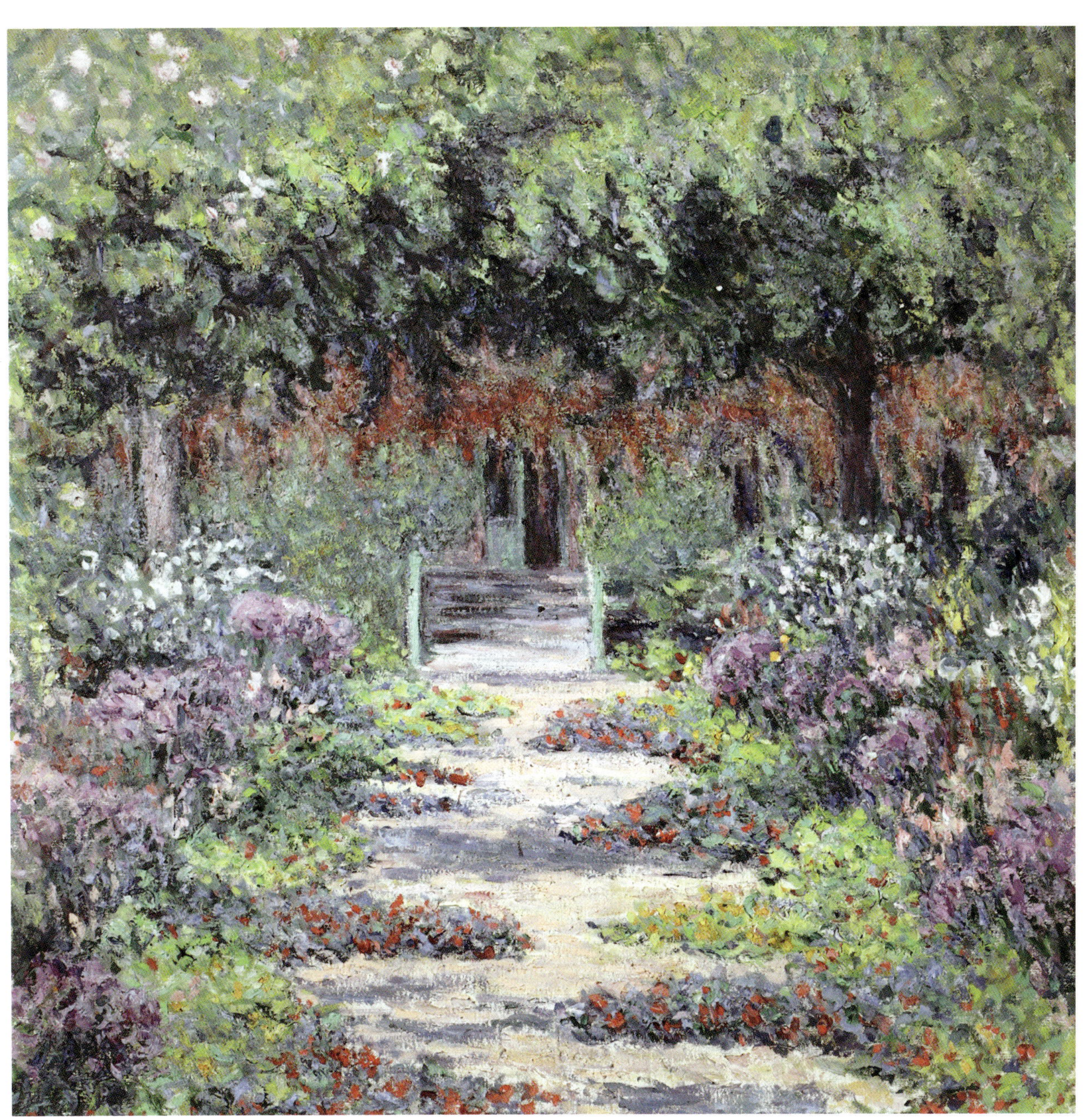

BLANCHE HOSCHEDÉ-MONET
The Garden of Giverny
(The Path under the Rose Arches) (*Le Jardin*
de Giverny [L'Allée des rosiers])
ca. 1918–24
Oil on canvas
26⅜ × 25⁹⁄₁₆ in. (67 × 65 cm)
Musée Clemenceau, Paris (2017.0.477)

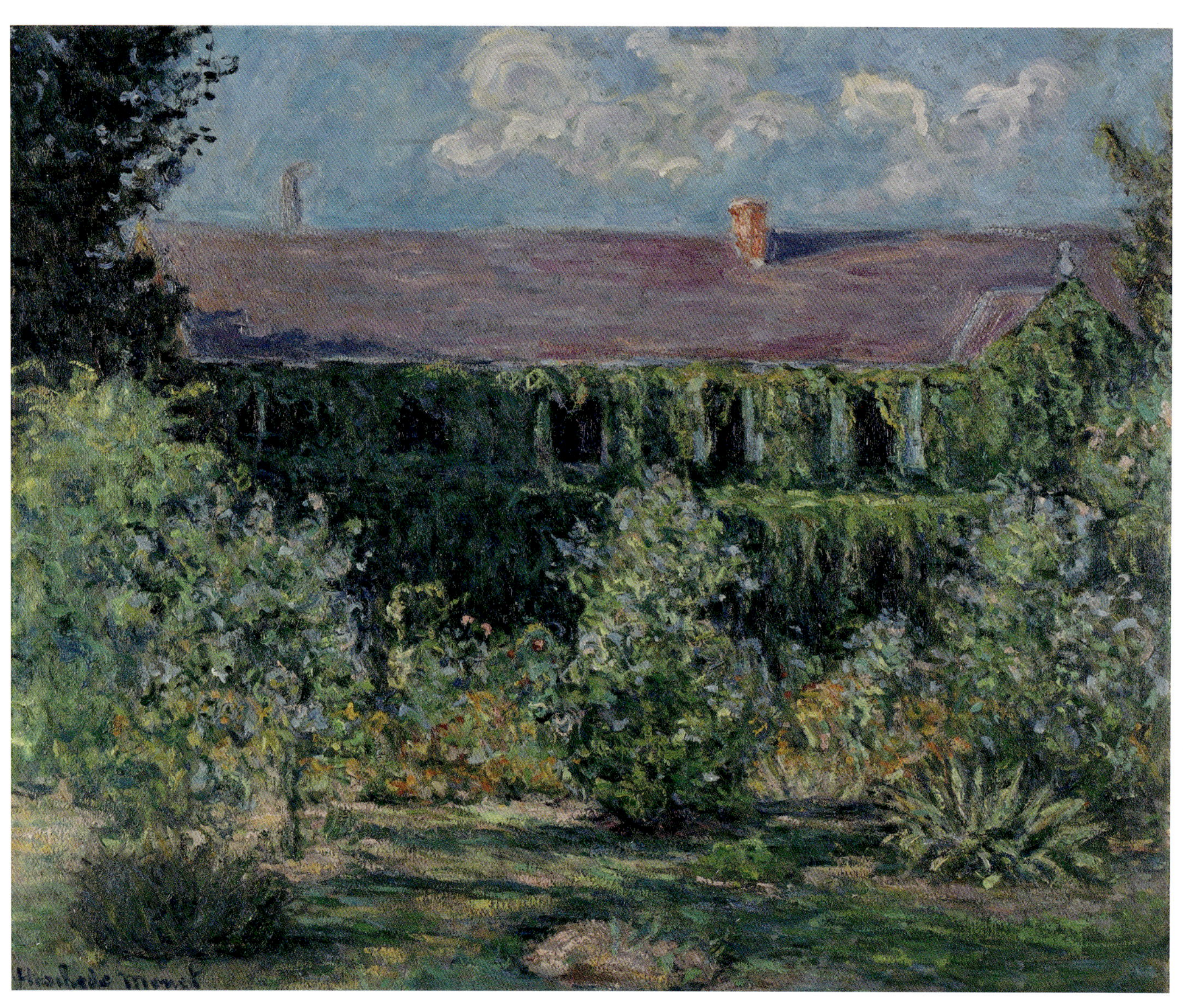

Pl. 25

BLANCHE HOSCHEDÉ-MONET
The House and Garden of Claude Monet, Giverny
(*La Maison et le jardin de Claude Monet, Giverny*)
after 1926
Oil on canvas
23 ⅝ × 28 ¾ in. (60 × 73 cm)
Musée Blanche Hoschedé-Monet, Vernon (79.89)

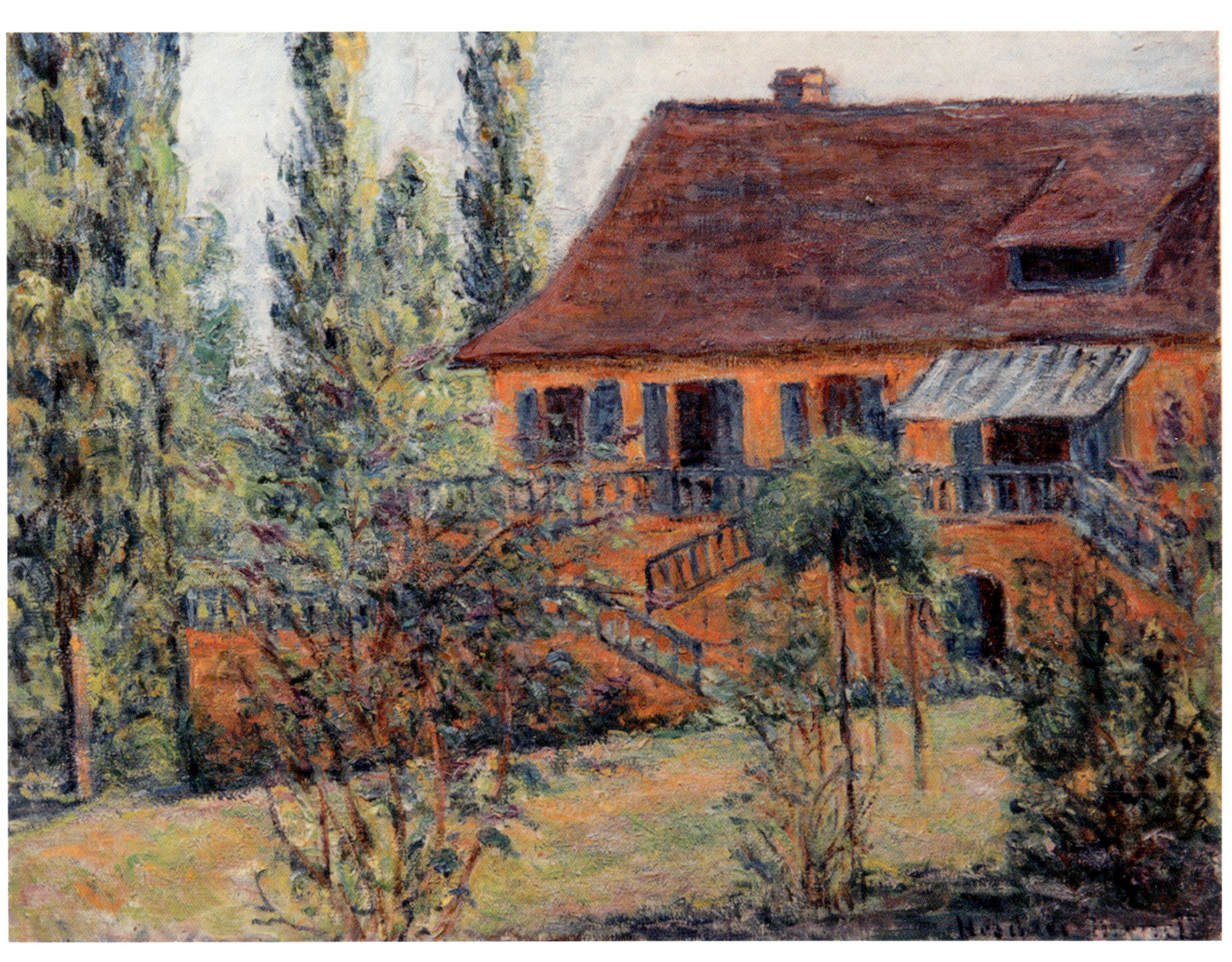

BLANCHE HOSCHEDÉ-MONET
The House, Sorel-Moussel
(*La Maison de Sorel-Moussel*)
n.d.
Oil on canvas
21¼ × 28¾ in. (54 × 73 cm)
Musée Marmottan Monet, Paris, legs Michel
Monet, 1966 (inv. 5063)

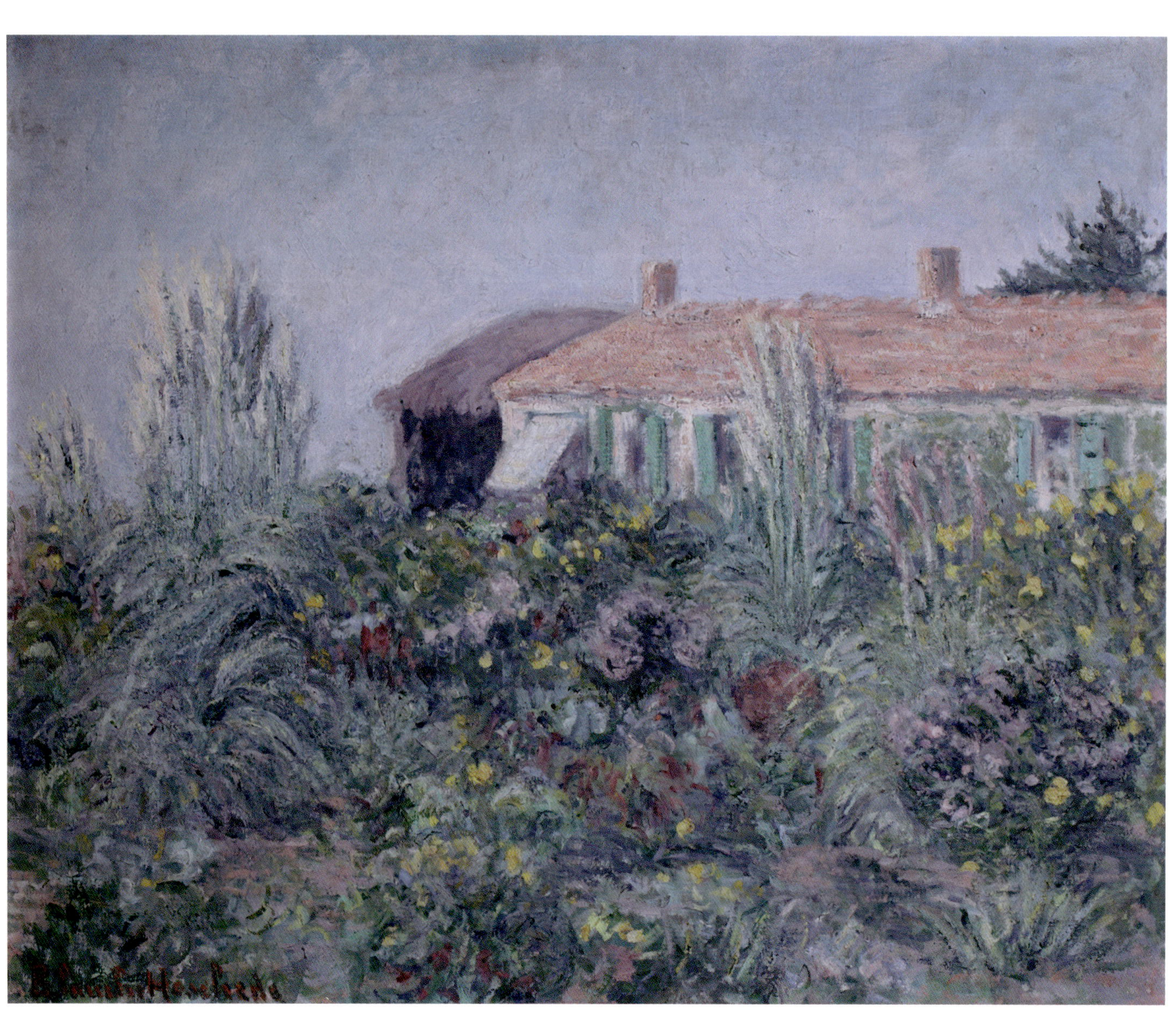

Pl. 27

BLANCHE HOSCHEDÉ-MONET
*Belébat: Home and Garden of Georges
Clemenceau*
(*Belébat: maison et jardin de Clemenceau*)
ca. 1927–29
Oil on canvas
21⅝ × 25⁹⁄₁₆ in. (55 × 65 cm)
Musée Clemenceau, Paris (2017.0.236)

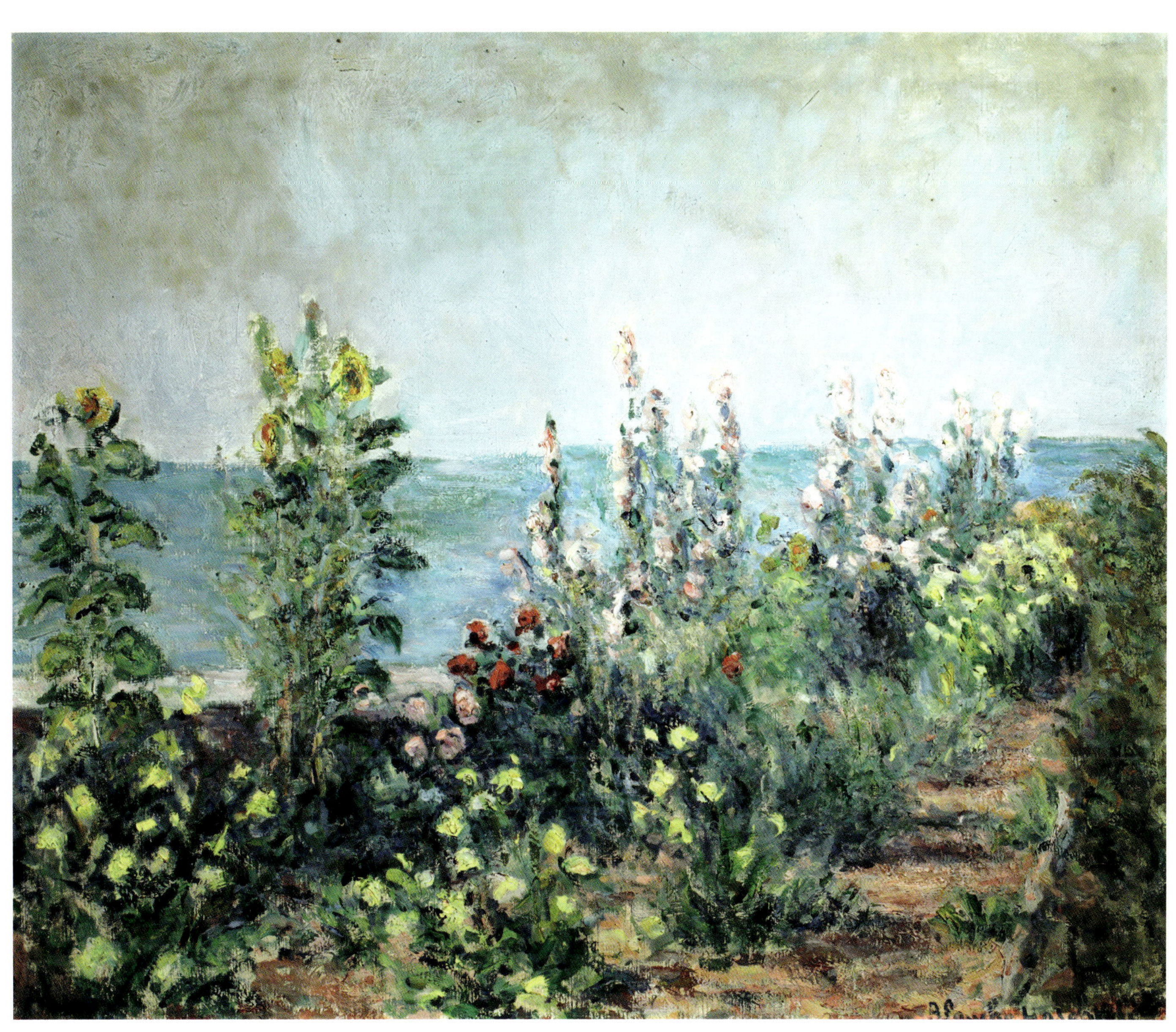

Pl. 28

BLANCHE HOSCHEDÉ-MONET
Belébat: Garden of Georges Clemenceau
(*Belébat: le jardin de Clemenceau*)
ca. 1927–29
Oil on canvas
24 7⁄16 × 29 1⁄8 in. (62 × 74 cm)
Musée Clemenceau, Paris (2017.0.235)

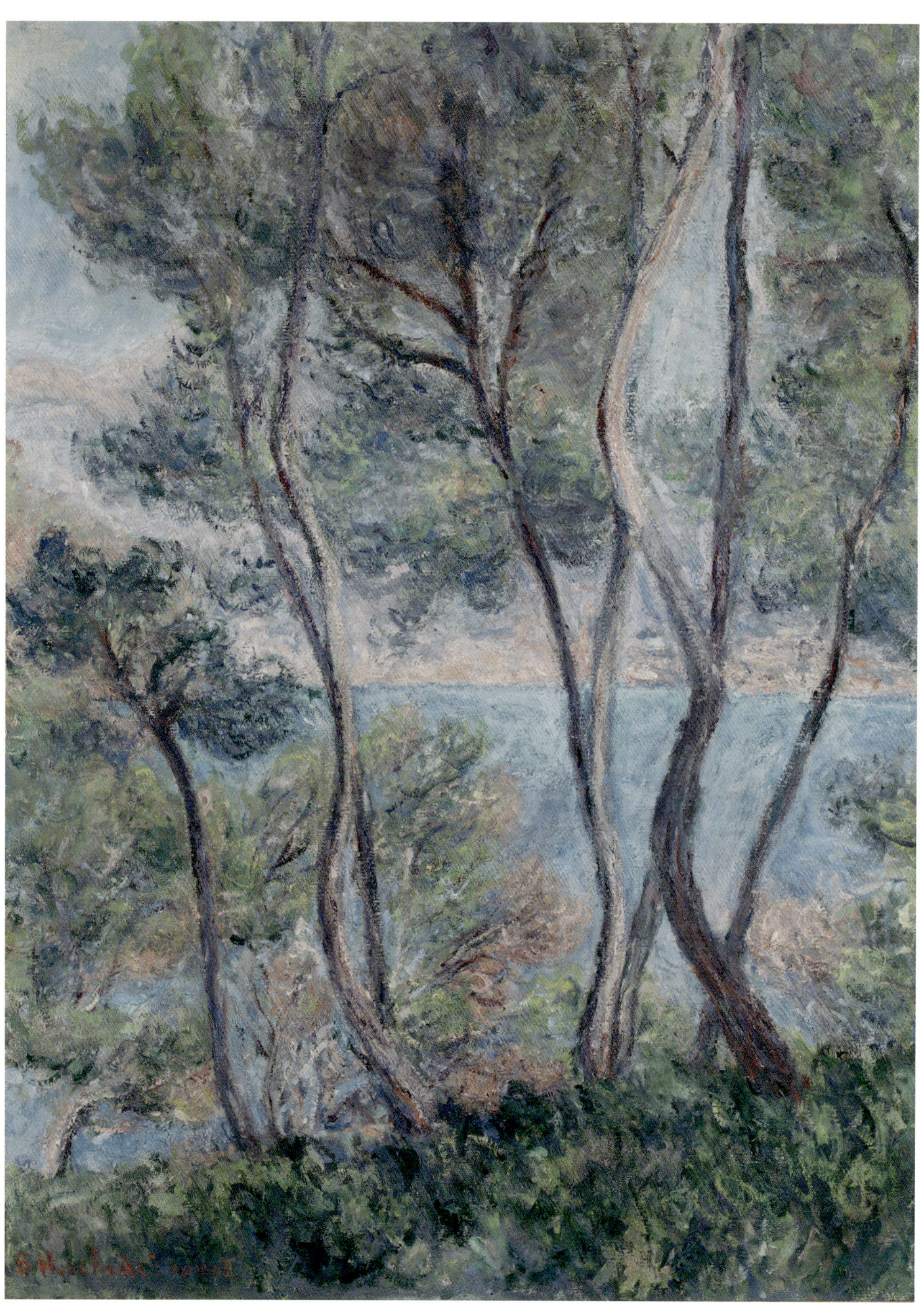

Pl. 29

BLANCHE HOSCHEDÉ-MONET
Maritime Pines (*Les Pins maritimes*)
1928
Oil on canvas
32 11/16 × 26 in. (83 × 66 cm)
Lycée Claude-Monet, Paris, on long-term loan
to the Musée des Impressionnismes Giverny
(D 2021.1.12)

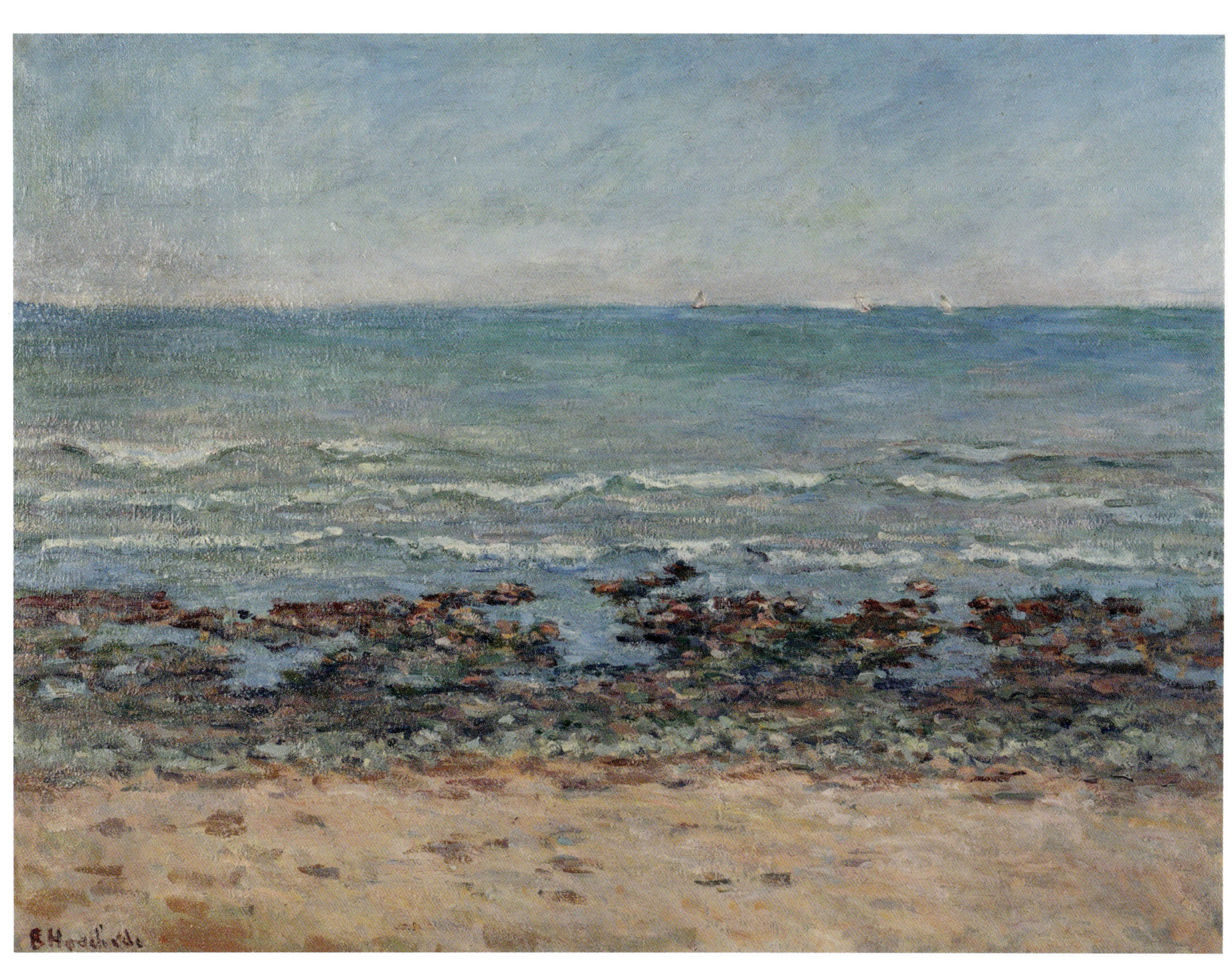

Pl. 30

BLANCHE HOSCHEDÉ-MONET
*The Beach at Diélette
(The English Channel) (La Plage
de Diélette [Manche])*
ca. 1932–39
Oil on canvas
21¼ × 28¾ in. (54 × 73 cm)
Musée Blanche Hoschedé-Monet,
Vernon (84.10.1)

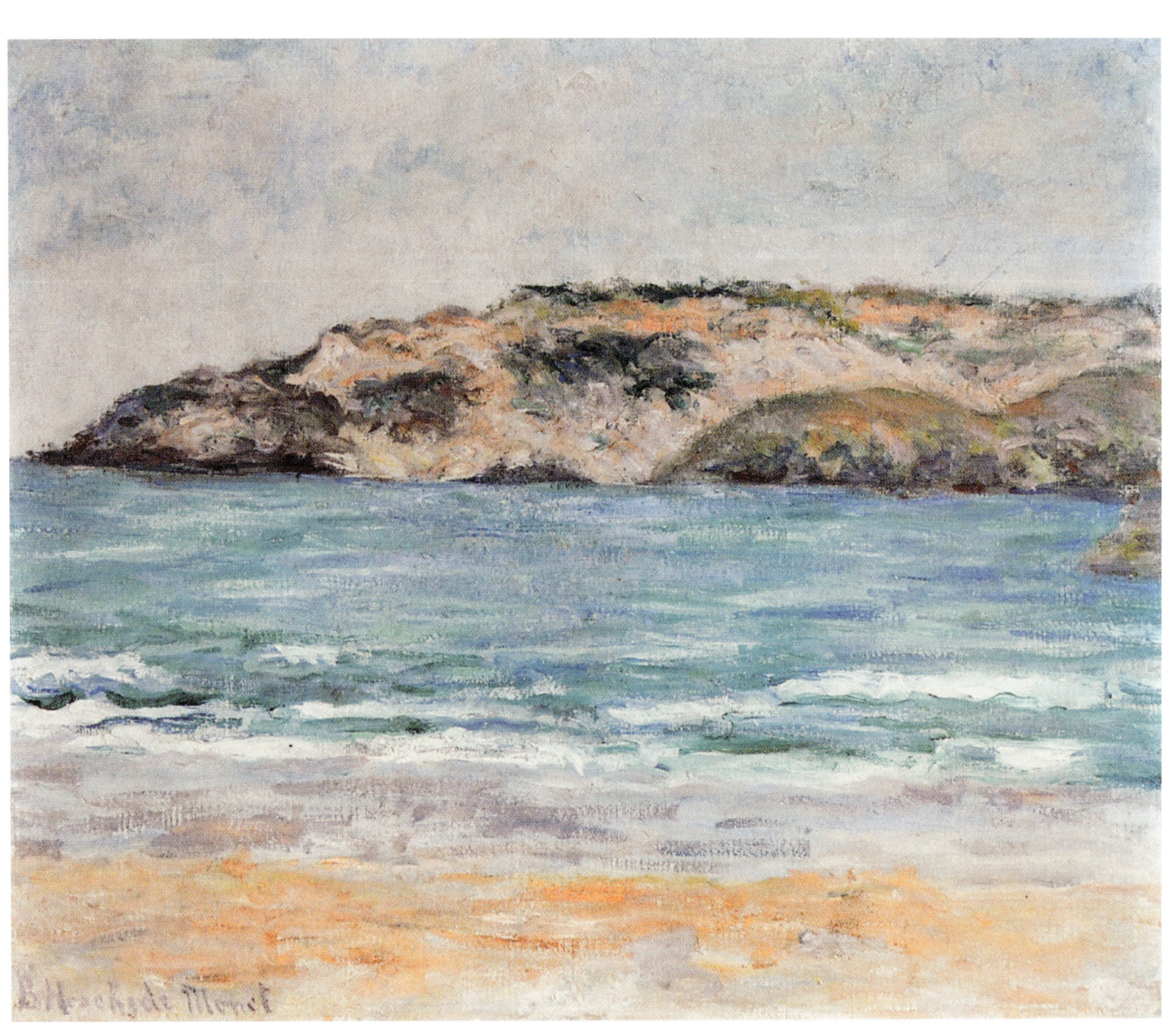

Pl. 31

BLANCHE HOSCHEDÉ-MONET
Seascape, Cotentin
(*Marine du Cotentin*)
n.d.
Oil on canvas
14 15/16 × 18 1/8 in. (38 × 46 cm)
Private collection, France

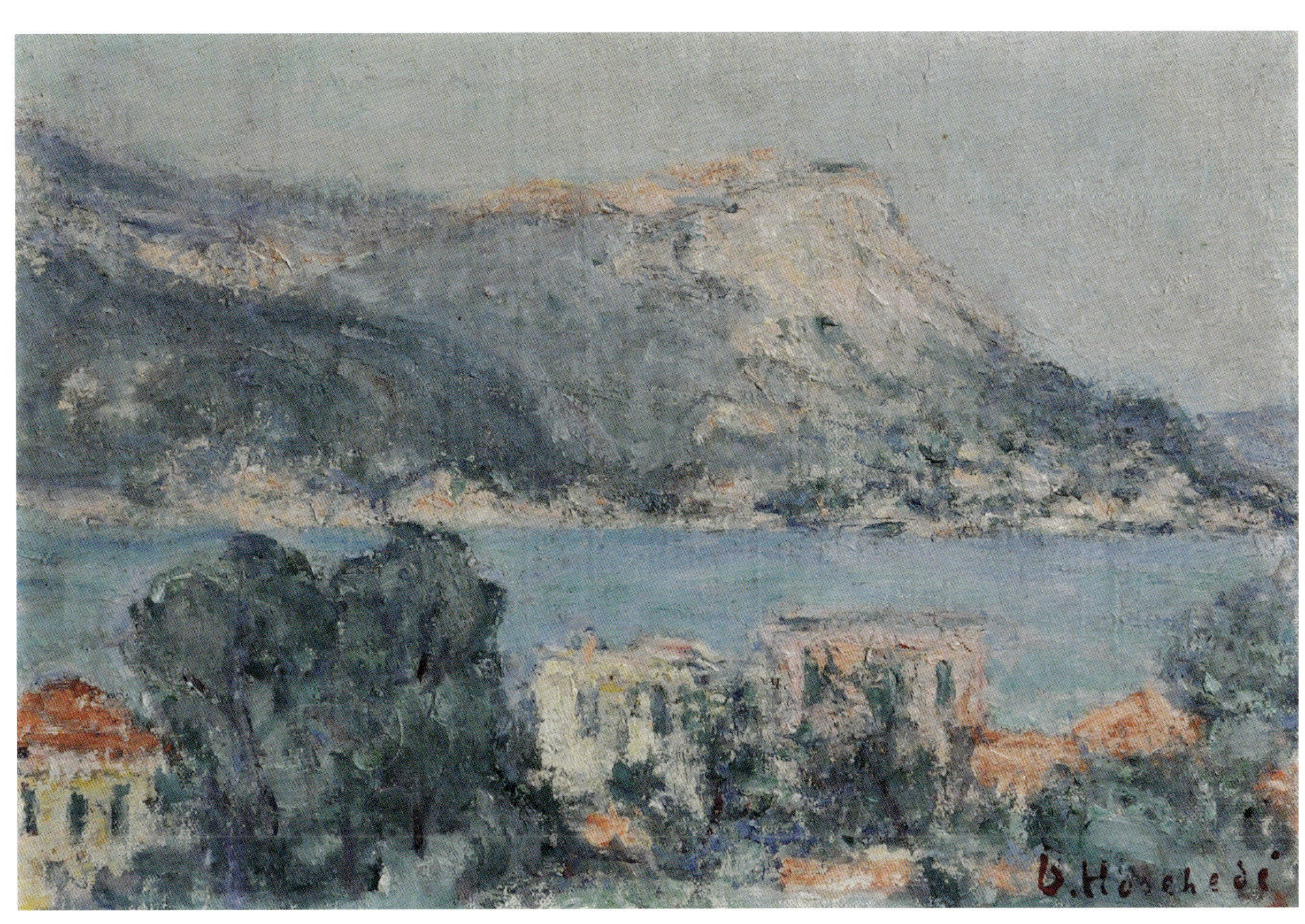

BLANCHE HOSCHEDÉ-MONET
View of Lake Bourget
(*Vue du Lac du Bourget*)
n.d.
Oil on canvas
9¼ × 13⅜ in. (23.5 × 34 cm)
Collection of Philippe Piguet

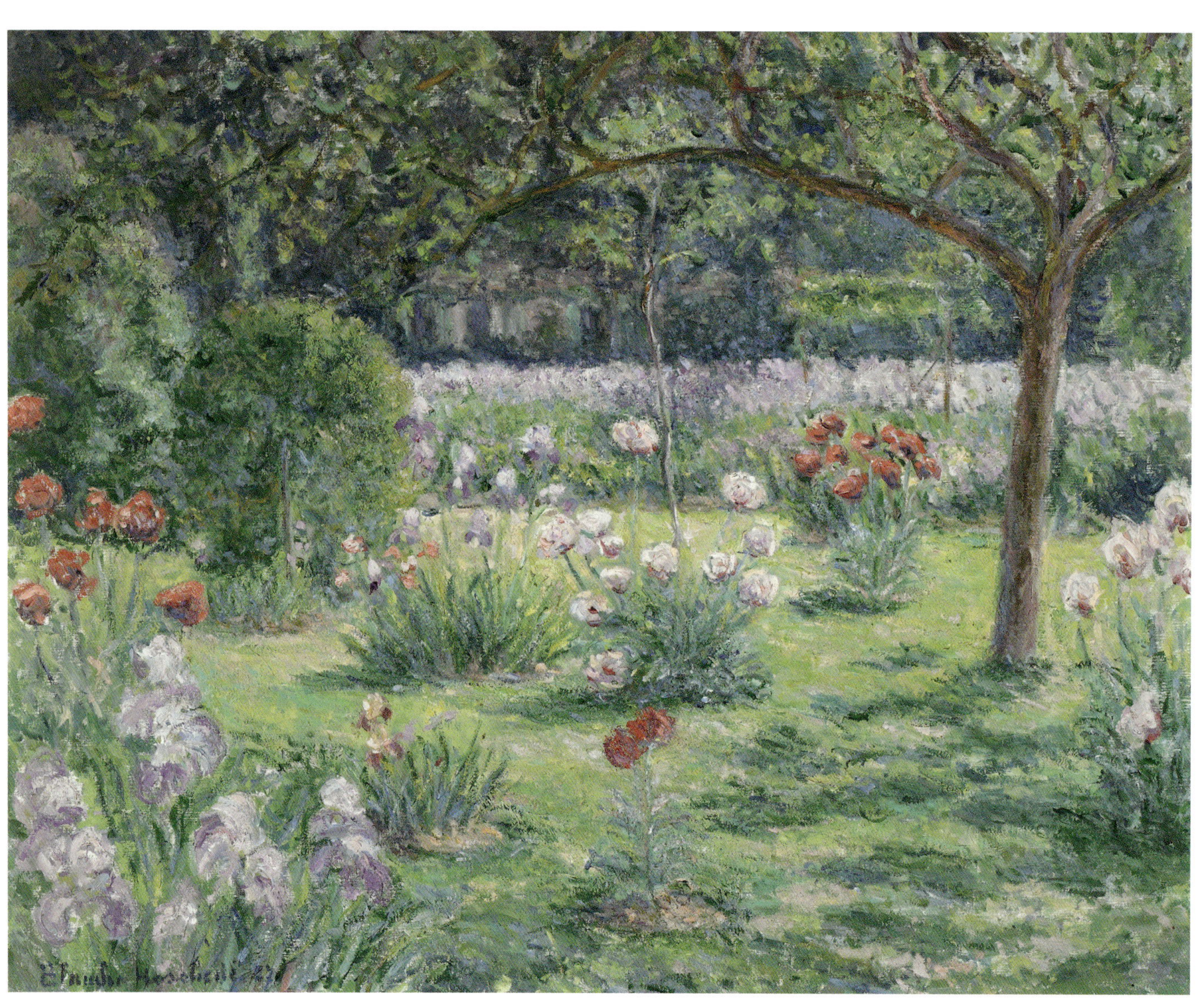

Pl. 33 (not in exhibition)

BLANCHE HOSCHEDÉ-MONET
Claude Monet's Garden, Giverny
(*Le Jardin de Claude Monet à Giverny*)
1927
Oil on canvas
28 $\frac{15}{16}$ × 36 $\frac{7}{16}$ in. (73.5 × 92.5 cm)
Musée d'Orsay, Paris, on long-term loan to the
Musée des Beaux-Arts, Rouen (D.1956.1)

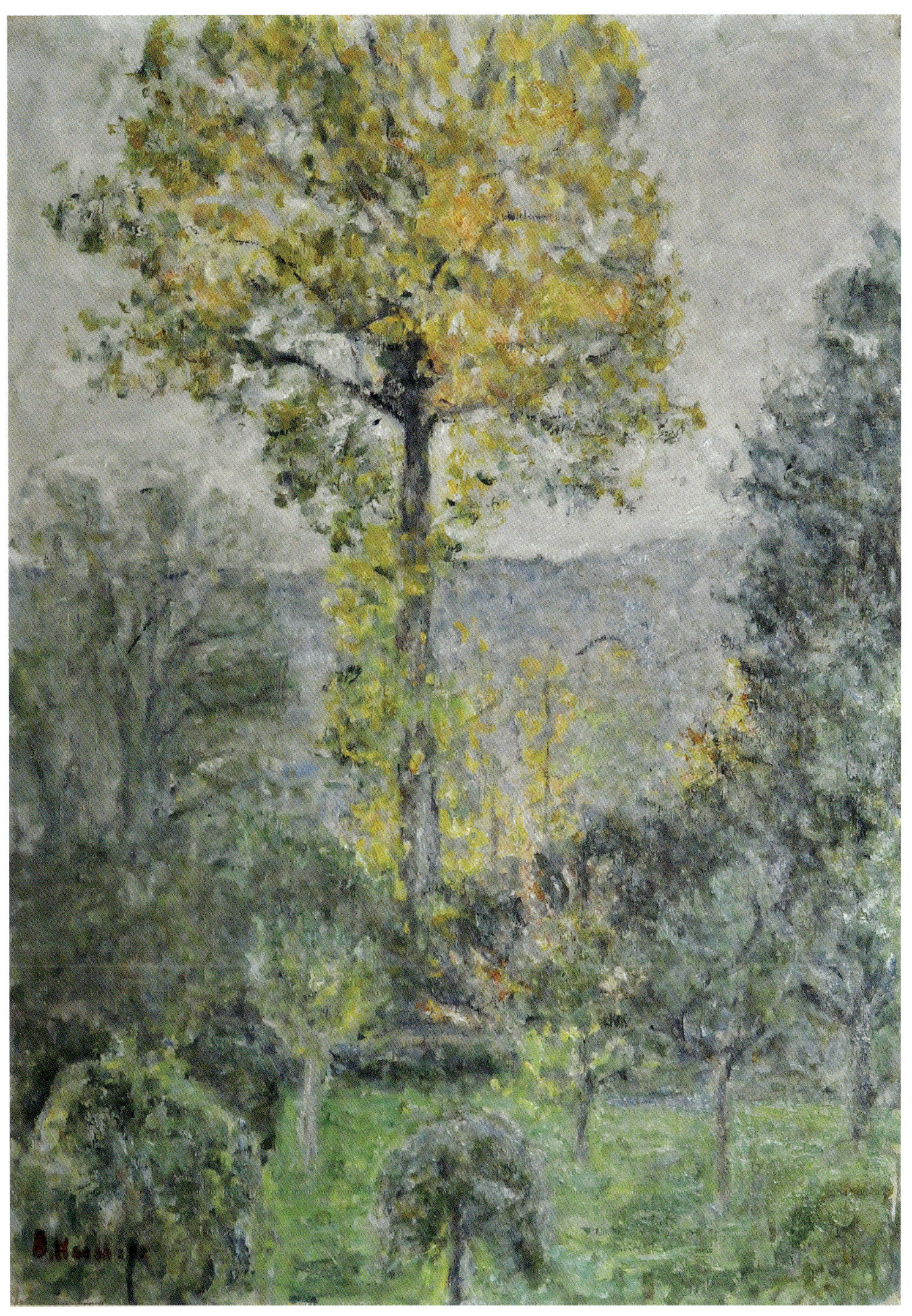

BLANCHE HOSCHEDÉ-MONET
The Yellow Poplar
(*Le Peuplier jaune*)
n.d.
Oil on canvas
25½ × 18⁷⁄₁₆ in. (64.7 × 46.8 cm)
Collection of Philippe Piguet

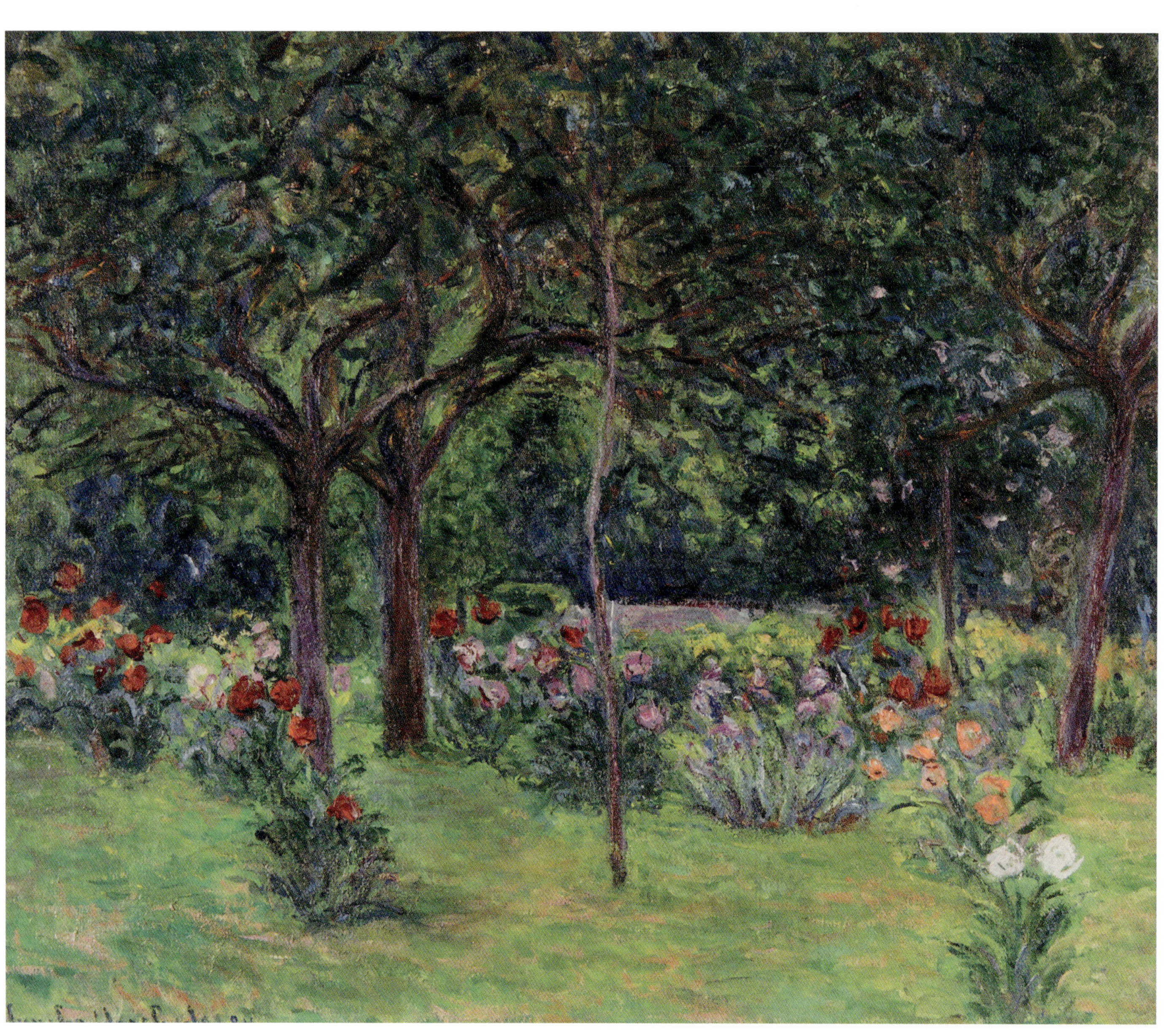

Pl. 35

BLANCHE HOSCHEDÉ-MONET
A Corner of Claude Monet's Garden
(*Coin du jardin de Claude Monet*)
1927
Oil on canvas
21¼ × 25⁹⁄₁₆ in. (54 × 65 cm)
Private Collection

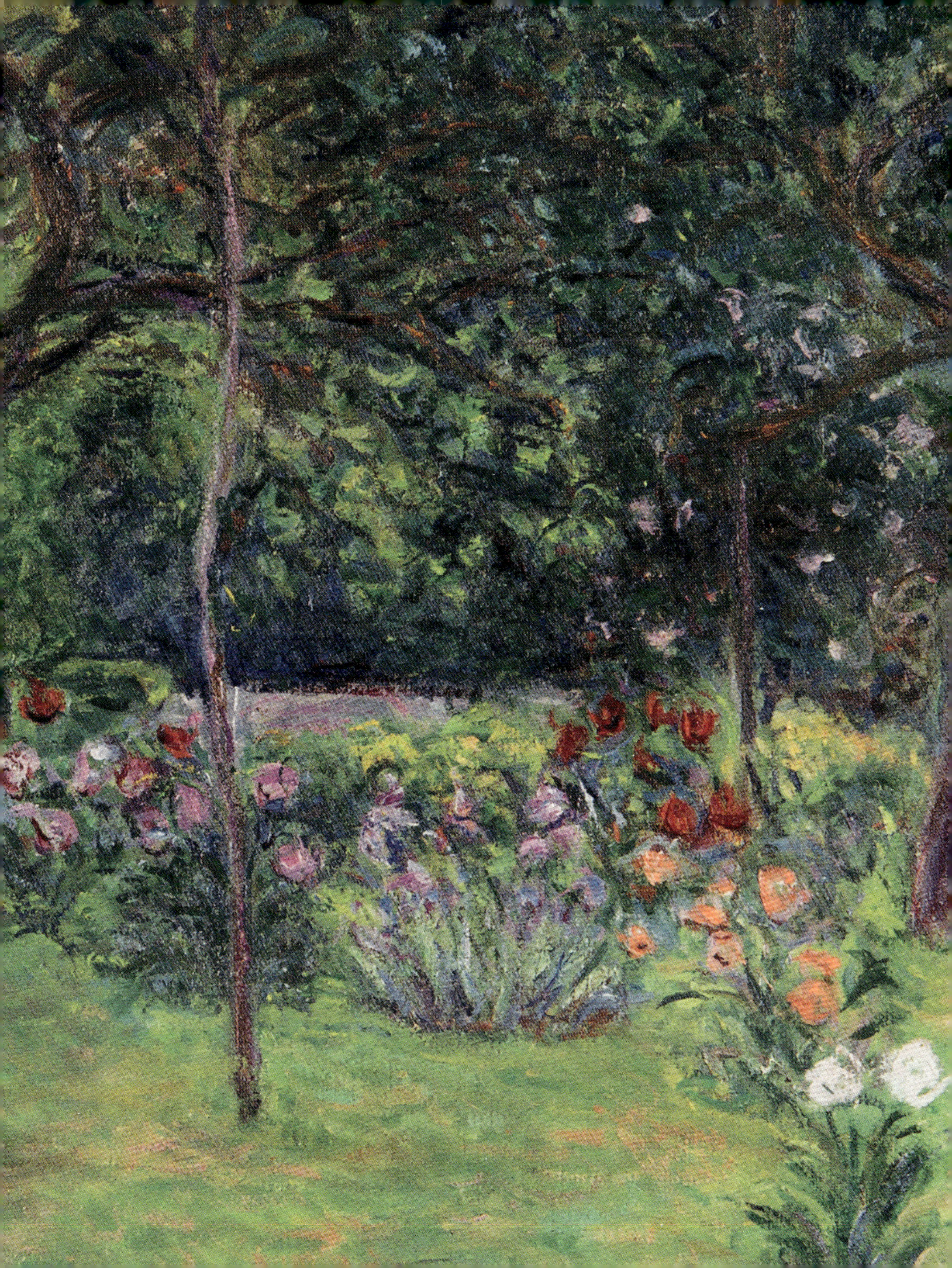

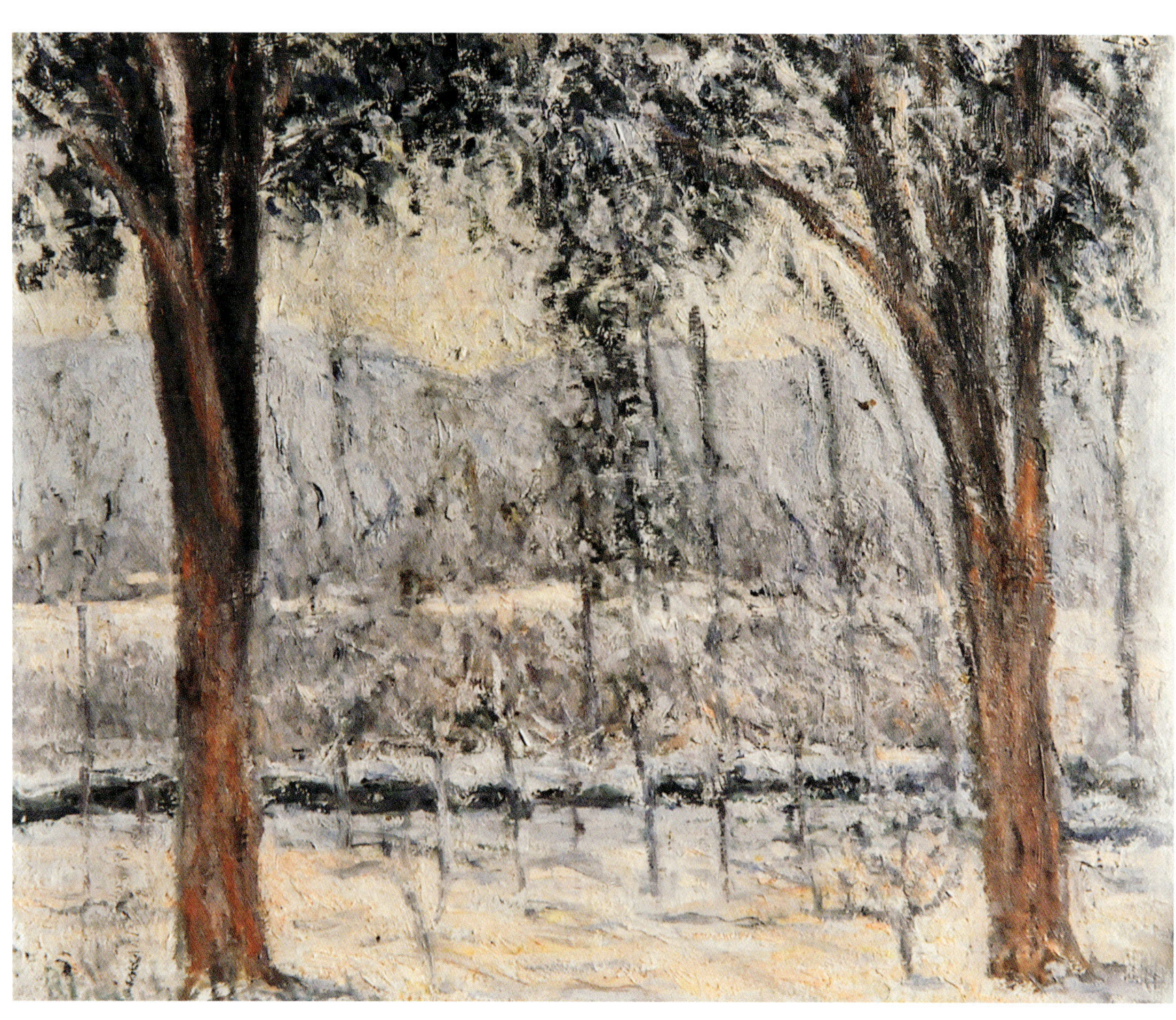

Pl. 36

BLANCHE HOSCHEDÉ-MONET
Landscape in the Snow
(A Corner of Claude Monet's Garden)
(*Paysage sous la neige [Un coin du jardin de Claude Monet]*)
after 1926
Oil on canvas
14 15/16 × 18 1/8 in. (38 × 46 cm)
Collection of Catherine Minot

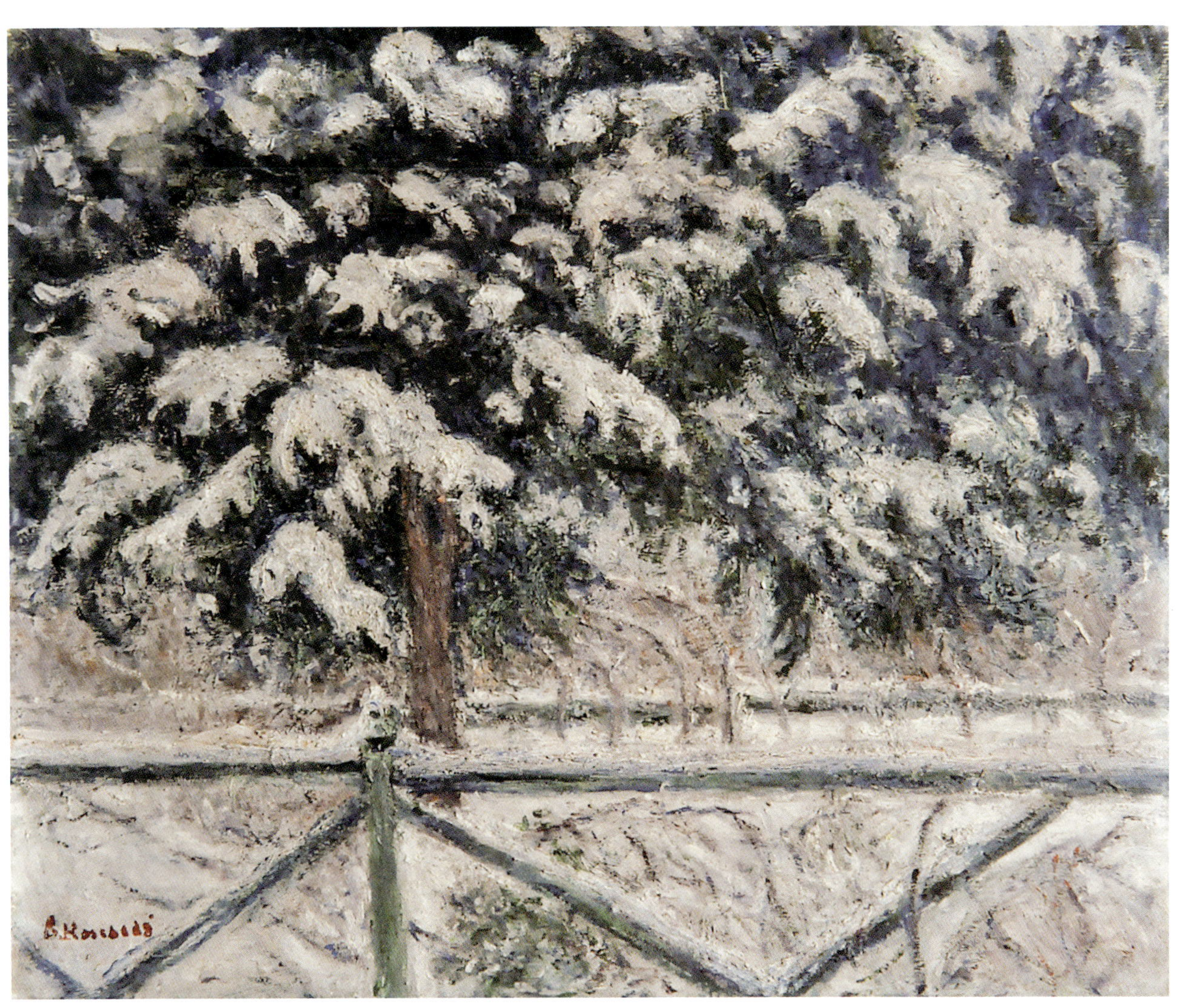

Pl. 37

BLANCHE HOSCHEDÉ-MONET
Balustrade and Fir Trees in the Snow
(*Balustrade et sapins sous la neige*)
n.d.
Oil on canvas
21¼ × 25⁹⁄₁₆ in. (54 × 65 cm)
Private collection

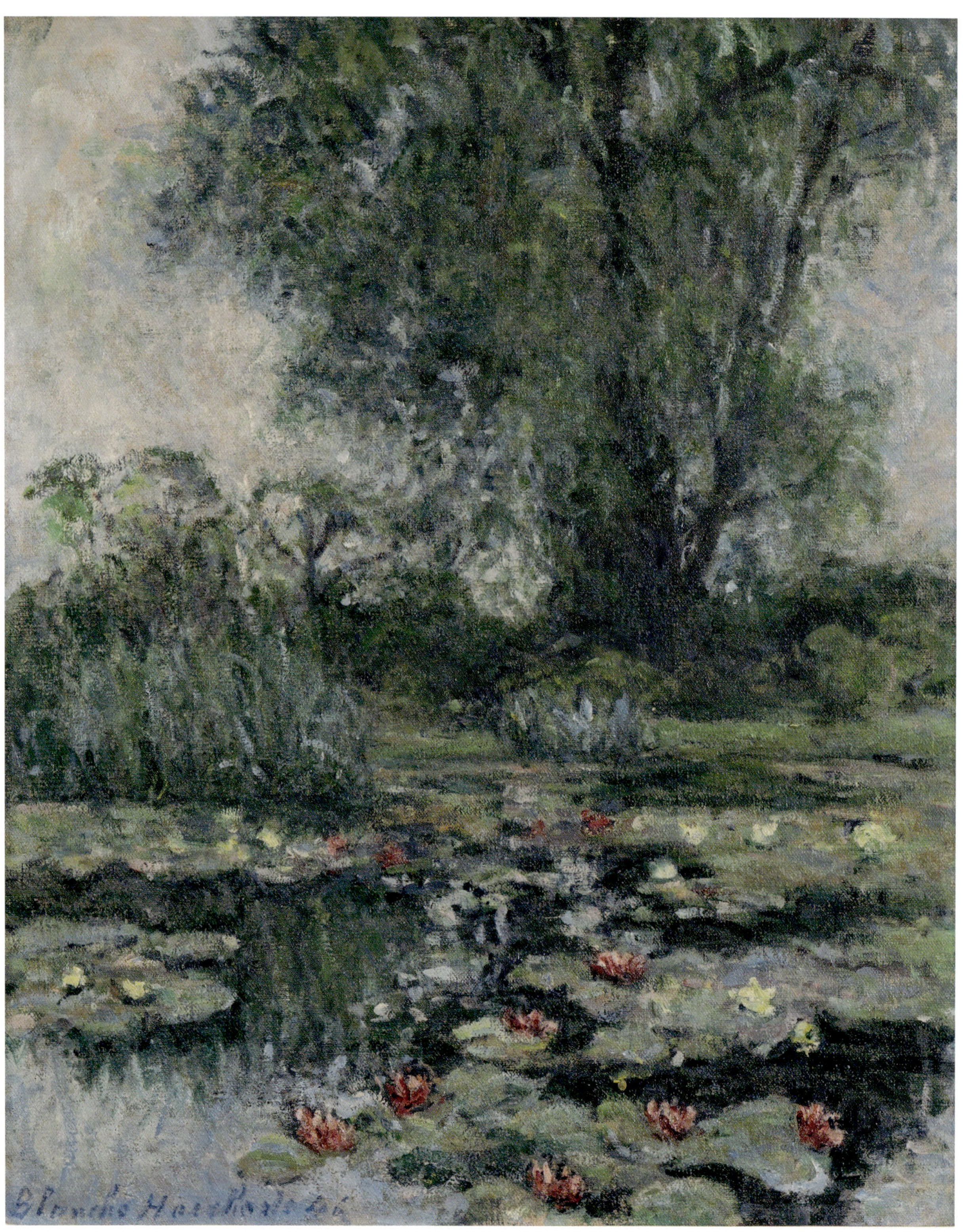

Pl. 38

BLANCHE HOSCHEDÉ-MONET
Water Lilies (*Nymphéas*)
ca. 1946
Oil on canvas
18 × 14⅞ in. (45.7 × 37.8 cm)
Collection of Gary Z. and Kathy J. Anderson

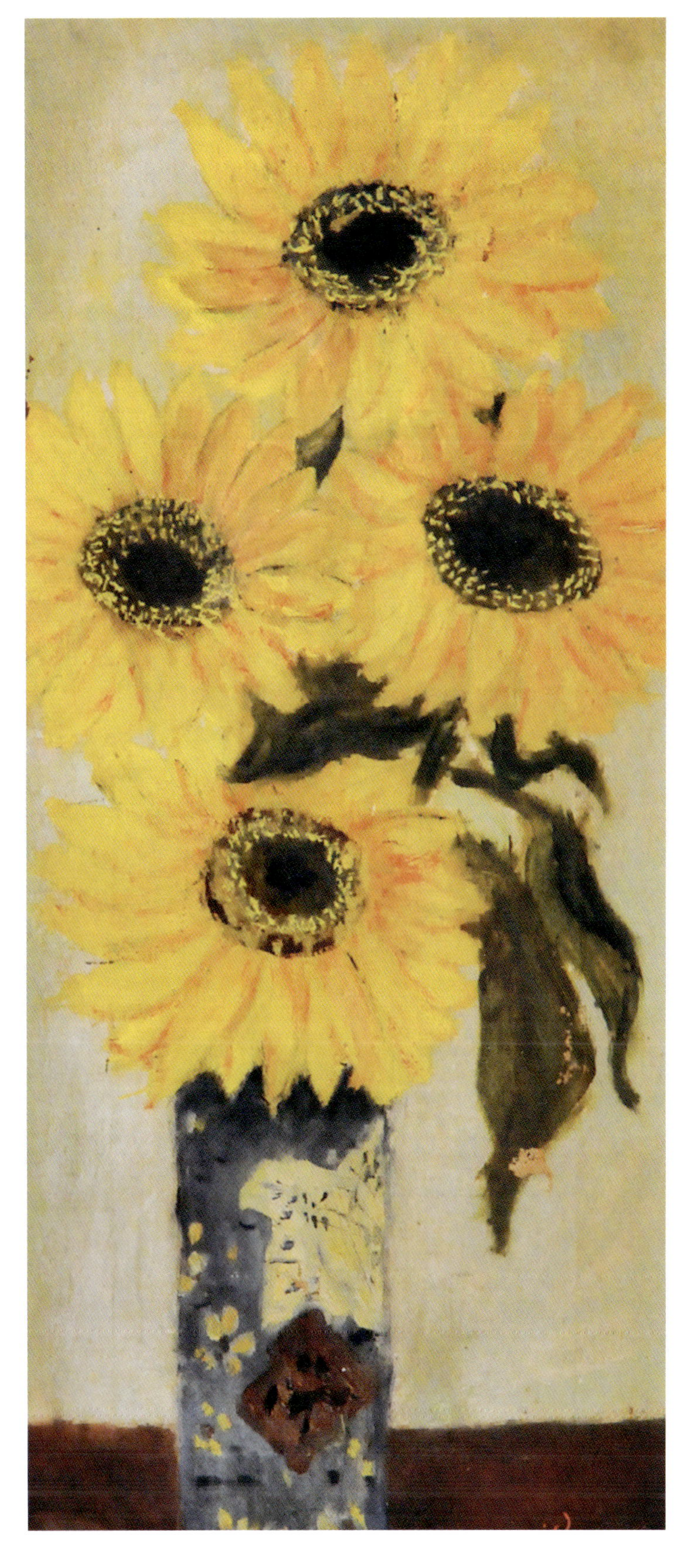

Pl. 39

BLANCHE HOSCHEDÉ-MONET
Four Sunflowers in a Vase
(*Quatre tournesols dans un vase*)
1878
Oil on canvas
23 5⁄8 × 11 in. (60 × 28 cm)
Private collection, France

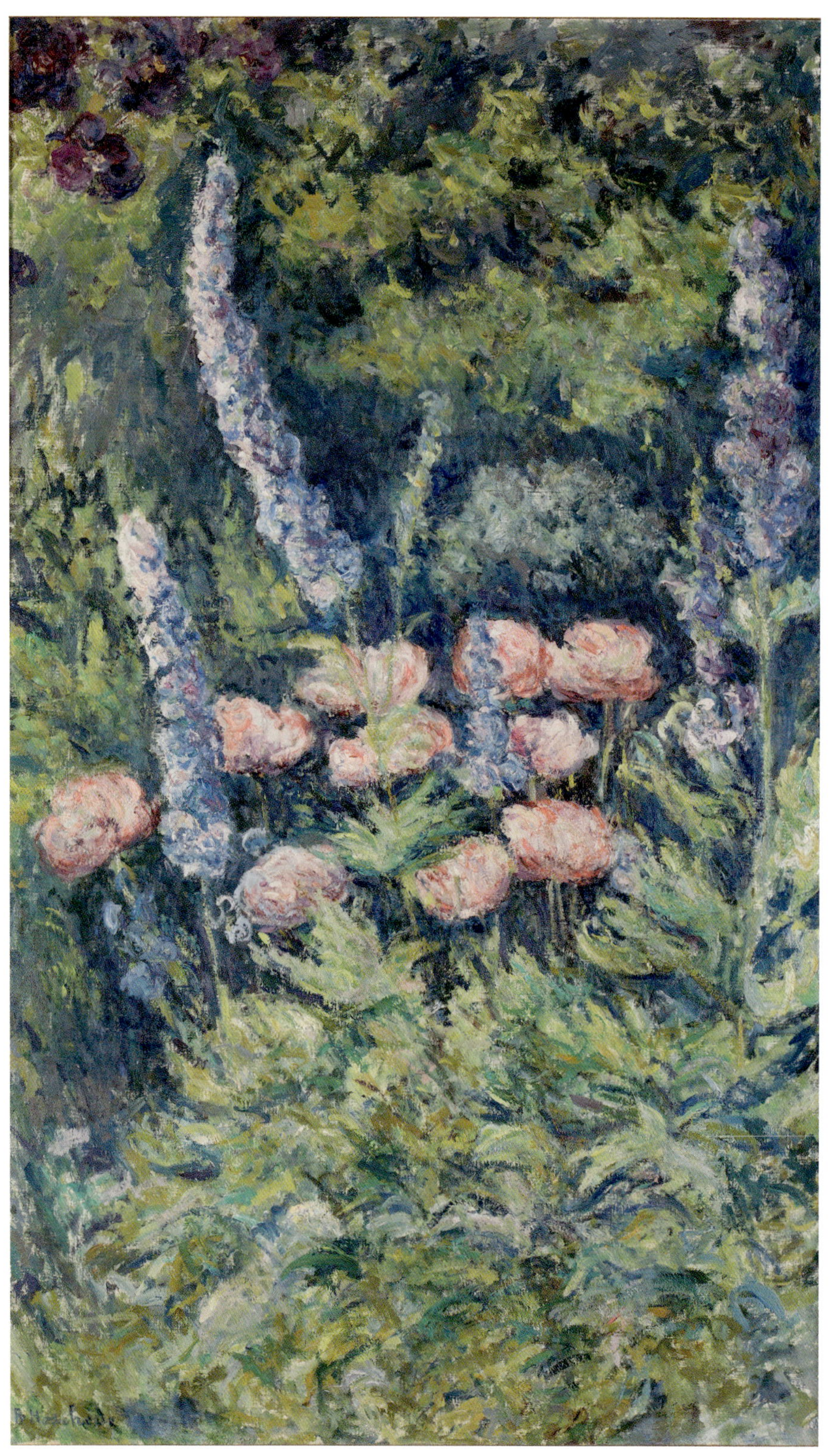

Pl. 40

BLANCHE HOSCHEDÉ-MONET
Lupins and Poppies
(*Lupins et pavots*)
1891
Oil on canvas
39⅜ × 23⅝ in. (100 × 60 cm)
Collection of the Village of Giverny, on long-term loan to the Musée des Impressionnismes Giverny (MDIG D 2009.1.1)

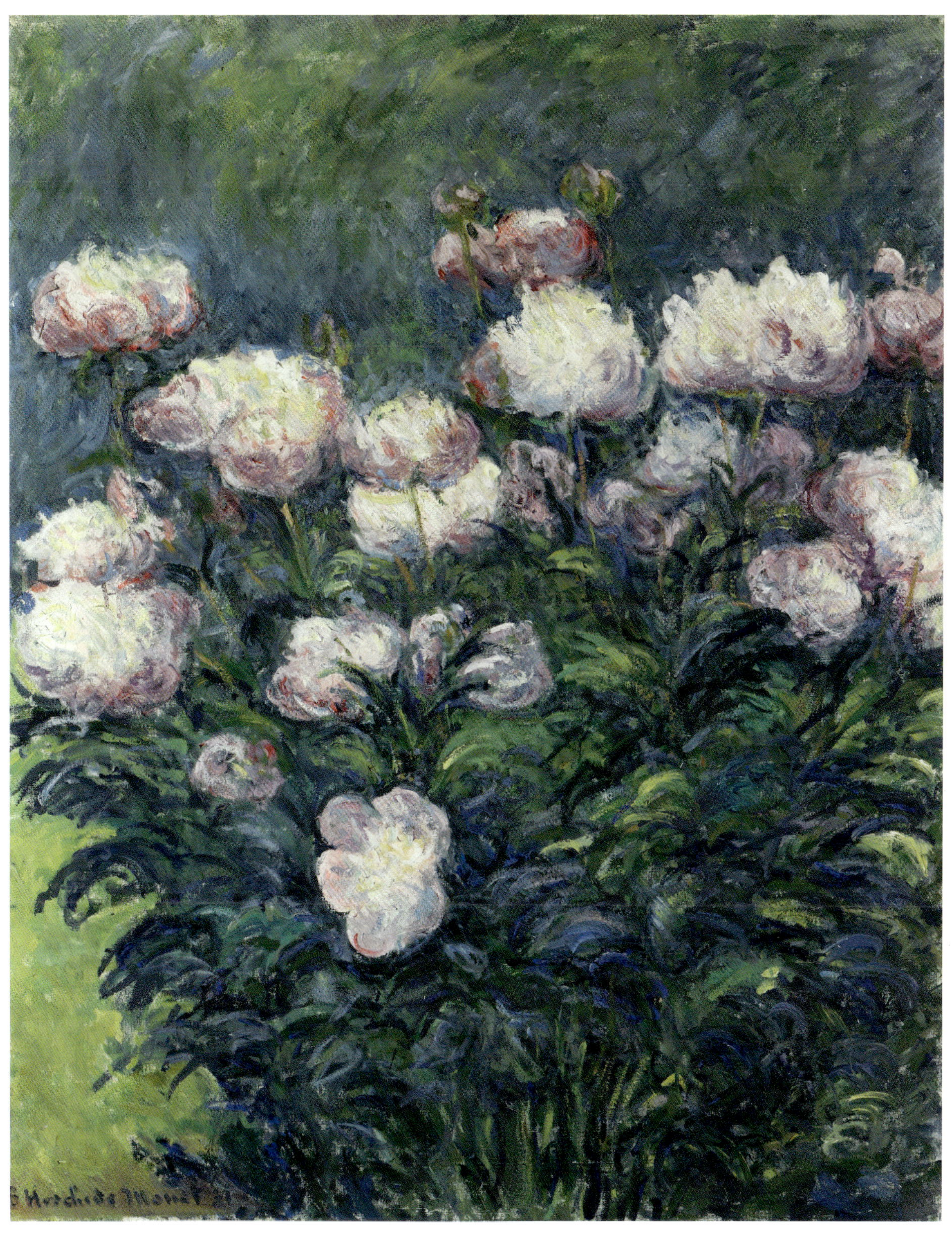

BLANCHE HOSCHEDÉ-MONET
Peonies (*Pivoines*)
1931
Oil on canvas
31⅞ × 25⁹⁄₁₆ in. (81 × 65 cm)
Musée d'Orsay, Paris, on long-term loan to the
Musée des Beaux-Arts, Rouen (D.1956.2)

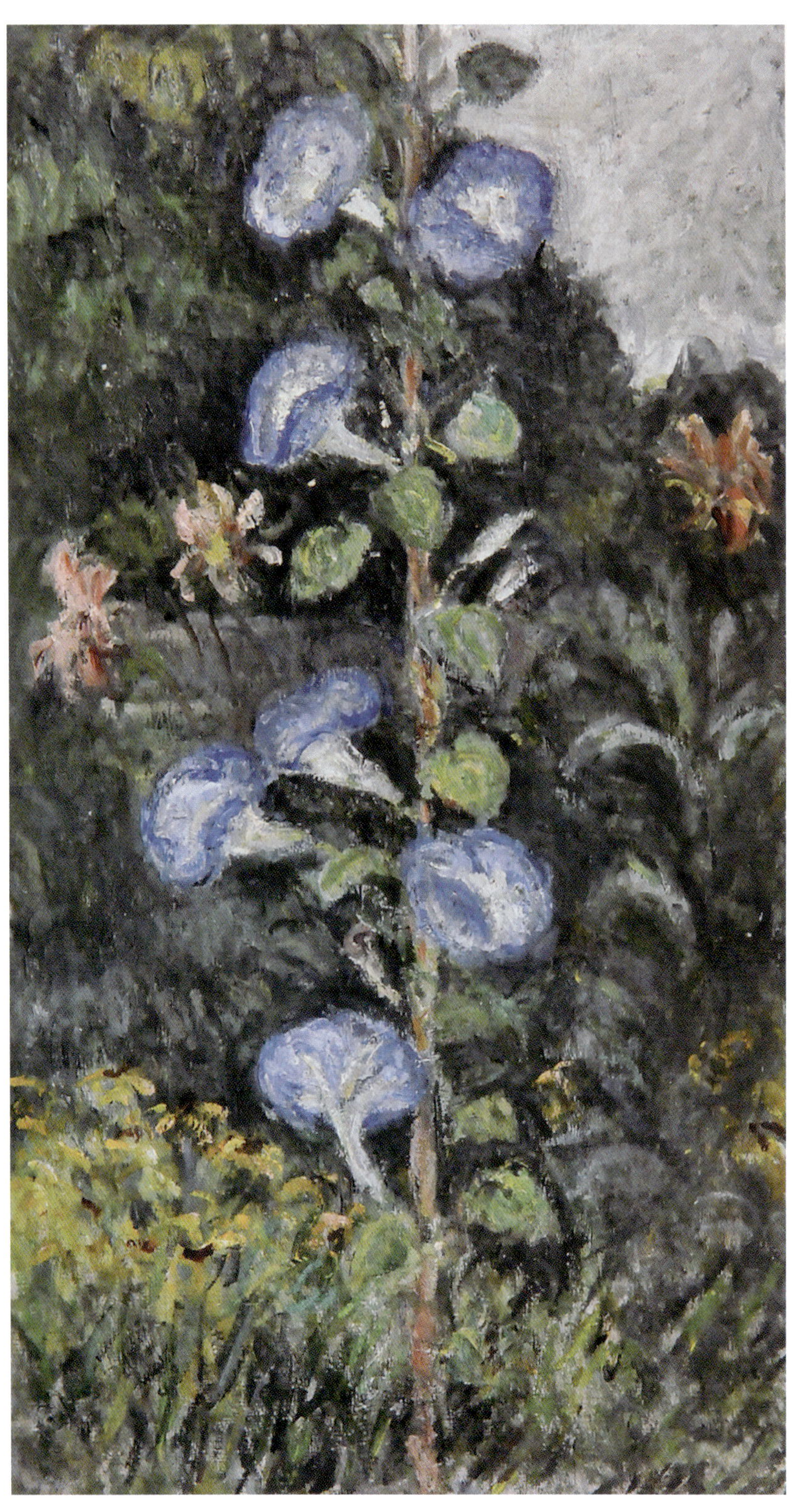

Pl. 42

BLANCHE HOSCHEDÉ-MONET
Convolvulus (Morning Glory)
(*Volubilis [Ipomées]*)
n.d.
Oil on canvas
31½ × 17 11/16 in. (80 × 45 cm)
Private collection, France

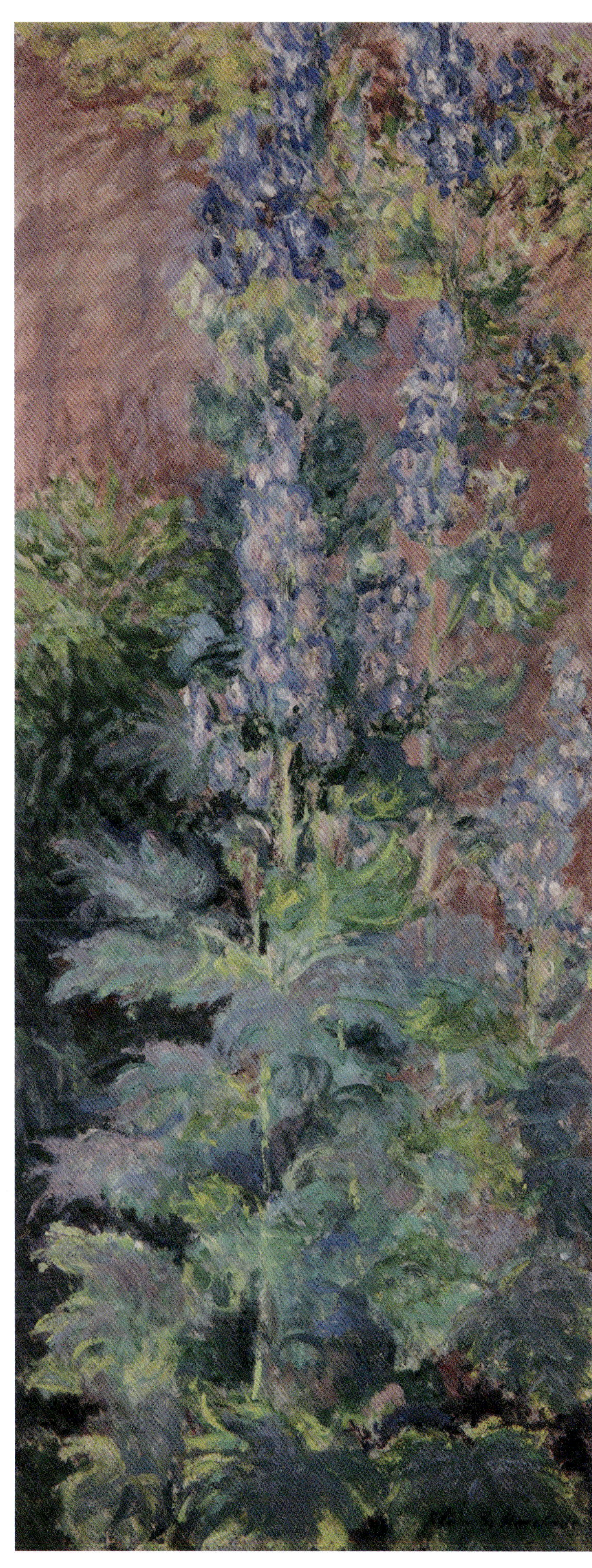

Pl. 43

BLANCHE HOSCHEDÉ-MONET
Larkspur (*Pieds d'alouettes*)
n.d.
Oil on canvas
42⅛ × 17⁵⁄₁₆ in. (107 × 44 cm)
Private collection, France

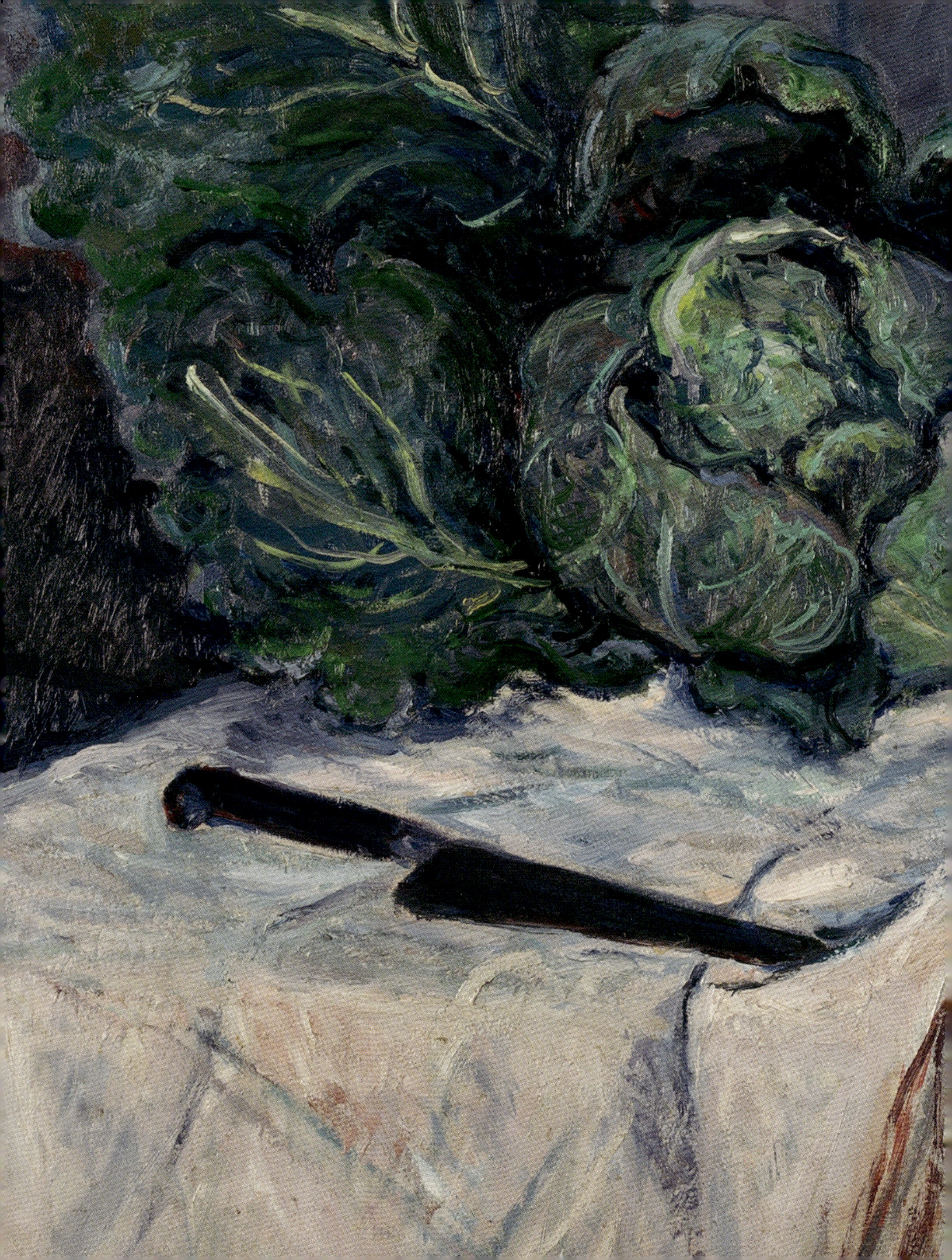

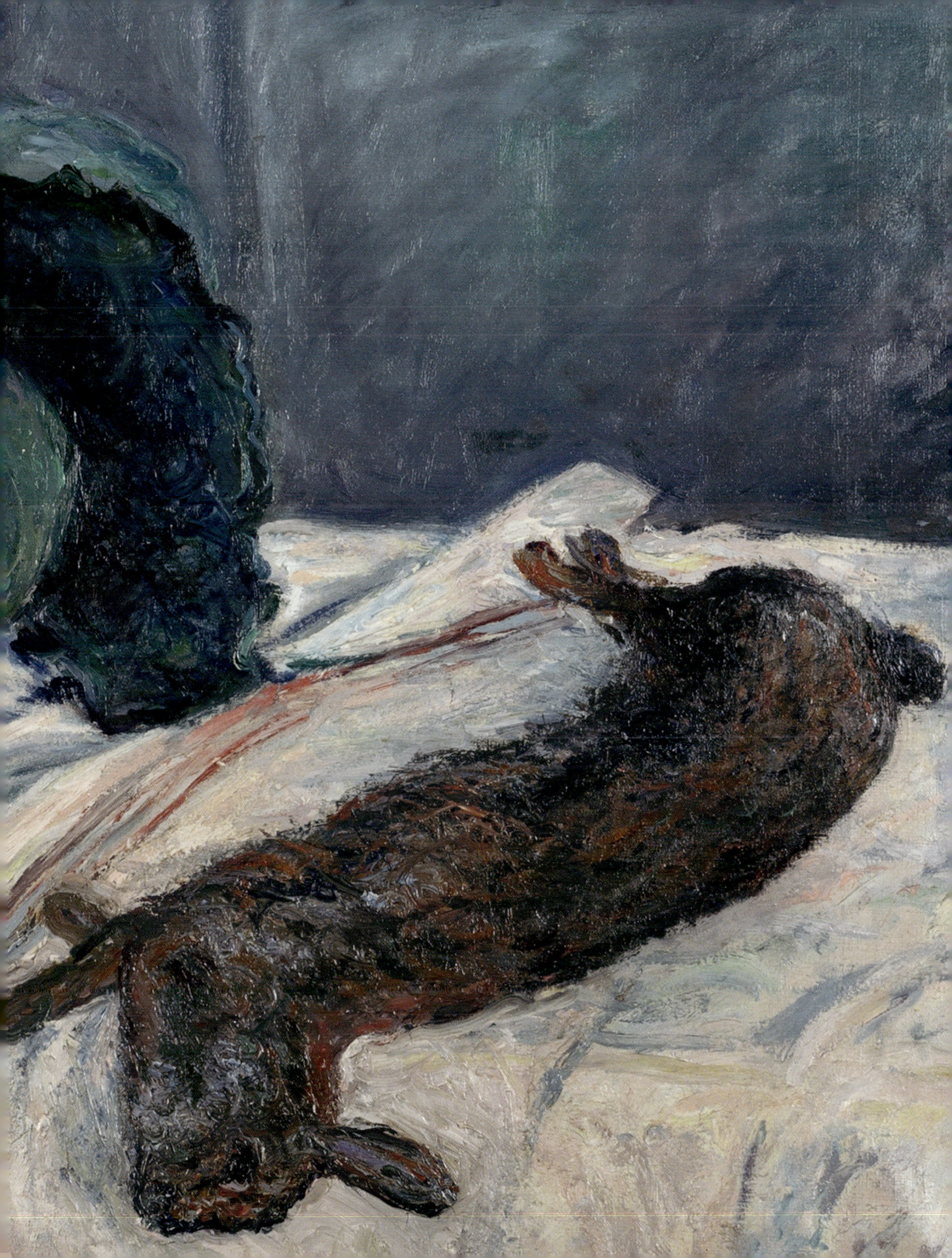

A CHRONOLOGY

Galina Olmsted

1865

Blanche Hoschedé is born in Paris on November 12, 1865, to Ernest and Alice (née Raingo) Hoschedé. She is the second oldest of their six children: Marthe (1864–1925), Blanche (1865–1947), Suzanne (1868–1899), Jacques (1869–1941), Germaine (1873–1968), and Jean-Pierre (1877–1961).

1876

Hoschedé-Monet meets Claude Monet for the first time, as a young girl at her family's summer estate, the Château de Rottembourg in Montgeron (fig. 34).

1878

Hoschedé-Monet completes her first painting, *Four Sunflowers in a Vase* (*Quatre tournesols dans un vase*) (pl. 39). Faced with significant financial difficulties, Ernest Hoschedé is forced to sell most of his art collection, as well as the Château de Rottembourg and the family apartment in Paris. The Hoschedé family moves to Vétheuil, where they share a home with Monet, his wife Camille Doncieux, and the two Monet sons, Jean and Michel.

1879

Doncieux dies after a prolonged illness on September 5.

1882

Having entered into a domestic partnership, Monet and Alice Hoschedé move their children to Pourville. Hoschedé-Monet begins to draw and paint *en plein air*, filling sketchbooks with views of the cliffs and surrounding landscapes (pl. 1).

1883

The Hoschedé and Monet families move to Giverny (fig. 35). Hoschedé-Monet begins to accompany Monet on his daily painting excursions, transporting their canvases and paints in a wheelbarrow.

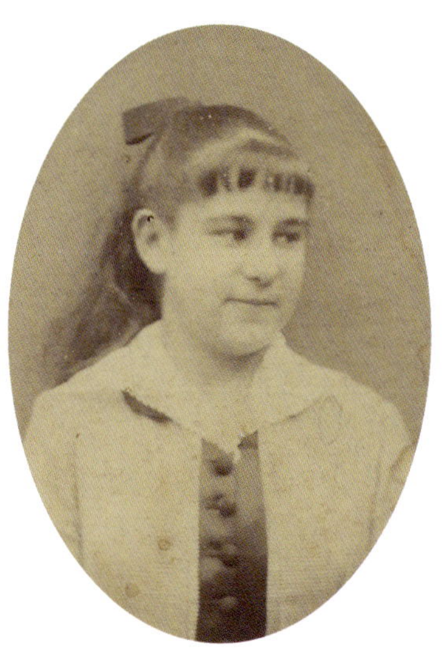

Fig. 34 Blanche Hoschedé at eleven years old, Montgeron, 1876. Collection of Philippe Piguet

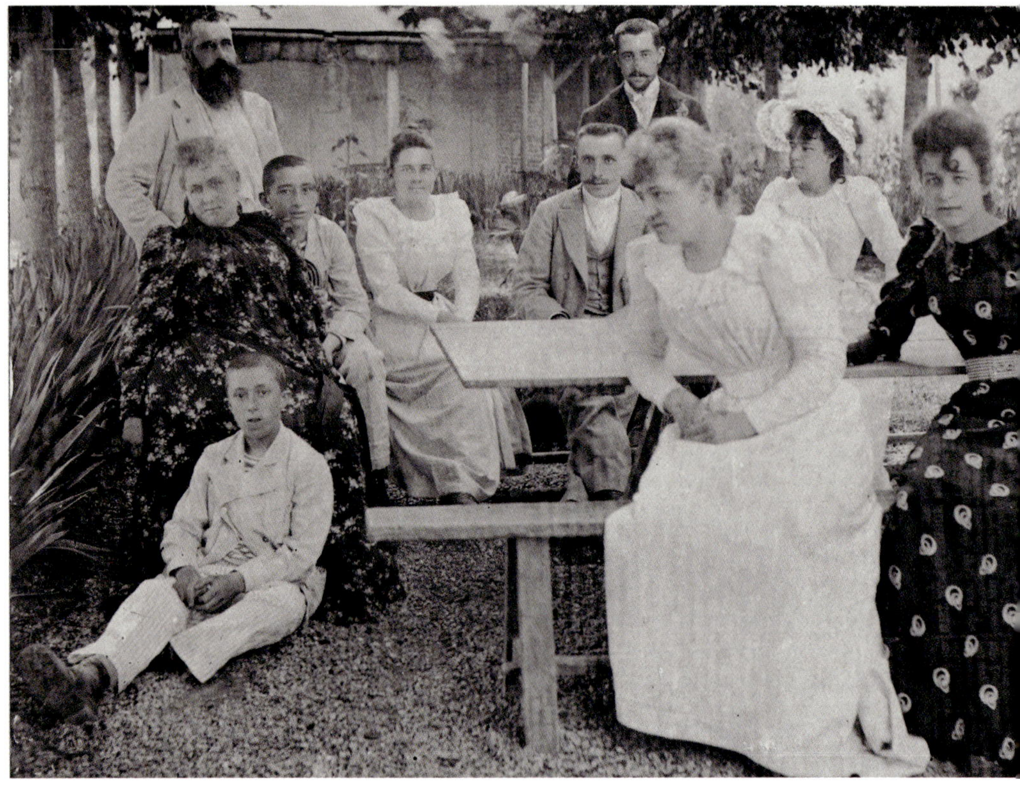

Hoschedé-Monet meets John Leslie Breck, an American painter who travels to Giverny to paint *en plein air*. The two become romantically involved but Monet forbids Hoschedé-Monet from marrying him.[1] Breck leaves France in 1892.

1888

Hoschedé-Monet submits an unidentified painting to the Salon des Artistes Français, with Monet's encouragement. It is rejected.

1890

Monet purchases the family home in Giverny. In the years ahead, he will build a greenhouse and multiple studios, excavate the lily pond, and plant extensive gardens throughout the property.

1891

Ernest Hoschedé dies in Paris on March 19. He is buried in Giverny, at his children's request.

Late in the year, Hoschedé-Monet accompanies Monet to England, where they visit her brother, Jacques Hoschedé, who was working as a ship broker in Lymington. Passing through London, they meet with John Singer Sargent and James McNeill Whistler, and see the famous Peacock Room which Whistler had designed for Fredrick Leyland.[2]

1892

Alice Hoschedé and Claude Monet marry on July 16. All six Hoschedé children become Monet's stepchildren. A few days later, on July 20, Suzanne Hoschedé, Blanche's sister, marries Theodore Earl Butler, an American artist who first visited Giverny in 1888 (fig. 36).

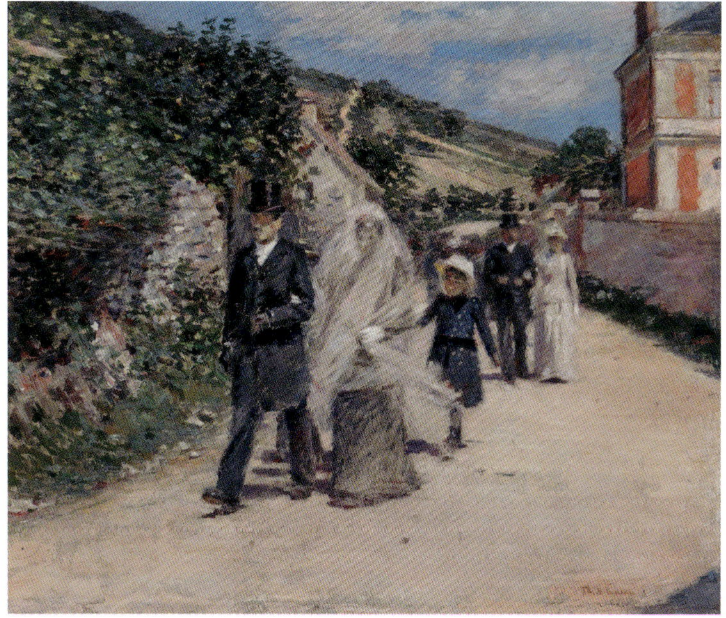

Fig. 35   The Hoschedé-Monet family, Giverny, ca. 1886. Collection of Philippe Piguet
From left to right and back to front: Claude Monet, Jean Monet; Alice Hoschedé, Michel Monet, Blanche Hoschedé, Jacques Hoschedé, Germaine Hoschedé; Jean-Pierre Hoschedé, Marthe Hoschedé, Suzanne Hoschedé.

Fig. 36   Theodore Robinson, *The Wedding March*, 1892. Oil on canvas, 22⁵⁄₁₆ × 26½ in. (56.7 × 67.3 cm). Terra Foundation for American Art

Hoschedé-Monet and Monet continue their daily painting excursions, setting up their easels side by side. In the spring, they make a series of haystack paintings in the meadow near the family home, the future site of the water lily pond (figs. 3 and 4).

1896

In the summer, Hoschedé-Monet and Monet begin making paintings of the Seine river (figs. 37 and 38), working side by side from the riverbank and from boats.

1897

On June 9, Hoschedé-Monet marries Jean Monet, Monet's eldest son. Soon after, the couple moves to Rouen where Jean works as a chemist for his uncle, Léon Monet (fig. 39).

1899

Suzanne Hoschedé-Butler dies on February 6 after a short illness. Her sister Marthe helps to raise her children, James and Lily, as the widowed Butler returned to New York City.

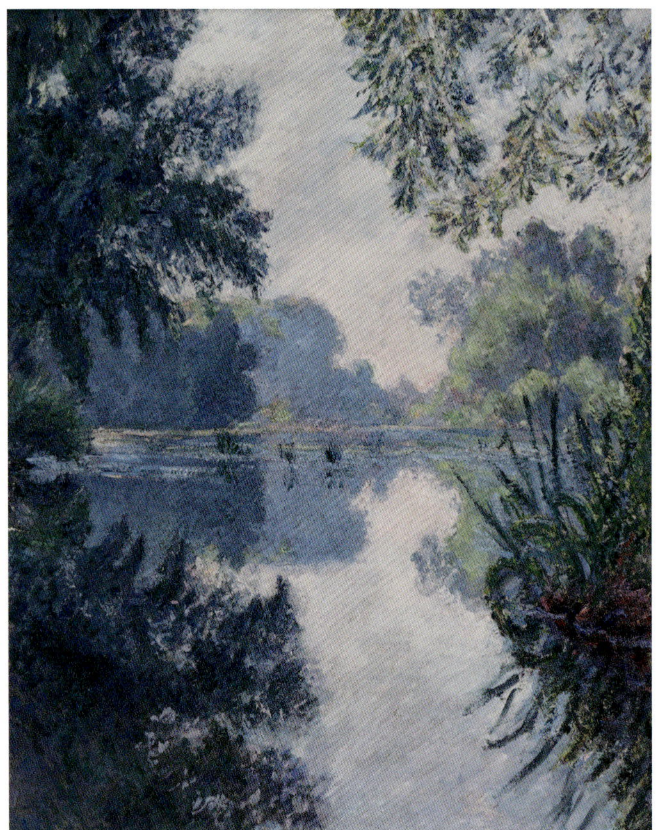

Fig. 37 Blanche Hoschedé-Monet, *Morning on the Seine (Matinée sur la Seine)*, ca. 1896. [See pl. 13]

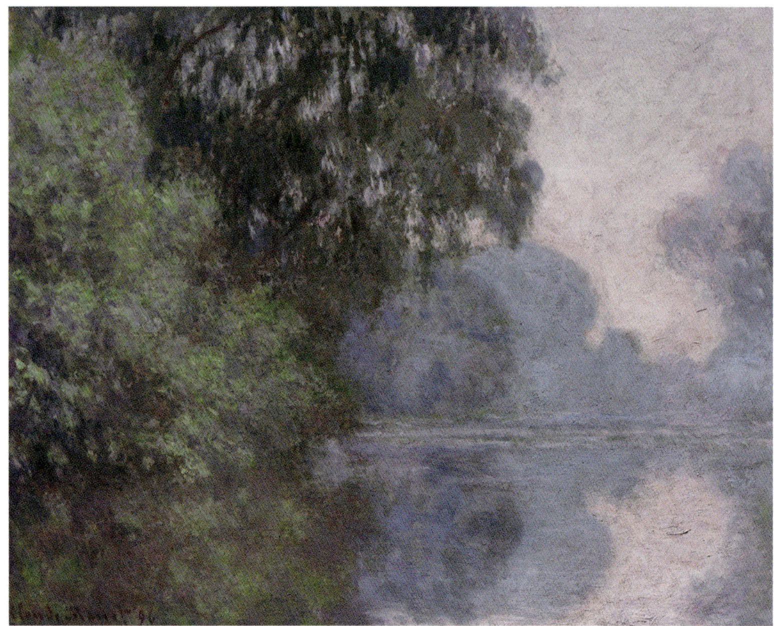

Fig. 38 Claude Monet, *Morning on the Seine, near Giverny*, 1896. Oil on canvas, 29 × 36⅝ in. (73.7 × 93 cm). Museum of Fine Arts Boston, Juliana Cheney Edwards Collection (39.655)

1900

Hoschedé-Monet and Jean travel to Switzerland for a belated honeymoon, where she makes several paintings.

After just six months in New York City, Theodore Earl Butler returns to Giverny and marries Marthe Hoschedé on October 31.

1905

Hoschedé-Monet exhibits her work for the first time at the Salon des Indépendants in Paris. She shows a group of seven paintings.

1906

Hoschedé-Monet returns to the Salon des Indépendants with a group of four paintings.

1907

Hoschedé-Monet exhibits three paintings at the Salon des Indépendants and participates in the first Salon de la Société des Artistes Rouennais, where she shows two paintings.

1908

Hoschedé-Monet sends a larger group of six paintings to the Salon de la Société des Artistes Rouennais.

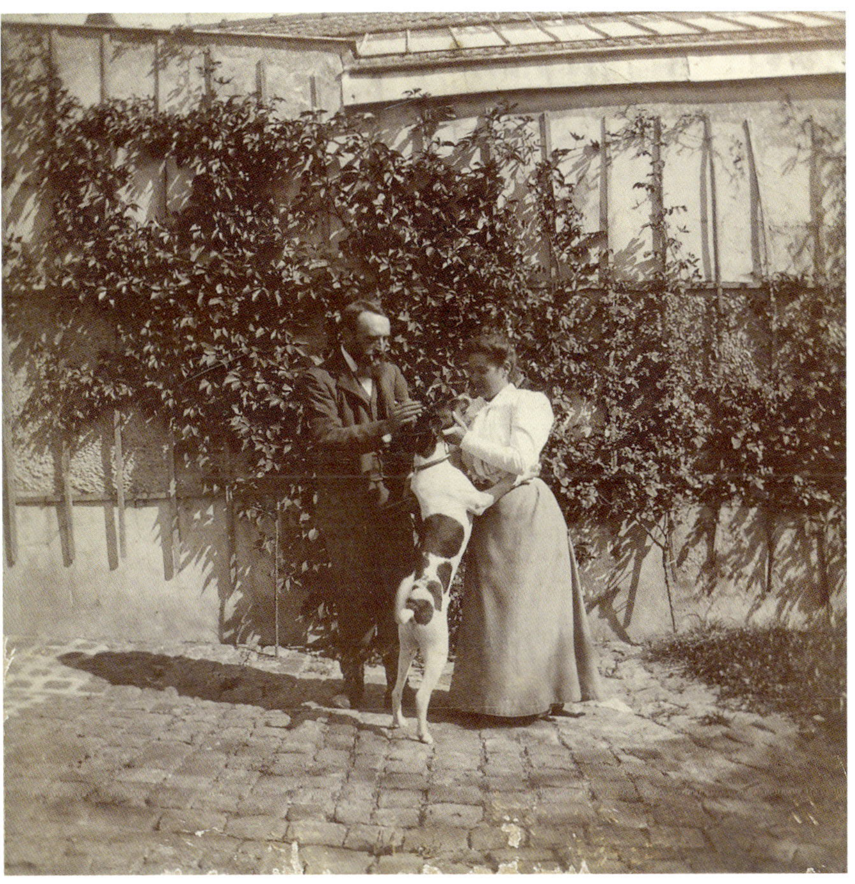

Fig. 39 Jean Monet and Blanche Hoschedé-Monet near their home in Rouen, rue du Renard, ca. 1897–1910. Collection of Philippe Piguet

1909

Hoschedé-Monet exhibits four paintings at the Salon de la Société des Artistes Rouennais. Monet exhibits *Les Nymphéas: Séries de paysages d'eau* at Durand-Ruel's gallery in Paris. The cycle is widely visited and admired. Monet remains preoccupied with water lilies for the remainder of his life and will work closely with Hoschedé-Monet on several large cycles.

1910

Hoschedé-Monet exhibits a group of six paintings at the Salon de la Société des Artistes Rouennais. Later that winter, Jean and his uncle have a falling-out over the family business. Jean resigns and the couple moves to Beaumont-le-Roger, closer to the family home in Giverny.

1911

Hoschedé-Monet participates in the fifth annual Salon de la Société des Artistes Rouennais, sending five paintings. On May 19, Alice Hoschedé dies in Giverny and Monet is widowed for a second time.

1912

In the summer, Jean Monet suffers a stroke and his health declines precipitously. Hoschedé-Monet becomes his primary caregiver.

1913

Hoschedé-Monet exhibits four paintings at the Salon de la Société des Artistes Rouennais. In May, she and Jean leave Beaumont-le-Roger, returning to Giverny where Monet bought them a small house, the Villa des Pinsons, at the edge of the village.

1914

Jean Monet dies on February 9 at just forty-six years old. Soon after, Jean-Pierre Hoschedé leaves Giverny to join the war effort and Michel Monet enlists as a volunteer. Marthe and Theodore Butler leave for the United States. Hoschedé-Monet moves back into the family home in Giverny to care for the property and for Monet, who is seventy-four years old.

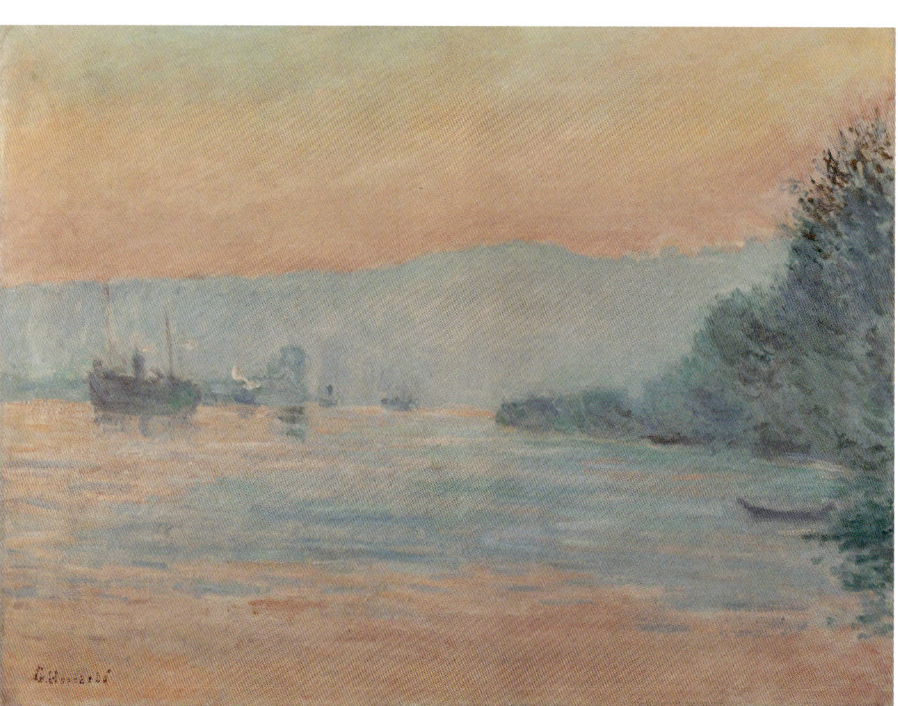

Fig. 40   Blanche Hoschedé-Monet, *The Seine near Rouen (La Seine près de Rouen)*, ca. 1897–1910. Oil on canvas, 21 ¼ × 28 ¾ in. (54 × 73 cm). Collection of Philippe Piguet

The art critic Gustave Geffroy writes to Hoschedé-Monet to say that he is "happy with your decision to stay with Monet, happy for him and happy for you. Suffering makes the reunion of those who remain all the more intimate and strong."[3]

1915

Between 1914 and his death in 1926, Monet was singularly dedicated to a large, decorative cycle of paintings of the water lily gardens which he referred to as his "grandes décorations." In 1915, he builds a third studio space to accommodate the oversized canvases (see fig. 29). Georges Clemenceau—a longtime friend of Monet and, later, the prime minister of France—is clear about Hoschedé-Monet's involvement in the series: "She worked on his canvases. She did the grounds [of the paintings] for him."[4]

1918

Monet begins drafting his plans to donate a cycle of water lily paintings to the French state, collaborating closely with Clemenceau on the renovation of the Orangerie in the Tuileries Gardens, right in the heart of Paris. Hoschedé-Monet works behind the scenes as a negotiator, able to navigate Monet's mercurial moods.

1925

Marthe Hoschedé dies on May 7, leaving Butler a widower for the second time.

1926

Monet dies in Giverny on December 5 at the age of eighty-six. Michel Monet asks Hoschedé-Monet to stay at the family home and to care for the property and its gardens. She agrees.

After Monet's death, twenty-two water lily panels are installed at the Musée de l'Orangerie in Paris, a gift from the artist to the nation of France.

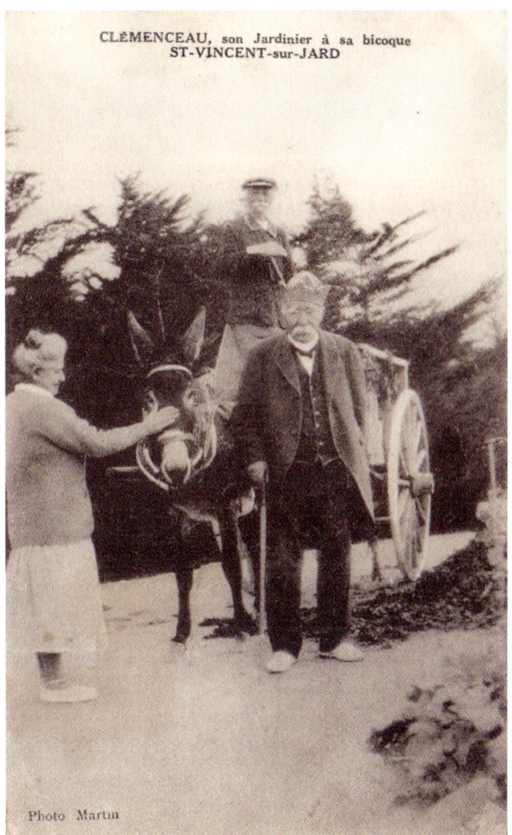

Fig. 41 Blanche Hoschedé-Monet and Georges Clemenceau in Saint-Vincent-sur-Jard, 1927–29. Collection of Philippe Piguet

In November, the first solo exhibition of Hoschedé-Monet's work opens at the Galerie Bernheim-Jeune in Paris. Although some art historians assert that she did not paint between 1914 and 1926, she shows a group of paintings less than one year after Monet's death. A small notice in the journal *Excelsior* reads, "Under the name Mme. Blanche Hoschedé, Mme Blanche Monet exhibits, on the rue du Faubourg-Saint-Honoré, a series of paintings—landscapes and flowers—with a very feminine sensibility."[5]

1927–1929

Hoschedé-Monet makes several trips to visit Georges Clemenceau at his home in Saint-Vincent-sur-Jard (fig. 41), producing paintings of the landscapes and seascapes nearby (pls. 27 and 28). She exhibits two paintings at the Salon des Indépendants in 1928 and 1929, and at the Salon de Vernon in 1929.

At the Salon des Indépendants in 1929, one critic described an early section of the exhibition: "Right away, we find ourselves in front of a landscape and a flowering garden by Mme Blanche Hoschedé-Monet. . . ."[6] Another critic wrote admiringly of her paintings: "Mme Blanche Hoschedé is, as we know, the daughter-in-law of Monet, and she does great honor to her teacher without copying him; delicate and sensitive talent."[7]

1930

Hoschedé-Monet travels to Italy with her youngest brother, Jean-Pierre, visiting Venice and Bassano del Grappa. This year, she also sends two paintings to the Salon des Indépendants.

1931

Her second solo exhibition opens in March at Bernheim-Jeune. She exhibits thirty-one works separated into three sections: paintings of Giverny, scenes from her travels, and still lifes. Her group of still lifes includes several flower paintings, such as *Peonies (Pivoines)* (pl. 41).

1931–1935

She exhibits annually at the Salon des Indépendants and the Salon de la Société des Artistes Rouennais, sending groups of two or three paintings each year.

1932–1939

Hoschedé-Monet travels extensively with family and friends, visiting Diélette, Aix-en-Provence, Saint-Jean-Cap-Ferrat, Kervoyal-Damgan, and the French Alps. She takes her paints and canvases with her on these various travels and continues her practice of painting *en plein air*. When in Giverny, her subjects mainly include her home, still lifes, and views of the garden on the family property.

1940

Hoschedé-Monet leaves Giverny in the summer due to wartime bombings in and around Paris following Germany's invasion of France. She travels first with her family to Gipcy and then to Aix-en-Provence. She returns to Giverny before 1942 to find the property and its gardens largely undamaged.

She sends two paintings to the Salon de Vernon. In autumn, another solo exhibition of her work opens in Paris, this time at the Galerie Alfred Daber.

In March, a large solo exhibition featuring forty-six paintings opens at Galerie d'Art Drouot Provence in Paris. One critic writes for the wartime journal *Combat*, "Blanche Hoschedé (Galerie Drouot Provence) is the daughter-in-law of Monet and 'no one, they tell us, better knows or better sustains the tradition of Giverny.' Evidently, and the landscapes by this artist are full of good qualities. But they don't make us forget Monet. . . ."[8]

In the winter, Hoschedé-Monet decides to visit one of her nieces in Nice. While there, she falls gravely ill and dies on December 8. She is buried in Giverny on December 20, in the family tomb alongside her parents, Alice and Ernest Hoschedé, her husband, Jean Monet, and her father-in-law, Claude Monet.

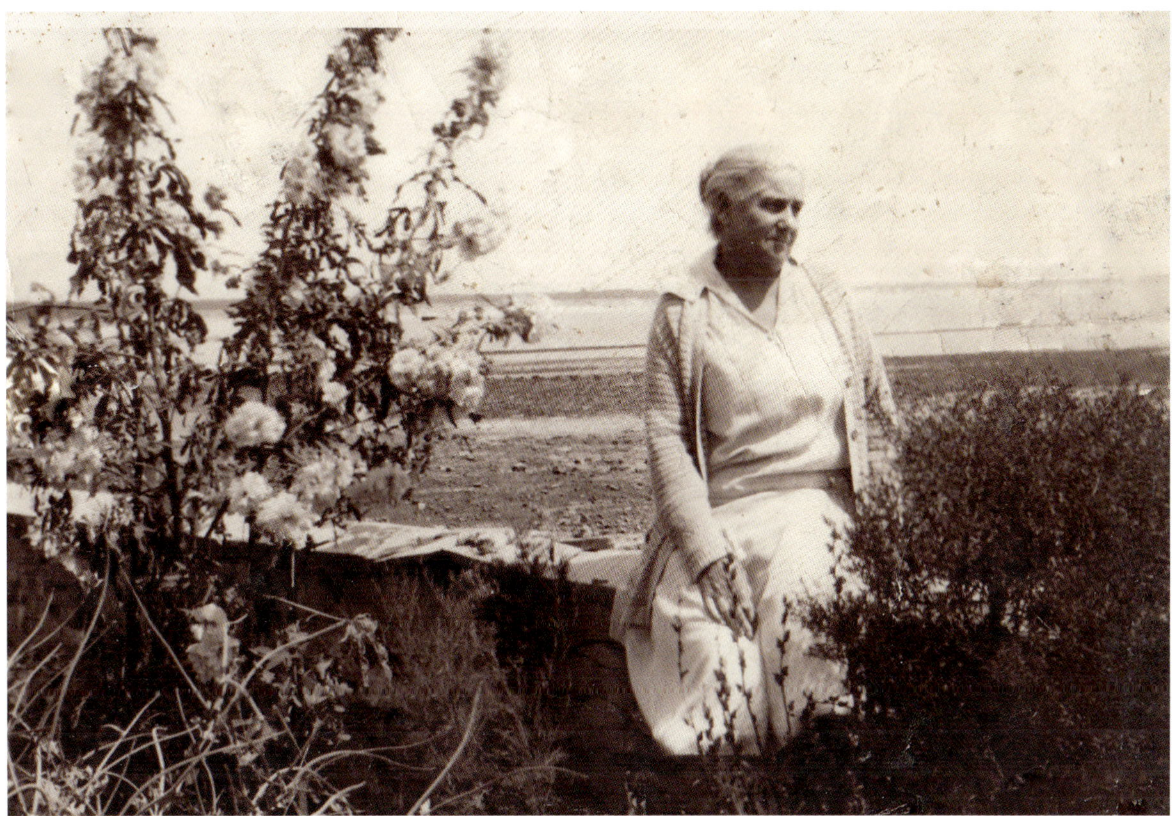

Fig. 42 Blanche Hoschedé-Monet sitting on a small wall, 1927–1929. Collection of Philippe Piguet

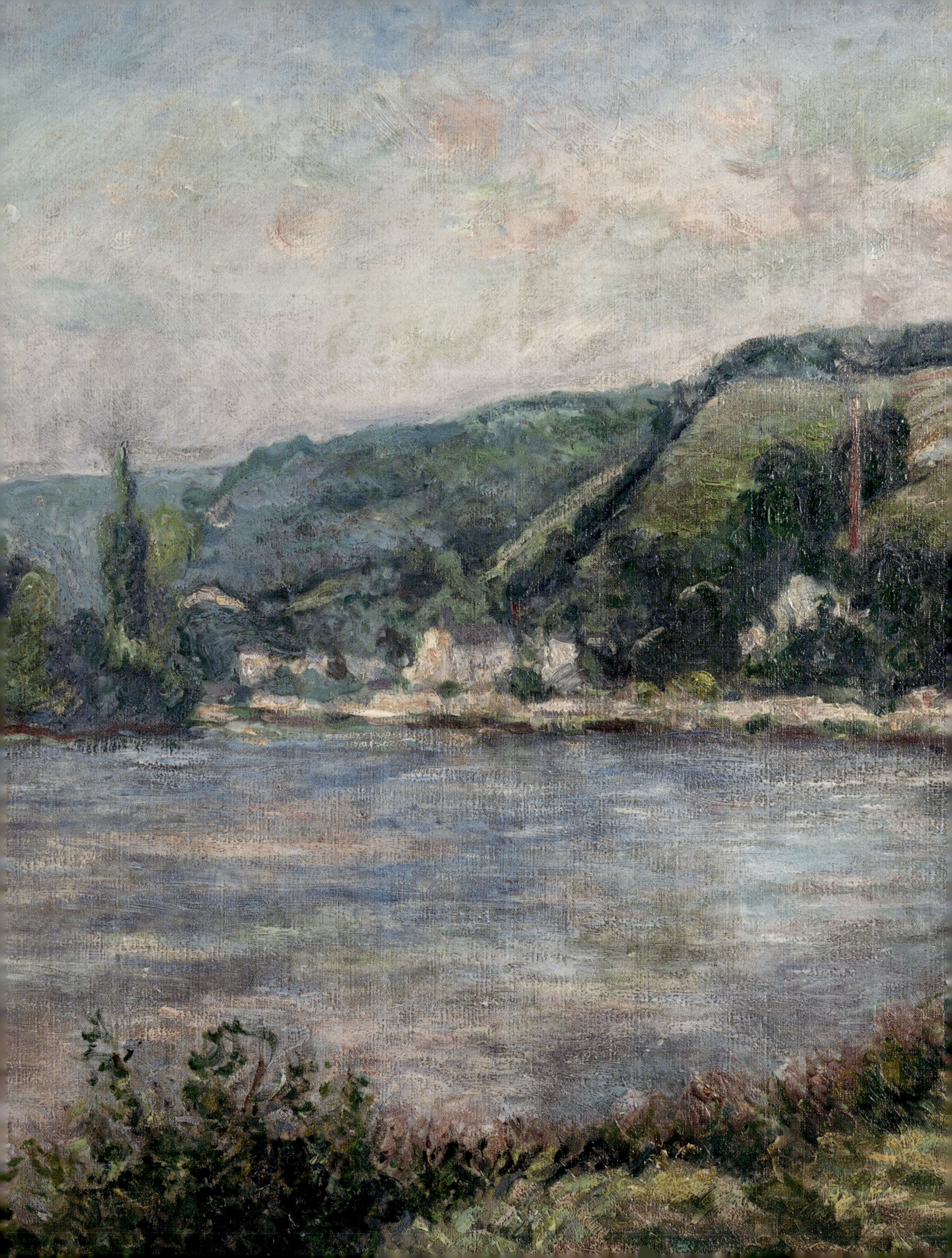

ENDNOTES

Peintre impressionniste

1. American Art Association, *Works in Oil and Pastel by the Impressionists of Paris* (New York: Press of J.J. Little & Co., 1886). The best source for understanding this first exhibition in the United States is Jennifer A. Thompson, "Durand-Ruel and America," in *Inventing Impressionism: Paul Durand-Ruel and the Modern Art Market*, ed. Sylvie Patry (New Haven, CT: Yale University Press, 2015), 134–51.

2. Greta [pseudonym], "Boston Art and Artists," *Art Amateur* 17 (October 1887): 93, as cited in Nina Lubbren, "Breakfast at Monet's: Giverny in the Context of the European Artists' Colonies," in *Impressionist Giverny: A Colony of Artists, 1885–1915*, ed. Katherine M. Bourguignon (Giverny: Musée d'Art Américain; Chicago: Terra Foundation for American Art, 2007), 29–43, n. 47.

3. Katherine M. Bourguignon, "Giverny: A Village for Artists," in Bourguignon, *Impressionist Giverny*, 17–28, esp. 17.

4. "Offert à Blanche pour ses vingt ans," as documented in Marie Berhaut, *Gustave Caillebotte: Catalogue raisonné des peintures et pastels* (Paris: Wildenstein Institute, 1994), 71, no. 31.

5. The following entries are noted in Monet's account book, dated February 23–24 and 26: "M. Caillebotte / *Figures en plein air* 200 F / M. Caillebotte peintre / *Les Dahlias* 600 F / *Pochade Argenteuil* 200 F," Musée Marmottan Monet, Paris, MM 5160 [1], fol. 10, as cited in Anne Distel, ed., *Gustave Caillebotte: Urban Impressionist* (New York: Abbeville Press, 1994), 312.

6. Daniel Wildenstein, *Claude Monet: Biographie et catalogue raisonné*, 4 vols. (Lausanne: La Bibliothèque des Arts, 1974–91), 1: 83.

7. "J'avais onze ans mais je me souviens de son arrivée à Montgeron chez mes parents. On me l'avait annoncé comme un grand artiste ayant les cheveux longs. Cela m'avait frappée et j'ai eu de suite de la sympathie car on sentait qu'il aimait les enfants." Jean-Pierre Hoschedé, *Blanche Hoschedé-Monet, peintre impressionniste* (Rouen: Lecerf, 1961), 7–8.

8. Hoschedé, *Blanche Hoschedé-Monet, peintre impressionniste*, 9.

9. The 1874 and 1878 sales of the Hoschedé collection included three and twenty paintings by Monet, respectively. These sales are first described in the scholarship by Merete Bodelsen, "Early Impressionist Sales 1874–94 in the Light of Some Unpublished 'Procès-Verbaux,'" *The Burlington Magazine* 110, no. 783 (1968): 331–49.

10. Wildenstein, *Claude Monet*, 3: no. 1383 and nos. 1472–88.

11. "Elle le fit en toutes circonstances, soit à l'atelier, soit au Jardin, soit l'accompagnant à ses motifs pour y transporter ses toiles et son chevalet en même temps que les siens. Ce transport elle le faisait à l'aide d'une brouette par des chemins plutôt illusoires, à travers champs et prairies parfois trempés de rosée. C'était le cas lorsque, par exemple, il s'agissait de motifs matinaux sur la Seine. Là encore elle aidait son beau-père en prenant volontiers les rames du canot." Hoschedé, *Blanche Hoschedé-Monet, peintre impressionniste*, 12.

12. Wildenstein, *Claude Monet*, 3: nos. 1362, 1363, 1364.

13. In a letter to Alice Hoschedé, dated November 12, 1885: "Je suis heureux de savoir que Blanche travaille; si elle voulait se donner un peu de peine, elle ferait bien, dites-le lui et qu'elle dessine, ce qu'elle ne fait jamais afin de s'habituer à mettre bien les choses en place." Cited in Sophie Fourny-Dargère, *Blanche Hoschedé-Monet, 1865–1947: Une artiste de Giverny* (Vernon and Rouen: Musée Municipal A.G. Poulain / Lecerf, 1991), 15, n. 10.

14. "July 3, 1892," in Theodore Robinson (1852–1896), *[Diaries] 1892–1896*, vol. 2, Frick Art Reference Library. Cited in Sona Johnston, *In Monet's Light: Theodore Robinson at Giverny* (Baltimore and London: The Baltimore Museum of Art / Philip Wilson Publishers, 2004), 190. This mention of a sale to Bertha and Potter Palmer on their 1892 trip to Giverny is one of Hoschedé-Monet's earliest known sales.

15. See Haley S. Pierce, "Blanche Hoschedé-Monet: Exhibition History," in this volume, pp. 134–37.

16. As cited in Hoschedé, *Blanche Hoschedé-Monet, peintre impressionniste*, 30–31.

17. Hoschedé, *Blanche Hoschedé-Monet, peintre impressionniste*, 6.

The Last of the Impressionists

1. "Sans sa belle-fille, Claude Monet vivrait dans un isolement qui le tuerait; c'est elle qui nous le conserve en vie, la postérité ne devra pas l'oublier." René Gimpel, *Journal d'un collectionneur marchand de tableaux* (Paris: Calmann Lévy, 1963), 319, entry for July 17, 1926.

2. See especially Jean-Noël Jeanneney, Sophie Eloy, and Cécile Girardeau, *Monet/Clemenceau: Correspondance* (Paris: Musée de l'Orangerie; RMN-Grand Palais, 2019).

3. "On a fait tout cela suivant ses volontés, et c'est pourquoi, tant que nous vivrons, on ne changera rien à ce qui existe; nous veillerons que ce qu'il avait voulu reste tel. Sa volonté est formelle," cited in Jean-Pierre Hoschedé, *Blanche Hoschedé-Monet,*

peintre impressionniste (Rouen: Lecerf, 1961).

4. "Tenez vous ferme à vos pinceaux. C'est la grande affaire. Ils possèdent et possèderons [*sic*] la vertu de vous faire oublier le vide." Georges Clemenceau to Blanche Hoschedé-Monet, Saint-Vincent-sur-Jard, September 12, 1927, cited in Hoschedé, *Blanche Hoschedé-Monet, peintre impressionniste*, 64.

5. Galerie Durand-Ruel archives, Paris, listing the sale and purchase of paintings by Blanche Hoschedé-Monet.

6. "Madame Blanche Hoschedé n'a point fatigué ses contemporains par la publicité de son nom. Elle pourrait pourtant se prévaloir de bien des titres qui manquent . . . à certains spécialistes . . . de la réclame. Bien entendu, l'influence de Claude Monet est constamment présente dans ces paysages, ces natures mortes. Mais elle n'en étouffe pas moins la féminité qui s'y exprime avec beaucoup de fraicheur." Lucien Rebatet, *Le Petit Parisien*, November 7, 1942.

7. "Elle peint la mer brumeuse et les fleurs qui dansent." Georges Clemenceau to Marguerite Baldensperger, Belébat, Saint-Vincent-sur-Jard, August 31, 1927. Cited in Georges Clemenceau, *Lettres à une amie, 1923-1929* (Paris: Gallimard, 1970), 452.

8. The original quotation cites "son père" ("her father") when referring to Claude Monet, although he was actually Blanche's stepfather and father-in-law.

9. "Madame Blanche Hoschedé-Monet est mieux que l'héritière d'un beau nom. Fille du plus prestigieux coloriste de la fin du siècle dernier, elle a estimé que l'exemple donné par son père, Claude Monet, était encore à suivre, et que les aspects qu'il a aimés sont toujours dignes

d'être peints. Nous ne trouvons donc, dans les œuvres de Madame Blanche Hoschedé-Monet, nulle trace de cette fausse originalité par laquelle tant de dames peintres, désireuses de se faire un nom, cherchent à épater la galerie. Des œuvres de Madame Blanche Hoschedé-Monet, vous n'en verrez guère qu'au Salon sans jury, celui des Indépendants. Talent véritable, noblesse du cœur et de l'esprit s'accompagnent toujours d'une très grande modestie." Anon., "L'Art indépendant: Venise par Mme Blanche Hoschedé-Monet," *Le Peuple*, June 19, 1935.

10. "les jardins sont sérieusement endommagés, en particulier par les hivers rigoureux." Louise Damasse, "Journal de guerre," handwritten notebooks, 1986, Musée Blanche Hoschedé-Monet, Vernon.

The Painter Hits Pause

1. For the Thornley-Monet Portfolio, see James A. Ganz, "Monet in Print," in *The Unknown Monet: Pastels and Drawings*, ed. James A. Ganz and Richard Kendall (Williamstown, MA: Sterling and Francine Clark Art Institute, 2007), 218–37 and 273–78.

2. Daniel Wildenstein, *Claude Monet: Biographie et catalogue raisonné* (Lausanne and Paris: La Bibliothèque des Arts, 1974–91), 3: no. 1330.

3. Ganz, "Monet in Print," 226.

4. Although difficult to date, this portrait has been placed in 1888 by comparing it to a similar painting by Breck. Royal W. Leith and Jeffrey R. Brown, "John Leslie Breck: His Life and Career," in *John Leslie Breck: American Impressionist* (Charlotte, NC: Mint Museum of Art, 2021), 51–53.

5. The records for women artists staying at the Hôtel Baudy in Giverny include such nationalities as British, Australian, Canadian,

Scottish, Norwegian, German, Polish, and Russian, as well as French and American. See Katherine M. Bourguignon, ed., *Impressionist Giverny: A Colony of Artists, 1885–1915* (Giverny: Musée d'Art Américain; Chicago: Terra Foundation for American Art, 2007), 203–12.

6. Following the death of Claude Monet's first wife, Camille, in 1879, Monet entered into a domestic partnership with Alice Hoschedé. The couple would later marry in 1892, although the Monet and Hoschedé families had been living together since 1878.

7. Ibid. For Cassatt, see p. 204; for MacMonnies, p. 209. Cassatt and MacMonnies were painting the two major tympanum murals for the central hall of the Woman's Building, *Modern Woman* and *Primitive Woman*, respectively.

8. Blanche Hoschedé-Monet's account book for the period 1890–47, Museé Marmottan Monet, Paris, 5160.2013.4.

9. "I saw some things by Mlle. Blanche, she has improved greatly since I saw her work last – a spring landscape, sold to Potter Palmer quite charming – Monet said she ought to work away from him – they both like to work together." Theodore Robinson, "July 3, 1892," in *[Diaries] 1892-1896*, vol. 2, Frick Art Reference Library. Cited in Sona Johnston, *In Monet's Light: Theodore Robinson at Giverny* (Baltimore and London: The Baltimore Museum of Art / Philip Wilson Publishers, 2004), 190.

10. Wheeler had founded a school for young women in Providence, Rhode Island, in 1889 and frequently brought students abroad to study art and art history. Bourguignon, *Impressionist Giverny*, 49, 52.

11. *Evening Star* (Washington, DC), June 20, 1915, 47.

12. ". . . ma sœur fit pour lui un grand sacrifice, celui de renoncer à peindre."

Jean-Pierre Hoschedé, *Claude Monet, ce mal connu: Intimité familiale d'un demi-siècle à Giverny, de 1883 à 1926* (Geneva: Pierre Cailler Éditeur, 1960), 1: 93.

13. Clemenceau quoted in Jean-Pierre Hoschedé, *Blanche Hoschedé-Monet, peintre impressionniste* (Rouen: Lecerf, 1961), 15. Clemenceau referred to Blanche Hoschedé-Monet in this way and in various iterations in many letters to Claude Monet following her return to Monet's side after her husband's death in 1914.

14. The saga of the *Water Lilies* is documented in Hoschedé, "Historique des décorations des Nymphéas," in *Claude Monet, ce mal connu,* 2: 11–26, and in Daniel Wildenstein, *Monet: The Triumph of Impressionism* (Cologne: Taschen, 2023, first published 1996), 519–600 *passim.*

15. https://www.youtube.com/watch?v=1eGda3a3lWg. See Wildenstein, *Monet: Triumph,* 525–27, and Sacha Guitry, "Random Memories," in *If Memory Serves: Memoirs of Sacha Guitry* (New York: Doubleday, 1935), 263–76.

16. Jean Renoir, *Renoir, My Father* (New York: New York Review of Books, 2001, first published 1958). For palette, see 359–62; for large canvas invention, see 428.

17. Ibid., 430.

18. Jeanne Fevre, *Mon oncle Degas* (Geneva: Pierre Cailler, 1949).

19. See Henri Loyrette, *Degas* (Paris: Fayard, 1991), 666, and Nancy Mowll Mathews, *Cassatt and Her Circle: Selected Letters* (New York: Abbeville Press, 1984), 328–29.

20. Loyrette, *Degas,* 667.

21. A discussion of the Degas segment of the film and Fevre's role in it can be found in Philip Hoy, *M. Degas Steps Out* (Oxfordshire and Baltimore: The Waywiser Press, 2022), 59–65.

22. Nancy Mowll Mathews, *Mary Cassatt: A Life* (New Haven: Yale University Press, 1998), 315, and Suzanne Glover Lindsay et al., *Edgar Degas: Sculpture,* The Collections of the National Gallery of Art, Systematic Catalogue (Washington, DC: National Gallery of Art, 1910), 116–19.

23. For the frontispiece of *Mon oncle Degas,* Fevre reproduced a photograph she identified as Clozier reading to Degas, although it is now thought to be *Louise Halévy Reading to Degas* (ca. 1895). Since Fevre knew Clozier so well, this must have been a familiar sight in the Degas household.

24. Cassatt's cataracts were diagnosed in 1914; she began having operations on them in 1915 and several more times between 1917 and 1921, but her eyesight never improved enough for her to paint again. Mathews, *Cassatt: A Life,* 305, 310–11.

25. Located in Le Mesnil-Théribus, in the Seine et Oise region northwest of Paris, she was not far from Pissarro and Monet. It is worth noting that she too had a pond and often used it for inspiration.

26. Mathews, *Cassatt and Her Circle,* 317.

27. Valet was a German national and had to leave France in the fall of 1914 after the war broke out, but they had worked on the exhibition up to that point and many others as well in their long association. Mathews, *Cassatt: A Life,* 306–8, 317.

28. Blanche Hoschedé married Claude Monet's eldest son, Jean, on June 9, 1897.

29. "At times silent and withdrawn, at other times incoherent and rambling, he showed little awareness of reality." Claire Joyes, *Monet at Giverny* (New York: Mayflower Books, 1975), 39.

30. Janine Burke discusses all the documentary evidence surrounding this issue in "La Nymphéa: Monet, Blanche Hoschedé and Giverny," in *Source: Nature's Healing Role in Art and Writing* (Sydney: Allen & Unwin, 2009), 279–312, especially 309–10.

31. 1912–26, presumably including the two years that Hoschedé-Monet was caring for her ailing husband.

32. *Exposition Blanche Hoschedé (Mme. Blanche Monet),* November 7–18, 1927, MM. Bernheim-Jeune, Éditeurs d'Art, Paris. An invitation card but no catalogue survives for this exhibition, so it is not known what paintings she exhibited. See Philippe Piguet, *Blanche Hoschedé-Monet: Un regard impressionniste* (Vernon and Paris: Musée de Vernon / Intensité Éditions, 2017), 44.

33. "I saw some things by Mlle. Blanche, she has improved greatly since I saw her work last – a spring landscape, sold to Potter Palmer quite charming – Monet said she ought to work away from him – they both like to work together." Theodore Robinson, "July 3, 1892," in *[Diaries] 1892-1896,* vol. 2, Frick Art Reference Library. Cited in Johnston, *In Monet's Light,* 190.

34. Alice and James Butler (called Lily and Jimmy or Jim), children of Suzanne Hoschedé and Theodore Butler (raised by Marthe Hoschedé Butler) both studied art in the United States during their residence there from 1913 to 1921. Richard Love, *Theodore Earl Butler: Emergence from Monet's Shadow* (Chicago: Haase-Mumm Publishing Company, 1985), 359, 401, 407, and Philippe Piguet, *Saga familiale: Monet, Hoschedé-Monet et les Butler* (Vernon: Musée de Vernon, 2022), 14, 20.

35. This painting has previously been published undated, see Philippe Piguet, *Blanche Hoschedé-Monet: Un destin impressionniste* (Louviers: Musée de Louviers;

Bonsecours: Éditions Point de vues, 2010), p. 74, BHM 8.

36. For photographs of the changing profile of the wisteria on the Japanese bridge, see especially Françoise Heilbrun, "The Patriarch of Giverny in Front of the Camera," in *Monet's Garden in Giverny*, ed. Marina Ferretti Bocquillon (Giverny: Musée des Impressionnismes Giverny, 2009), 31–38. See also Piguet, *Blanche Hoschedé-Monet: Un destin impressionniste*, p. 77, BHM 31. Many Hoschedé-Monet paintings of the lily pond and bridge have been on the market in recent years; see https://www.artnet.com/artists/blanche-hosched%C3%A9-monet/ (retrieved March 29, 2024) for paintings that have not yet been published as part of her known body of work.

37. See Piguet, *Blanche Hoschedé-Monet: Un destin impressionniste*, p. 74, BHM 10.

38. Blanche Hoschedé-Monet, *Le Jardin et la maison de Monet à Giverny*, before 1924, oil on canvas, 28¹³⁄₁₆ × 36⅝ in. (73.2 × 93 cm), Musée des Augustins, Toulouse (67 37 1); see https://www.augustins.org/fr/notice/67-37-1-le-jardin-et-le-maison-de-monet-a-giverny-9bf31c05-ffcb-4443-aa19-3e803100911d (retrieved March 24, 2024).

In the Light of Claude Monet

1. "A ma sœur Blanche, en reconnaissance de ce qu'elle fut auprès de Monet, de ce qu'elle fit pour sa mémoire." Jean-Pierre Hoschedé, *Claude Monet, ce mal connu*, 2 vols. (Geneva: Pierre Cailler Éditeur, 1960).

2. Clemenceau quoted in Jean-Pierre Hoschedé, *Blanche Hoschedé-Monet, peintre impressionniste* (Rouen: Lecerf, 1961), 15. Clemenceau referred to Blanche Hoschedé-Monet in this way and in various iterations in many letters to Claude Monet following her return to Monet's side after her husband's death in 1914.

3. "Peintre impressionniste. Pas dans l'ombre mais dans la lumière de Claude Monet." Ibid., title and inscription on the cover page.

4. "C'est en 1876 que j'ai vu Monet pour la première fois. J'avais onze ans mais je me souviens de son arrivée à Montgeron chez mes parents. On me l'avait annoncé comme un grand artiste ayant les cheveux longs. Cela m'avait frappée et j'ai eu de suite de la sympathie car on sentait qu'il aimait les enfants." Hoschedé, *Blanche Hoschedé-Monet, peintre impressionniste*, 7–8. Claude Monet was invited by Ernest Hoschedé, Blanche's father and a great collector and champion of the new generation, to work at the Château de Rottembourg at Montgeron in Essonne, where he created a group of large panel paintings meant to adorn the walls of the family home.

5. Falling upon economic hardship, the Hoschedé family moved to Vétheuil in 1878 where they lived with Claude Monet, his wife Camille, and their two sons. Following Camille's death, Claude Monet and Alice Hoschedé entered into a domestic partnership, moving their families to Pourville in 1882 before settling in Giverny in 1883.

6. "Blanche accompagnait toujours Monet sur le lieu de son travail, portant ses toiles, son matériel et le sien aussi . . . elle travaillait dans son voisinage . . . sans jamais peindre le même motif que lui." Hoschedé, *Claude Monet, ce mal connu*, 1: 91.

7. "Monet regardait ce qu'elle avait peint, lui faisait ses compliments, ou plus souvent, lui indiquait ce qu'il jugeait mauvais, mal construit, mais jamais je ne l'ai entendu lui dire comment il fallait faire." Ibid.

8. "Mademoiselle Blanche Hoschedé obligé de venir à Paris après demain 13 mai voudrait profiter de son séjour pour aller au Champ de Mars. Je lui promets de l'y conduire et vous prierai d'obtenir un moyen d'entrer. . ." Claude Monet to Gustave Geffroy, May 11, 1891, Delphine Frémeaux sale, Rouen, December 20, 2020.

9. Philippe Piguet, *Saga familiale: Monet, Hoschedé-Monet et les Butler* (Vernon: Musée de Vernon, 2022), 16, note 12. A letter dated December 16, 1891, from Blanche Hoschedé to her mother, Alice Hoschedé (collection of Philippe Piguet), states: "Après le déjeuner, nous avons été avec lui [Sargent] voir les Paons de Whistler." The Peacock Room is now installed in the Freer Gallery of Art, National Museum of Asian Art, Smithsonian, Washington, DC.

10. "Il me tarde de voir ce qu'elle aura fait en mon absence et surtout d'après ce que tu m'en dis." Claude Monet to his wife Alice Hoschedé, Sandviken, February 26, 1895, collection of Philippe Piguet.

11. Blanche Hoschedé-Monet's sketchbook, 1882–84, fol. 25, collection of Philippe Piguet, on loan to the Musée des Impressionnismes Giverny.

12. For a comprehensive study of Blanche Hoschedé-Monet's paintings, refer to Philippe Piguet, *Blanche Hoschedé-Monet: Un destin impressionniste* (Musée de Louviers / Bonsecours: Éditions Point de vues, 2010).

13. Daniel Wildenstein, *Claude Monet: Biographie et catalogue raisonné* (Lausanne: La Bibliothèque des Arts, 1974–91), 3: no. 1331.

14. ". . .on peut dire que Monet a trouvé le courage de survivre et de vivre et la force de travailler, par

la présence de celle qui devint sa fille dévouée, lui gardant sa maison intacte, l'encourageant à reprendre ses outils de peintre, recevant ses amis comme le faisait autrefois sa mère." Hoschedé, *Claude Monet, ce mal connu*, 1: 92.

15. "...par sa seule présence, la guérisseuse morale la plus dévouée, la plus attachée qu'il soit possible d'imaginer." Ibid.

16. Philippe Piguet, *Saga familiale: Monet, Hoschedé-Monet et les Butler* (Vernon: Musée de Vernon, 2022), 16, note 10. "[Monet] a rapporté un album de photographies de chez [Galerie Georges] Petit contenant des Corot, Millet, et Delacroix. Blanche était impayable avec son parti pris de Delacroix contre Corot...." Alice Hoschedé-Monet in a letter to her daughter Germaine Hoschedé, Giverny, March 20, 1890, collection of Philippe Piguet.

17. See Philippe Piguet, *Blanche Hoschedé-Monet: Un destin impressionniste* (Louviers: Musée de Louviers; Bonsecours: Éditions Point de vues, 2010), p. 87, BHM 121.

18. See Piguet, *Blanche Hoschedé-Monet: Un destin impressionniste*, p. 86, BHM 116.

19. "pas dans l'ombre mais dans la lumière de Claude Monet." Hoschedé, *Claude Monet, ce mal connu*, 2: 1.

A Chronology

1. "Miss Brady passed on her way to the river and back. She had heard a *potin* [rumor] that Blanche Hoschedé was about to marry (an American)," October 18, 1892. Theodore Robinson (1852–1896), *[Diaries] 1892–1896*, vol. 1, Frick Art Reference Library.

2. Philippe Piguet, *Saga familiale: Monet, Hoschedé-Monet et les Butler* (Vernon: Musée de Vernon, 2022), 16, note 12. A letter dated December 16, 1891 from Blanche Hoschedé to her mother, Alice Hoschedé (collection of Philippe Piguet), states: "Après le déjeuner, nous avons été avec lui [Sargent] voir les Paons de Whistler." The Peacock Room is now installed in the Freer Gallery of Art, National Museum of Asian Art, Smithsonian, Washington, DC.

3. "... je suis heureux de votre décision de rester avec Monet, heureux pour lui et heureux pour vous. Le malheur fait la réunion plus intime et plus forte de ceux qui restent." Gustave Geffroy to Blanche Hoschedé-Monet, Tuesday [unknown] 1914, published in Jean-Pierre Hoschedé, *Blanche Hoschedé-Monet, peintre impressionniste* (Rouen: Lecerf, 1961), 42.

4. "Elle travaillait à ses toiles. Elle lui faisait ses fonds." Jean Martet, *M. Clemenceau peint par lui-même* (Paris: A. Michel, 1929), 52–53.

5. "Sous le nom de Mme Blanche Hoschedé, Mme Blanche Monet expose, rue du Faubourg-Saint-Honoré, une série de peintures – paysages et fleurs – où s'affirme une sensibilité très feminine." Le Veilleur [pseudonym], "Pont des Arts," *Excelsior*, November 11, 1927, n.p.

6. "Tout de suite nous nous trouvons devant un paysage et un jardin fleuri, de Mme Blanche Hoschedé-Monet...." L'Imagier [pseudonym], "Le Salon des Indépendants. Aujourd'hui, vernissage," *L'Œuvre*, January 18, 1929, n.p.

7. "Mme Blanche Hoschedé, comme on sait la belle-fille de Monet, fait grand honneur à son maître sans le copier; talent délicat et sensible." Arsène Alexandre, "Le Salon des Indépendants," *Le Figaro*, January 19, 1929, 1.

8. "Blanche Hoschedé (Galerie Drouot Provence) est la belle-fille de Monet et 'personne, nous dit-on, ne connaît et ne continue mieux la tradition de Giverny'. Évidemment, et les paysages de cette artiste sont pleins de qualités. Mais ils ne font pas oublier Monet...." C.E. "Tour d'expositions," *Combat: organe du Mouvement de libération française*, April 2, 1947, 2.

WORKS IN THE EXHIBITION

Haley S. Pierce

Blanche Hoschedé-Monet
French, Paris 1865–1947 Nice

Four Sunflowers in a Vase (*Quatre tournesols dans un vase*)
1878
Oil on canvas
23 ⅝ × 11 in. (60 × 28 cm)
Private collection, France
Pl. 39

Sketchbook
1882–84
4 ½ × 7 ⅞ × ¹³⁄₁₆ in. (11.5 × 20 × 2 cm)
Collection of Philippe Piguet, on long-term loan to the Musée des Impressionnismes Giverny (MDIG D 2009.1.1)
Pl. 1

Les Petites-Dalles
ca. 1884–85
Oil on canvas
23 ⅝ × 31 ⅞ in. (60 × 81 cm)
Private collection
Pl. 3

Trees in the Fog (*Arbres dans le brouillard*)
ca. 1888
Oil on canvas
20 ¹⁄₁₆ × 32 ¹¹⁄₁₆ in. (51 × 83 cm)
Private collection
Pl. 7

Lupins and Poppies (*Lupins et pavots*)
1891
Oil on canvas
39 ⅜ × 23 ⅝ in. (100 × 60 cm)
Collection of the Village of Giverny, on long-term loan to the Musée des Impressionnismes Giverny (MDIG D 2009.1.1)
Pl. 40

The Ice Floes at Vernon (*Les Glaçons à Vernon*)
ca. 1893
Oil on canvas
19 ¹¹⁄₁₆ × 28 ¾ in. (50 × 73 cm)
Collection of Marc and Nicole Piguet
Pl. 8

Haystack at Giverny (*Meule à Giverny*)
ca. 1893
Oil on canvas
19 ⅞ × 32 ½ in. (50.5 × 82.6 cm)
Collection of Alice and Rick Johnson
Pl. 4

The Weeping Willows on the Lily Pond at Giverny (*Les Saules sur l'étang de Giverny*)
ca. 1893–97
Oil on canvas
23 ¾ × 32 in. (60.3 × 81.3 cm)
Columbus Museum of Art, Columbus, Ohio: Museum Purchase, through exchange (2013.051)
Pl. 12

The Small Grainstacks (*Les Moyettes*)
ca. 1894
Oil on canvas
18 ⅛ × 22 ¹⁄₁₆ in. (46 × 56 cm)
Collection of Alice and Rick Johnson
Pl. 5

Morning on the Seine (*Matinée sur la Seine*)
ca. 1896
Oil on canvas
28 ¾ × 23 ¹³⁄₁₆ in. (73 × 60.5 cm)
Collection of Alice and Rick Johnson
Pl. 13

The Bank of the Seine (*Bord de la Seine*)
ca. 1897–1910
Oil on canvas
23 ¾ × 29 in. (60.3 × 73.7 cm)
Collection of Gary J. and Kathy Z. Anderson
Pl. 17

The Seine at Croisset (*La Seine à Croisset*)
ca. 1897–1910
Oil on canvas
19 ¹¹⁄₁₆ × 32 ⁵⁄₁₆ in. (50 × 82.7 cm)
Private collection
Pl. 18

View of Rouen (*Vue générale de Rouen*)
ca. 1900
Oil on canvas
23 ⅝ × 28 ¾ in. (60 × 73 cm)
Private collection
Pl. 14

View of the Port of Rouen (The Ferry Bridge) (*Vue du port de Rouen [Le pont transbordeur]*)
ca. 1900
Oil on cardboard
9 ⁷⁄₁₆ × 13 ¾ in. (24 × 35 cm)
Collection of Philippe Piguet
Pl. 15

Le Poujol, Hérault – Evening (*Le Poujol, Hérault – le soir*)
ca. 1907–11
Oil on canvas
23 ⅝ × 28 ¾ in. (60 × 73 cm)
Collection of Jean-Loup Piguet
Pl. 21

Normandy Landscape, Beaumont-le-Roger (*Paysage normand, Beaumont-le-Roger*)
ca. 1910–13
Oil on canvas
19 ⅛ × 28 ¾ in. (48.5 × 73 cm)
Collection of Mrs. Catherine Fernandez Herry
Pl. 22

The Garden of Giverny (The Path under the Rose Arches) (*Le Jardin de Giverny [L'Allée des rosiers]*)
ca. 1918–24
Oil on canvas
26 ⅜ × 25 ⁹⁄₁₆ in. (67 × 65 cm)
Musée Clemenceau, Paris (2017.0.477)
Pl. 24

The House and Garden of Claude Monet, Giverny (*La Maison et le jardin de Claude Monet, Giverny*)
after 1926
Oil on canvas
23 ⅝ × 28 ¾ in. (60 × 73 cm)
Musée Blanche Hoschedé-Monet, Vernon (79.89)
Pl. 25

Landscape in the Snow (A Corner of Claude Monet's Garden) (*Paysage sous la neige [Un coin du jardin de Claude Monet]*)
after 1926
Oil on canvas
14 ¹⁵⁄₁₆ × 18 ⅛ in. (38 × 46 cm)
Collection of Catherine Minot
Pl. 36

A Corner of Claude Monet's Garden (*Coin du jardin de Claude Monet*)
1927
Oil on canvas
21¼ × 25⁹⁄₁₆ in. (54 × 65 cm)
Private collection
Pl. 35

Still Life with Cabbage and Rabbit (*Nature morte au chou et au lapin*)
1927
Oil on canvas
25⁹⁄₁₆ × 31⅞ (65 × 81 cm)
Musée Blanche Hoschedé-Monet, Vernon (85.4.1)
Pl. 23

Belébat: Home and Garden of Georges Clemenceau (*Belébat: maison et jardin de Clemenceau*)
ca. 1927–29
Oil on canvas
21⅝ × 25⁹⁄₁₆ in. (55 × 65 cm)
Musée Clemenceau, Paris (2017.0.236)
Pl. 27

Belébat: Garden of Georges Clemenceau (*Belébat: le jardin de Clemenceau*)
ca. 1927–29
Oil on canvas
24⁷⁄₁₆ × 29⅛ in. (62 × 74 cm)
Musée Clemenceau, Paris (2017.0.235)
Pl. 28

Maritime Pines (*Les Pins maritimes*)
1928
Oil on canvas
32¹¹⁄₁₆ × 26 in. (83 × 66 cm)
Lycée Claude-Monet, Paris, on long-term loan to the Musée des Impressionnismes Giverny (D 2021.1.12)
Pl. 29

The Beach at Diélette (The English Channel) (*La Plage de Diélette [Manche]*)
ca. 1932–39
Oil on canvas
21¼ × 28¾ in. (54 × 73 cm)
Musée Blanche Hoschedé-Monet, Vernon (84.10.1)
Pl. 30

Water Lilies (*Nymphéas*)
ca. 1946
Oil on canvas
18 × 14⅞ in. (45.7 × 37.8 cm)
Collection of Gary J. and Kathy Z. Anderson
Pl. 38

The Small Grainstacks (*Les Moyettes*)
n.d.
Oil on canvas
18⅛ × 22¹⁄₁₆ in. (46 × 56 cm)
Private collection
Pl. 6

Giverny in the Snow (*Giverny sous la neige*)
n.d.
Oil on canvas
23⁷⁄₁₆ × 28¾ in. (59.5 × 73 cm)
Collection of Jean-Loup Piguet
Pl. 9

The Duboc Farm, Giverny (*La Ferme Duboc, Giverny*)
n.d.
Oil on canvas
28¾ × 21⁷⁄₁₆ in. (73 × 54.5 cm)
Collection of Philippe Piguet
Pl. 10

The Hill, Giverny (*La Côte à Giverny*)
n.d.
Oil on canvas
21⁷⁄₁₆ × 28¾ in. (54.5 × 73 cm)
Private collection
Pl. 11

Meadows downstream from Rouen (*Prés en aval de Rouen*)
n.d.
Oil on canvas
20⅞ × 30⁵⁄₁₆ in. (53 × 77 cm)
Collection of Jean-Loup Piguet
Pl. 19

The House, Sorel-Moussel (*La Maison de Sorel-Moussel*)
n.d.
Oil on canvas
21¼ × 28¾ in. (54 × 73 cm)
Musée Marmottan Monet, Paris, legs Michel Monet, 1966 (inv. 5063)
Pl. 26

Seascape, Cotentin (*Marine du Cotentin*)
n.d.
Oil on canvas
14¹⁵⁄₁₆ × 18⅛ in. (38 × 46 cm)
Private collection, France
Pl. 31

View of Lake Bourget (*Vue du Lac du Bourget*)
n.d.
Oil on canvas
9¼ × 13⅜ in. (23.5 × 34 cm)
Collection of Philippe Piguet
Pl. 32

The Yellow Poplar (*Le Peuplier jaune*)
n.d.
Oil on canvas
25½ × 18⁷⁄₁₆ in. (64.7 × 46.8 cm)
Collection of Philippe Piguet
Pl. 34

Balustrade and Fir Trees in the Snow (*Balustrade et sapins sous la neige*)
n.d.
Oil on canvas
21¼ × 25⁹⁄₁₆ in. (54 × 65 cm)
Private collection
Pl. 37

Convolvulus (Morning Glory) (*Volubilis [Ipomées]*)
n.d.
Oil on canvas
31½ × 17¹¹⁄₁₆ in. (80 × 45 cm)
Private collection, France
Pl. 42

Larkspur (*Pieds d'alouettes*)
n.d.
Oil on canvas
42⅛ × 17⁵⁄₁₆ in. (107 × 44 cm)
Private collection, France
Pl. 43

The Port of Argenteuil (*Le Bassin
d'Argenteuil*)
1874
Oil on canvas
21¾ × 25⅞ in. (55.2 × 65.7 cm)
Sidney and Lois Eskenazi Museum of Art,
Indiana University, Bloomington, IN (76.15)
Pl. 16

Cliff Walk at Pourville (*Promenade sur
la falaise, Pourville*)
1882
Oil on canvas
26⅛ × 32⁷⁄₁₆ in. (66.5 × 82.3 cm)
Art Institute of Chicago, Mr. and Mrs. Lewis
Larned Coburn Memorial Collection
(1933.443)
Pl. 2

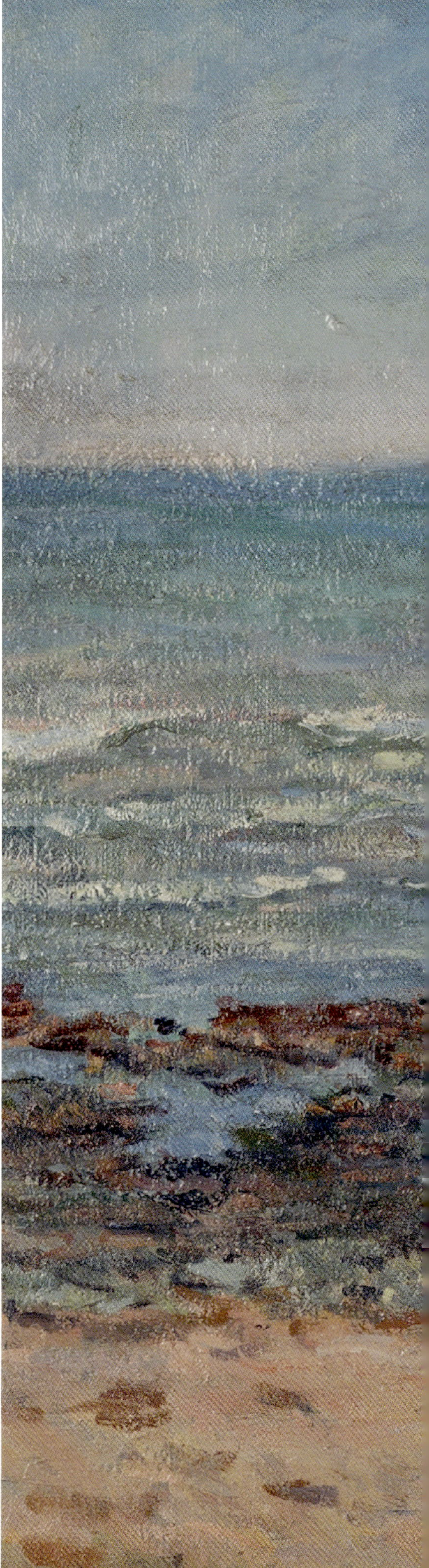

Detail of Pl. 30

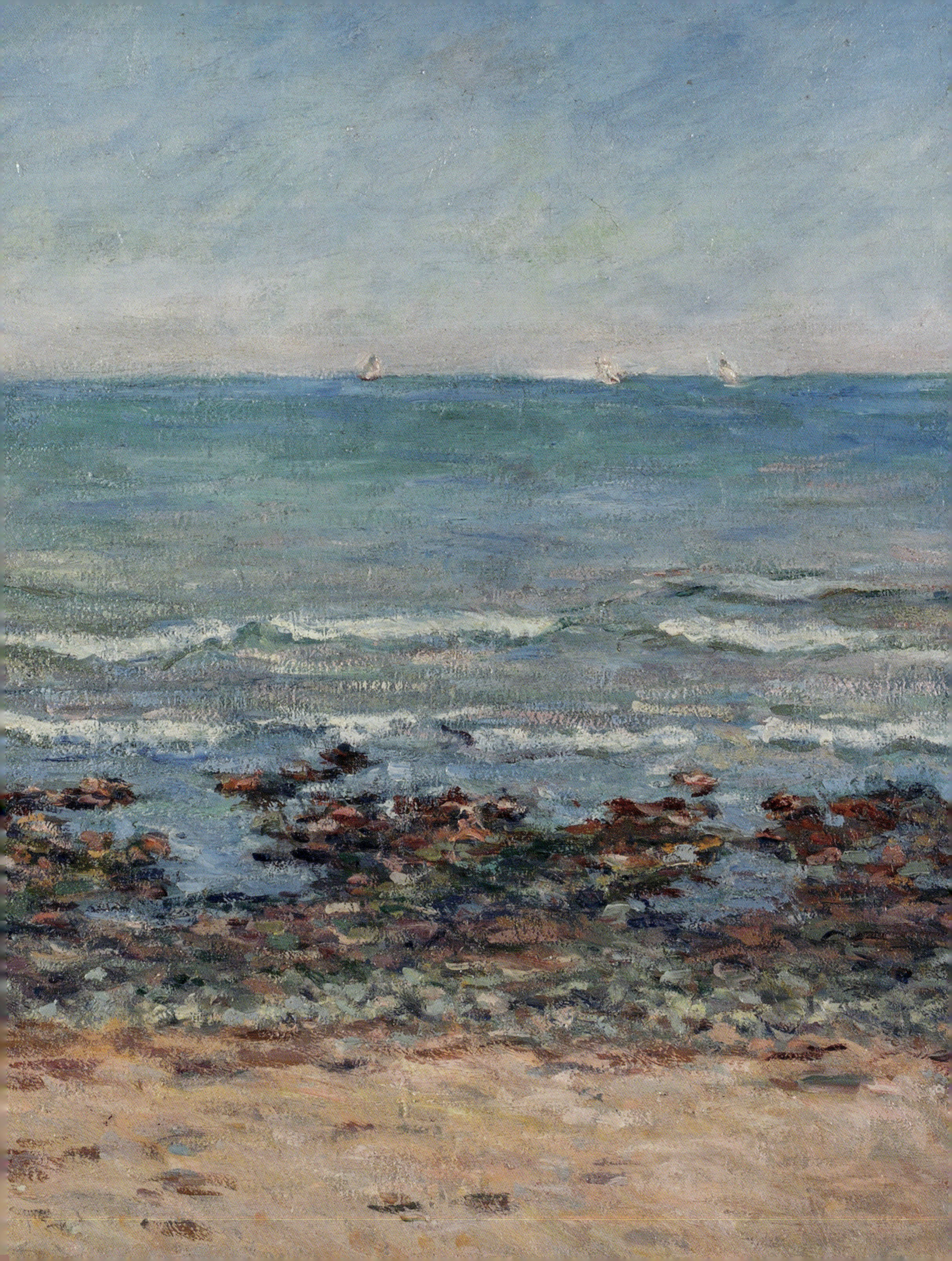

BLANCHE HOSCHEDÉ-MONET EXHIBITION HISTORY

Haley S. Pierce

Notes to reader:
All locations are in France unless otherwise specified.
Exhibitions after 1947 are posthumous.
Blanche Hoschedé-Monet has been abbreviated to BHM.

* Indicates a solo exhibition, featuring only Blanche Hoschedé-Monet;
all others listed are group exhibitions, including Blanche Hoschedé-Monet
among other artists.

1905
Salon des Indépendants
Grandes Serres de l'Alma et des Invalides, Cours la Reine, Paris, March 24–April 30
BHM exhibits seven paintings

1906
Salon des Indépendants
Grandes Serres de l'Alma et des Invalides, Cours la Reine, Paris, March 20–April 30
BHM exhibits four paintings

1907
Salon des Indépendants
Grandes Serres de l'Alma et des Invalides, Cours la Reine, Paris, March 20–April 30
BHM exhibits three paintings

Salon de la Société des Artistes Rouennais
Musée des Beaux-Arts, Rouen, April 7–May 5
BHM exhibits two paintings

1908
Salon de la Société des Artistes Rouennais
Musée des Beaux-Arts, Rouen
BHM exhibits six paintings

1909
Salon de la Société des Artistes Rouennais
Musée des Beaux-Arts, Rouen
BHM exhibits four paintings

1910
Salon de la Société des Artistes Rouennais
Musée des Beaux-Arts, Rouen
BHM exhibits six paintings

1911
Salon de la Société des Artistes Rouennais
Musée des Beaux-Arts, Rouen
BHM exhibits five paintings

1913
Salon de la Société des Artistes Rouennais
Musée des Beaux-Arts, Rouen
BHM exhibits four paintings

Blanche Hoschedé (Mme. Blanche Monet) *
MM. Bernheim-Jeune, Éditeurs d'Art, Paris, November 7–18

1928
Salon des Indépendants
Grand Palais des Champs-Élysées, Avenue Alexandre III, Paris, January 20–February 29
BHM exhibits two paintings

1929
Salon des Indépendants
Grand Palais des Champs-Élysées, Avenue Alexandre III, Paris, January 18–February 28
BHM exhibits two paintings

Salon de Vernon
BHM exhibits two paintings

1930
Salon des Indépendants
Grand Palais des Champs-Élysées, Avenue Alexandre III, Paris, January 17–March 2
BHM exhibits two paintings

1931
Salon des Indépendants
Grand Palais des Champs-Élysées, Avenue Alexandre III, Paris, January 23–March 1
BHM exhibits two paintings

Blanche Hoschedé-Monet *
MM. Bernheim-Jeune, Éditeurs d'Art, Paris, March 9–20

Salon de la Société des Artistes Rouennais
Musée des Beaux-Arts, Rouen
BHM exhibits three paintings

1932
Salon des Indépendants
Grand Palais des Champs-Élysées, Avenue Alexandre III, Paris, January 22–February 28
BHM exhibits two paintings

Salon de la Société des Artistes Rouennais
Musée des Beaux-Arts, Rouen
BHM exhibits three paintings

1933
Salon des Indépendants
Grand Palais des Champs-Élysées, Avenue Alexandre III, Paris, January 20–February 26
BHM exhibits three paintings

Salon de la Société des Artistes Rouennais
Musée des Beaux-Arts, Rouen
BHM exhibits three paintings

1934
Salon des Indépendants
Grand Palais des Champs-Élysées, Avenue Alexandre III, Paris, February 2–March 11
BHM exhibits two paintings

Salon de la Société des Artistes Rouennais
Musée des Beaux-Arts, Rouen
BHM exhibits two paintings

1935
Salon des Indépendants
Grand Palais des Champs-Élysées, Avenue Alexandre III, Paris, January 18–March 3
BHM exhibits two paintings

Salon de la Société des Artistes Rouennais
Musée des Beaux-Arts, Rouen
BHM exhibits two paintings, not included in the exhibition catalogue

1942
Salon de Vernon
BHM exhibits two paintings

Blanche Hoschedé *
Galerie Alfred Daber, Paris, October 16–November 7

1947
Blanche Hoschedé *
Galerie d'Art Drouot Provence, Paris, March 14–April 14

1954
Salon des Indépendants
Grand Palais des Champs-Élysées, Avenue Alexandre III, Paris, April 14–May 9
Organized posthumously by Jean-Pierre Hoschedé, the artist's brother; six works exhibited by BHM

Blanche Hoschedé-Monet *
Galerie Zak, Paris, November 19–December 3

1957
Blanche Hoschedé-Monet *
Salle des Fêtes, Vernon, June 16–23
Organized by Jean-Pierre Hoschedé, the artist's brother

1959
Blanche Hoschedé-Monet, 1865–1947 / Henry Ottmann, 1877–1927
Musée des Beaux-Arts, Rouen, April 11–May 11

1960
Claude Monet and the Giverny Artists
Charles E. Slatkin Galleries, New York, NY, March 22–April 23

1966
Dame et Demoiselles: Blanche Hoschedé, Jeanne Baudot, Paule Gobillard
Galerie Durand-Ruel, Paris, June 16–July 29

Vingt ans d'acquisitions, 1948–1968
Musée des Augustins, Toulouse

1971
Monet et ses amis: Le legs Michel Monet, La donation Donop de Monchy
Musée Marmottan Monet, Paris, June

Blanche Hoschedé-Monet, 1865–1947 *
Galerie Robert Tuffier, Les Andelys, June 11–30

1988–89
Monet et ses amis
The Museum of Modern Art, Ibaraki, Mito, Japan, October 1–November 6, 1988; Fukushima Prefectural Museum of Art, Fukushima, Japan, November 12–December 25, 1988; Kyoto Municipal Museum of Art, Kyoto, Japan, January 24–February 28, 1989

1991
Blanche Hoschedé-Monet, 1865–1947: Une artiste de Giverny *
Musée Municipal A.G. Poulain (now Musée Blanche Hoschedé-Monet), Vernon, April 6–June 2

2004–5
Inspirations des bords de Seine: Maximilien Luce et les peintres de son époque
Musée de l'Hôtel-Dieu, Mantes-la-Jolie, October 30, 2004–March 7, 2005

2007–8
Impressionist Giverny: A Colony of Artists, 1885–1915
Musée d'Art Américain Giverny (now Musée des Impressionnismes Giverny), Giverny, April 1–July 1, 2007; San Diego Museum of Art, San Diego, CA, July 22–October 1, 2007

In Monet's Garden: Artists and the Lure of Giverny
Columbus Museum of Art, Columbus, OH, October 12, 2007–January 20, 2008; Musée Marmottan-Monet, Paris, February 12–May 11, 2008

2009
Le Jardin de Monet à Giverny: L'invention d'un paysage
Musée des Impressionnismes Giverny, Giverny, May 1–August 15

2010–11
Blanche Hoschedé-Monet: Un destin impressionniste *
Musée de Louviers, June 5–October 3, 2010

Monet and the Artists of Giverny: The Beginning of American Impressionism
Kitakyushu Municipal Museum of Art, Kitakyushu, Japan, October 9–November 28, 2010; Bunkamura Museum of Art, Tokyo, Japan, December 7, 2010–February 17, 2011; Okayama Prefectural Museum of Art, February 25–April 10, 2011

2013
Vernon et les bords de Seine au temps des impressionnistes
Musée Municipal A.G. Poulain (now Musée Blanche Hoschedé-Monet), Vernon, April 13–September 22

2017
Blanche Hoschedé-Monet: Un regard impressionniste *
Musée Municipal A.G. Poulain (now Musée Blanche Hoschedé-Monet), July 8–October 29

2020
Reflets d'une collection
Musée des Impressionnismes Giverny, Giverny, June 15–August 30

De l'aube au crépuscule: Couleur impressionniste
Musée de Louviers, July 10–November 15

L'Herbier secret de Giverny: Monet et Hoschedé en botanistes
Muséum d'Histoire Naturelle, Rouen, July 15–November 15

2022
Saga familiale: Monet, Hoschedé-Monet et les Butler
Musée Municipal A.G. Poulain (now Musée Blanche Hoschedé-Monet), April 29–October 2

2023
Léon Monet: Frère de l'artiste et collectionneur
Musée du Luxembourg (Sénat), Paris, March 15–July 16

2025
Blanche Hoschedé-Monet in the Light *
Sidney and Lois Eskenazi Museum of Art, Indiana University, Bloomington, IN,
February 14–June 15

SELECTED BIBLIOGRAPHY

Bocquillon, Marina Ferretti, Vanessa Lecomte, and Gabrielle van Zuylen. *Le Jardin de Monet à Giverny: L'invention d'un paysage.* Giverny: Musée des Impressionnismes Giverny; Milan: 5 continents, 2009.

Bourguignon, Katherine M., ed. *Impressionist Giverny: A Colony of Artists, 1885–1915.* Giverny: Musée d'Art Américain; Chicago: Terra Foundation for American Art, 2007.

Bourguignon, Katherine M., et al. *Monet and the Artists of Giverny: The Beginning of American Impressionism.* Fukuoka, Japan: Nishinippon Shimbun, 2010.

Burke, Janine. "La Nymphéa: Monet, Blanche Hoschedé and Giverny," in *Source: Nature's Healing Role in Art and Writing*, 279–312. Sydney: Allen & Unwin, 2009.

Burke, Janine. "Monet's 'Angel': The Artistic Partnership of Claude Monet and Blanche Hoschedé-Monet." *Colloquy: Text, Theory, Critique.* No. 22 (December 2011): 68–80. https://www.monash.edu/__data/assets/pdf_file/0005/1764671/burke.pdf.

Clemenceau, Georges. *Lettres à une amie, 1923–1929.* Paris: Gallimard, 1970.

Fourny-Dargère, Sophie. *Blanche Hoschedé-Monet, 1865–1947: Une artiste de Giverny.* Vernon: Musée Municipal A.G. Poulain; Rouen: Lecerf, 1991.

Geffroy, Gustave. *Claude Monet: Sa vie, son œuvre.* Paris: G. Crès & Cie, 1924.

Gimpel, René. *Journal d'un collectionneur marchand de tableaux.* Paris: Calmann Lévy, 1963.

Hoschedé, Jean-Pierre. *Claude Monet, ce mal connu: Intimité familiale d'un demi-siècle à Giverny, de 1883 à 1926.* 2 vols. Geneva: Pierre Cailler Éditeur, 1960.

Hoschedé, Jean-Pierre. *Blanche Hoschedé-Monet, peintre impressionniste.* Rouen: Lecerf, 1961.

Houston, Joe, et al. *In Monet's Garden: Artists and the Lure of Giverny.* Columbus, Ohio: Columbus Museum of Art; Paris: Musée Marmottan Monet; London: Scala Publishers, 2007.

Jeanneney, Jean-Noël, Sophie Eloy, and Cécile Girardeau. *Monet/Clemenceau: Correspondance.* Paris: Musée de l'Orangerie; RMN-Grand Palais, 2019.

Johnston, Sona. *In Monet's Light: Theodore Robinson at Giverny.* Baltimore: The Baltimore Museum of Art; London: Philip Wilson Publishers, 2004.

Klein, Jacques-Sylvain, and Philippe Piguet. *Les Peintres de la Normandie.* Rennes: Éditions Ouest-France, 2019.

Lefebvre, Géraldine. *Léon Monet: Frère de l'artiste et collectionneur.* Paris: RMN-Grand Palais, 2023.

Manoeuvre, Laurent. *Les Pionnières: Femmes et impressionnistes.* Rouen: Éditions des Falaises, 2016.

Martet, Jean. *M. Clemenceau peint par lui-même.* Paris: A. Michel, 1929.

Piguet, Hubert. "Blanche Hoschedé-Monet (1865–1947), peintre impressionniste," in *Précis analytique des travaux de L'Académie des Sciences, Belles-Lettres et Arts de Rouen, 1985 et 1986*, 323–27. Fécamp: L. Durand & Fils, 1988.

Piguet, Philippe. *Blanche Hoschedé-Monet: Un destin impressionniste.* Louviers: Musée de Louviers; Bonsecours: Éditions Point de vues, 2010.

Piguet, Philippe. *Blanche Hoschedé-Monet: Un regard impressionniste.* Vernon: Musée de Vernon; Paris: Intensité Éditions, 2017.

Piguet, Philippe. *Saga familiale: Monet, Hoschedé-Monet et les Butler.* Vernon: Musée de Vernon, 2022.

Robinson, Theodore. *[Diaries] 1892–1896.* 4 vols. Frick Art Reference Library, New York.

Sciama, Cyrille, and Marie Delbarre. *Les Enfants de l'impressionnisme.* Giverny: Musée des Impressionnismes Giverny; Paris: Flammarion, 2023.

Wildenstein, Daniel. *Claude Monet: Biographie et catalogue raisonné.* 4 vols. Lausanne: La Bibliothèque des Arts, 1974–91.

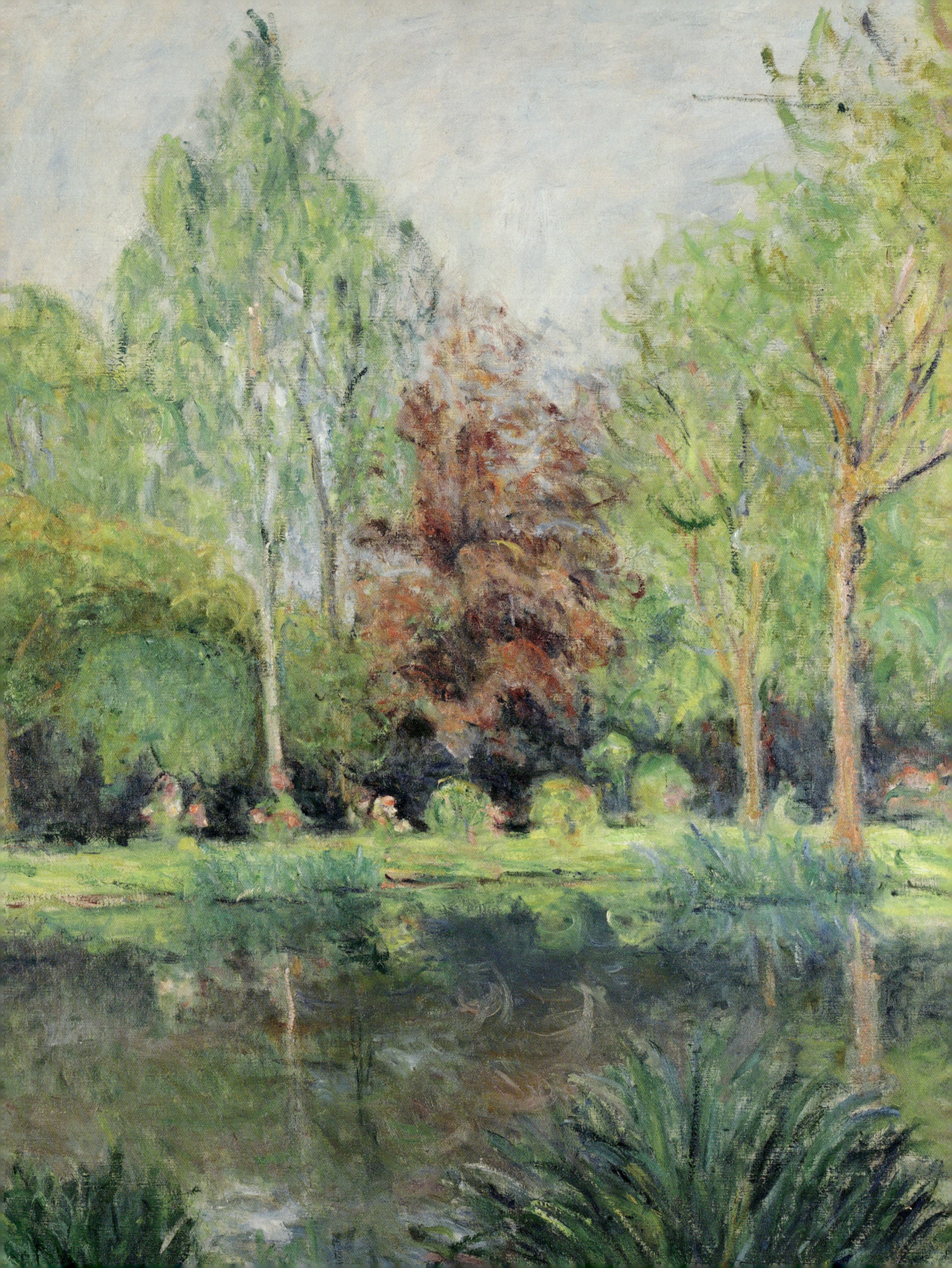

INDEX

Page numbers in *italics* refer to the illustrations

    Detail of Pl. 26

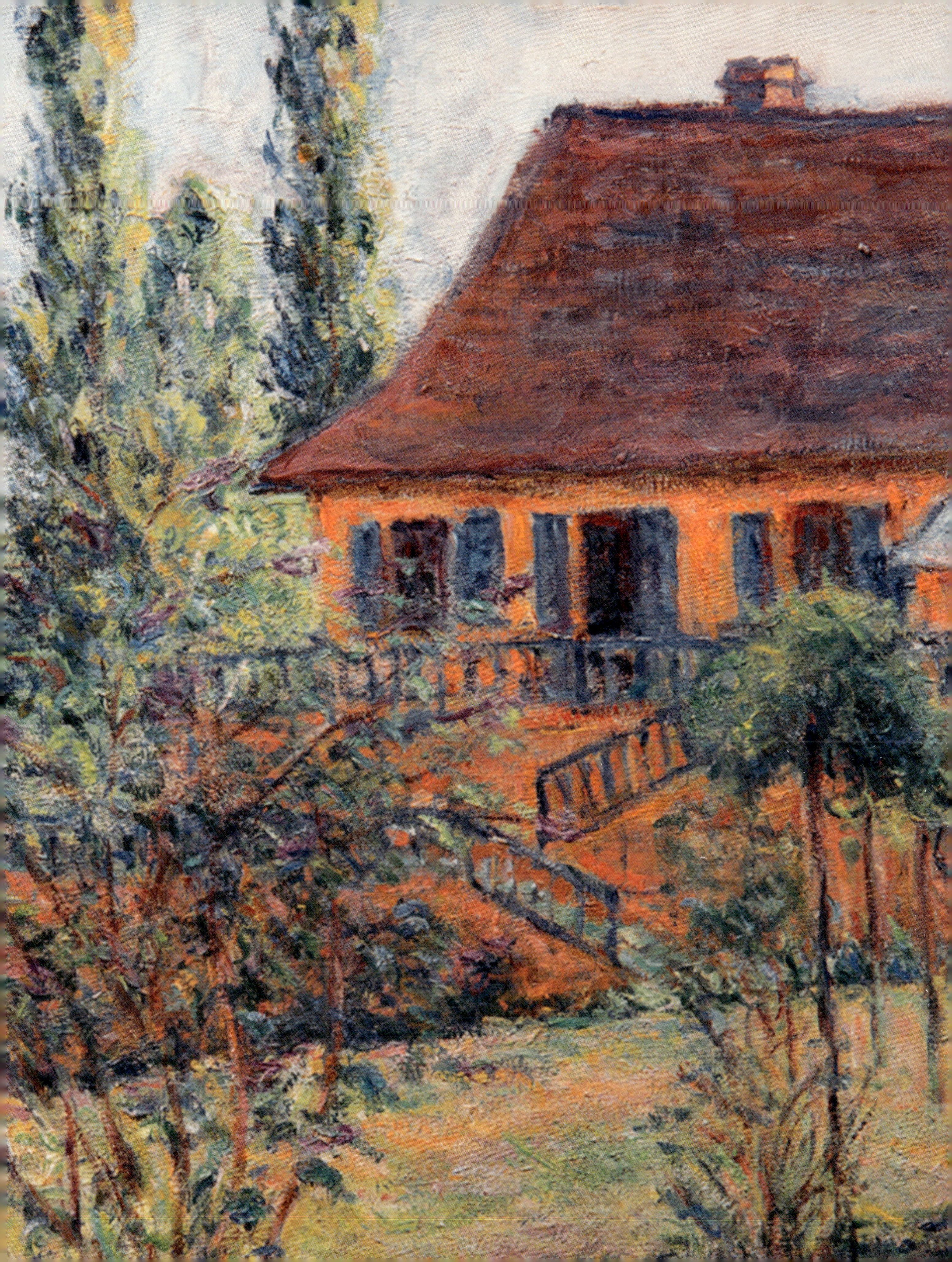